The Midland & Great Northern Joint Railway
and its Locomotives

A picture that was probably taken by the Midland Railway Photographer is this view at Peterborough, where the M&GN Joint line crossed over the Great Northern Railway and the Midland line from Manton. This is M&GN bridge No. 1, often referred to as New England or 'Rhubarb' Bridge. At the left of the picture we can see the connection to the Midland Railway's Wisbech sidings, but to the right of the Midland Railway's running lines everything belongs to the Great Northern Railway. What cannot be seen in the picture, as it is just behind the photographer, is Wisbech West Junction signal box – although signal wires and point rodding are clearly visible. R.J. ESSERY COLLECTION.

THE
MIDLAND & GREAT NORTHERN
JOINT RAILWAY
AND ITS LOCOMOTIVES

BOB ESSERY

With Contributions from
NIGEL DIGBY, DAVID JENKINSON
AND ALAN WELLS

LIGHTMOOR PRESS

This view of Sheringham was taken when the photographer was looking south west from the Down platform towards the original signal box, an Eastern & Midlands Railway type identical to Holt. The date is possibly 1894, when the Midland Railway Photographer was sent from Derby to take photographs of their new acquisition. The station is substantially in its E&M condition and the only change visible is what appears to be a GN-type tumbler signal as the Up starter. The permanent way is still flat-bottom rail, not replaced here until 1902. The station was rebuilt with beautiful platform canopies in 1896–97, and the Up waiting shelter seen here was 'moved' to Eye Green. Probably only the woodwork went, there being no need to take bricks to Eye Green! Taking centre stage is the E&M water crane, a lifting type developed from the L&F standpipes supplied by the original contractor, which are believed to have come from Ransomes & Rapier. It is not known if these lifting cranes were bought in or were products of the Melton Constable foundry. The station was further developed in 1905–6 to cater for the new Norfolk & Suffolk arrangements allowing the GER into the station. The old signal box was swept away, replaced by two new M&GN ones at each end of the altered layout. R.J. ESSERY COLLECTION.

CONTENTS

© Bob Essery and Lightmoor Press 2009.

Locomotive drawings by Alan Wells.

Designed by Nigel Nicholson. Cover design by Neil Parkhouse.

British Library Cataloguing-in-Publication Data. A catalogue
record for this book is available from the British Library.
ISBN 9781 899889 37 2

LIGHTMOOR PRESS
Unit 144B, Lydney Trading Estate, Harbour Road, Lydney, Gloucestershire GL15 5EJ
www.lightmoor.co.uk
Lightmoor Press is an imprint of Black Dwarf Lightmoor Publications Ltd.

Printed by TJ International, Padstow, Cornwall.

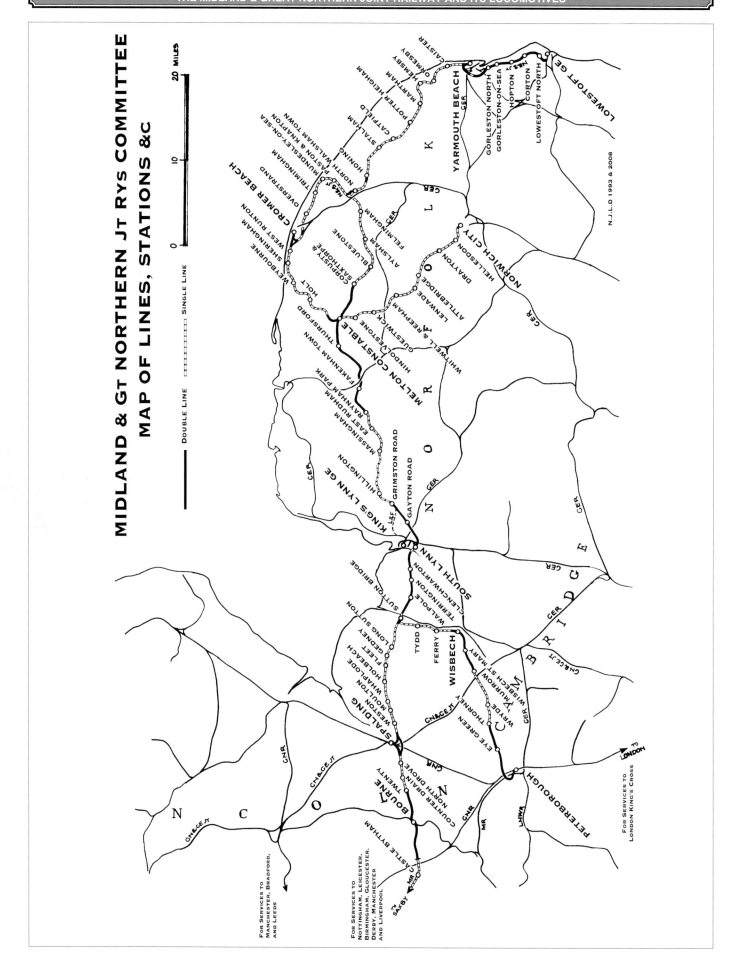

MIDLAND & Gt NORTHERN Jt Rys COMMITTEE
MAP OF LINES, STATIONS &c

DOUBLE LINE ▭▭▭▭ SINGLE LINE

0   10   20 MILES

N.J.L.D 1993 & 2008

INTRODUCTION

In the early 1980s, the late David Jenkinson and I, frustrated by the lack of a detailed summary of Midland Railway locomotives, resolved to do something about it – the result was a four volume series (*An Illustrated Review of Midland Locomotives*) published by Wild Swan Publications between 1984 and 1989. The explanation of why we concentrated on the Johnson and later years of the company's history is given in the introduction of Volume One so it need not be repeated. Since then, my good friend David Hunt has recorded elsewhere the story of a number of Kirtley classes and added to our knowledge of the story of the pre-Johnson period. When David Jenkinson and I were considering the format of our work we were conscious that we ought to include the London Tilbury & Southend Railway locomotives, which became Midland stock in 1912, and the locomotive stock of the two joint lines that were under Midland Railway control, namely the Somerset & Dorset and Midland & Great Northern Joint Railways.

These three concerns suggested themselves as the logical theme for an extra add-on to the main Midland series, and the only decision was whether to cover them in one large book or separate them into three smaller compilations. After much thought we planned to adopt the latter course, partly because their activities were widely separated geographically, partly because the locomotive story was noticeably different in each case, but especially because it seemed to us that the three companies' locomotive stock concerned might well need more by way of general explanation, not least in terms of the very nature of the systems on which they ran. The variety of types to be considered in these proposed three books probably equalled all

those of the parent Midland Company during the period we intended to cover and this, added together with the points mentioned above, prompted us to adopt a different method of treatment from the main series. In each case we planned to start with a slightly more extended explanation of the particular system on which the engines ran; then we proposed to consider the 'inherited' locomotive position at the point when each of the three concerns first came under Midland design influence, and, lastly, we intended to look at the locomotives which were subsequently added to the lists – either for specific use on the systems concerned, or whose design originated from one or other of them (for example, the 'Tilbury' tanks).

We planned to start this series with what was, in terms of corporate identity, the newest of the three, the Midland & Great Northern Joint Railway. This was perhaps the least known of the three concerns in locomotive terms to most enthusiasts – and certainly true in terms of our own records – so from the outset we must record our deepest gratitude for the considerable contribution made to our story by Alan M. Wells, a noted authority on the M&GN, who made freely available his photographic collection and notes, along with many beautiful and accurate drawings of M&GN locomotives which he had produced over the years. Many of these drawings are reproduced in these pages, and we freely acknowledge that without his help our efforts would probably have been far less complete and certainly less well illustrated. Combined with his never-failing courtesy, advice and guidance as we went along, it has been our pleasure and privilege to have had his help. Others whose contribution must be acknowledged are Phil Atkins, John Edgington and the library staff of the NRM,

Plate 1
Johnson 4-4-0 No. 54 is seen here leaving Gedney for South Lynn with a passenger train circa 1909. The engine is in original condition. The first three coaches are ex-Midland railway vehicles but the photographer recorded no other details. Note the GN type 'somersault' signal and the Whittaker tablet exchange apparatus at the bottom of the platform ramp. E.E. Boltz.

while our good friend Bernard Matthews has continued to allow us total access to his magnificent photographic collection. Stephen Summerson read the manuscript, corrected errors and generally devoted considerable time to help ensure that the story was both complete and as accurate as possible.

Apart from a few minor alterations, the above was written in the early 1990s; but, for a variety of reasons, David and myself never completed the work on the M&GN project. The first development towards completing our 'Midland' project came in 2000 when Ian Allan asked me if I could write the story of the London Tilbury & Southend Railway and its locomotives. Although I had done some research on the locomotive stock of this line it offered me the opportunity to start from scratch, and in many ways the final M&GN manuscript has been based upon this experience. At the time, David Jenkinson was involved with other interests and he was happy for me to 'go it alone', so the 2001 publication was a solo effort. Recently, when in conversation with Lightmoor Press about the Somerset & Dorset and Midland & Great Northern Joint, I was asked if I would complete the manuscript on the M&GN for publication. My feeling was it should be completed, but I would try to retain the written contributions from both the late David Jenkinson and the late Alan Wells, together with his drawings. Therefore text written by David and I or David and Alan will appear as 'we' but recent additions from my pen will appear in the singular. I can only hope that readers will understand why this has been done and not find it confusing. There was also another factor to be considered. During the period between David Jenkinson and I setting aside our work and my being asked

LEFT: **Plate 2**
This delightful picture was taken at Whaplode station and shows a junior member of staff – probably a Lad Porter – engaged in lamping duties, the legend on his cap is MID&GN. R.J. ESSERY COLLECTION.

BELOW: **Plate 3**
Beyer Peacock 4-4-0 No. 33 heads a Down Cromer train at Holt. The train mostly consists of ex-GNR carriages with an E&M third as second vehicle. The original Westinghouse brake has been replaced by vacuum brake but the photograph was taken before the locomotive was reboilered in 1908. E.E. BOLTZ.

to complete it, Nigel Digby produced his *A Guide to the Midland & Great Northern Joint Railway* that was published by Ian Allan in 1993. Therefore it seemed to me that I should endeavour to compliment his work rather than to duplicate what he produced.

The locomotive drawings in this book are by Alan Wells; most have been reproduced at a scale of 7mm:1 foot, suitable for the 0-gauge modeller. Unless referenced otherwise, the map extracts are from the Midland Railway Distance Diagrams.

Before the manuscript went to the publishers I asked Nigel Digby and John Hobden of the M&GN Circle to read it and I am most grateful for their comments. In particular I must record my thanks to Nigel Digby who, in addition making many useful suggestions and providing much additional material – especially Appendix D and E – completely revised and rewrote the livery chapter that had originally been the work of David Jenkinson and Alan Wells, to ensure that it contained the fruits of the research into the subject that has taken place in recent years. Finally, I would like to conclude by saying that although I am fully responsible for the final version of this story, I should acknowledge the immense contribution from both David and Alan by dedicating this book to their memory; I hope they would have approved the final product.

Bob Essery, December 2007

ABOVE: **Plate 4**
This example of a M&GN trespass notice, believed to have been painted white with black letters, is included to show the style used by the company, but unfortunately it is not known where it was photographed. R.J. ESSERY COLLECTION.

BELOW: **Plate 5**
A note on the original print states that this is the 1.28pm express from Cromer to King's Cross leaving Melton Constable. When the picture was taken the train was passing Melton West signal box and was on the line to Lynn; the line behind the signal box is from Cromer. The train is made up of GNR stock and the train engine, Johnson 4-4-0 No. 46, which has just taken over the train, will work through to Peterborough. ALAN WELLS COLLECTION.

Plate 6
This delightful undated picture was taken at Cromer and shows the driver and fireman on the cab of an unidentified Johnson 4-4-0. The limited protection for the engineman from bad weather is evident and this was not the most comfortable of engine cabs, but nevertheless the driver has the look of a satisfied man while there is a questioning look in the fireman's eyes. Just visible on the inside of the cab side sheet above the driver's head we can see the plate or painted area that carried the driver's name. The oblong plate had concave corners and the background was painted black, the letters and lining were in yellow. Alan Wells Collection.

CHAPTER 1

THE NATURE OF JOINT LINES

Joint lines as such ceased to have a meaning following the nationalisation of the big four railway companies in 1948, but hitherto they had represented an interesting feature of the British railway scene from the very earliest years. Therefore, before introducing the complexity of the locomotive stock that originally came into 'joint ownership', it is appropriate to spend a little time considering just what a joint railway was, beginning with the concept of a joint line – as opposed to 'running powers', which are not the same thing.

In the early years of railway development during the nineteenth century, competition between rival concerns was, to say the least, at times rather keen! The result was that two or more different railways frequently served many areas, often with their own separate stations in the towns that they served. This fierce competition continued right up until the grouping, and beyond if the old companies still found themselves as part of different members of the big four. Although keen to compete with each other, these rival companies at times found it made more sense if they joined forces with one another in order to either jointly construct or operate a section of line between them; both companies (sometimes it was more than two) enjoyed equal rights to run their trains and this practice was very distinct to the many other instances where 'running powers' existed. Running powers meant that one company possessed the legal right, which was not always exercised, to work their trains over the lines of another company, but without there being any question of part ownership of the line.

A good example of the complexity of joint ownership and running powers was to be found at Carlisle Citadel station. Before 1923 two companies, namely the London & North Western and the Caledonian, jointly owned the station, but 'running powers' were enjoyed by five other railways, namely the Midland, the North British, the Glasgow & South Western, the North Eastern and the Maryport & Carlisle. This complex ownership of lines was only partially tidied up in 1923. Joint lines varied in size and importance; there were many points of contact between two or more companies during the pre-group period and, while some of the jointly owned lines were but short lengths of track, others were sizable systems.

The 1923 grouping reduced the number of jointly owned lines simply because in several instances the 'joint owners' found themselves to be part of the same enlarged group. But the joint lines with locomotive stock, in which we are interested here, did not fall into this category. Although this book is concerned only with the M&GN, there was also the Somerset & Dorset Joint Railway in England, and the Midland Railway, on its quest to enlarge its sphere of influence, crossed the Irish Sea to acquire interests in Ireland and part of its system in 1922 included the County Donegal Joint Committee, a narrow gauge railway in the North West of Ireland. With a track mileage of ninety-one miles, this company, which owned a number of locomotives, was one of the top six joint lines in the British Isles. Finally we should mention the Severn & Wye Joint, a complicated network of railways whose origins have been fully documented by

Plate 1
Notwithstanding the modest nature of the train, the locomotive is running under express passenger train headcode and is approaching Peterborough. When this picture was taken, probably around 1920, No. 77 had received an extended smokebox and new chimney. W.L. GOOD.

Plate 2
Taken at Sutton Bridge Junction, this picture shows No. 57, a Johnson 4-4-0, after it had been rebuilt with a 'G7' boiler, with an express to Leicester. ALAN WELLS COLLECTION.

Ian Pope and Paul Karau in books published by Wild Swan. In 1894 the GWR and the Midland Railway acquired the thirty-nine route miles of this system and, as was recorded in chapter 2 of *Midland Locomotives, Volume 3*, the locomotive stock was divided between the two companies.

When one expresses the joint lines in route mileage terms then there were four systems whose tracks were in three figures. Of these the largest was the M&GN. Second in size, but arguably the most important in a total railway sense, was the Cheshire Lines Committee, a system jointly owned by the Great Northern, Great Central and Midland railways. However, since this system, while owning both passenger and freight rolling stock, did not possess any locomotives, it does not figure in our story. The third largest joint line was in fact a system jointly owned by the Great Northern and Great Eastern railways, but again no locomotives were employed in joint ownership and the 1923 grouping saw this line become part of the newly formed London & North Eastern Railway. Fourth in size, but, as far as latter-day enthusiasts are concerned, first in popularity, is the Somerset & Dorset Joint Railway.

Although this work deals with the M&GN, the reader's attention should be drawn to the similarity of the two lines where the Midland Railway had a direct locomotive input. Both the S&DJR and the M&GN enjoyed common Midland Railway ownership, and on both joint lines the Midland Railway was responsible for the motive power affairs of the joint company. There were many points of similarity between these two systems: both had their own locomotive superintendents who maintained the system's stock of locomotives; each line had its own distinctive livery and we explore this aspect

in greater depth in due course; and, naturally, each line had its own locomotive works as well – Highbridge for the S&DJR and Melton Constable for the M&GN, each works being part of an efficient railway community pleasantly situated in open countryside.

The 1923 grouping saw the joint owners as parts of different companies, so joint ownership and operation was to continue until the 1948 nationalisation. However, certain changes were to take place during the 1930s. The first was the absorption of the S&DJR locomotive stock into that of the London Midland & Scottish Railway in 1930, while seven years later the M&GN locomotives became part of L&NER stock. In the case of the S&DJR, a total renumbering took place, but the M&GN stock was placed on the duplicate list by having a zero placed before the original number. Although a number of S&DJR engines were withdrawn from service by the LM&SR fairly quickly, their demise was not as rapid as the fate of the M&GN engines, many of which were scrapped by the L&NER at an early date following the 1937 changes. The remaining locomotives were allocated with new numbers in 1946, but even then some never carried them. Although the 1948 nationalisation brought an end to this joint line activity, it could not destroy the affection which many enthusiasts felt for these lines and, while originally the S&DJR was by far the most popular, the M&GN enjoyed a very strong local following. The initials S&DJR and M&GN still arouse a feeling of nostalgia amongst many railway enthusiasts. There were of course many points of similarity between these two lines, and both were to suffer the economists' axe. The first to be affected was the M&GN whose system was to be largely closed in 1959, while the S&DJR was to continue for a few more years – until it too was closed in 1966.

CHAPTER 2

THE M&GN IN OUTLINE

Before we can begin to consider the locomotive stock of the M&GN, which the celebrated historian E.L. Ahrons once described as '*the quaintest assortment that ever adorned a railway of this length*', it is necessary to consider how the system developed into its final form. Only by understanding the history of the system can one appreciate how such a varied mix of motive power came to be in existence on 1st July 1893 when the new Joint Committee was incorporated. This final 'coming together' marked the conclusion of a complex story of independent lines, some of which had previously amalgamated with each other, and not all of which owned their own locomotives.

At its inception on 1st July 1893, the Midland & Great Northern Railways Joint Committee took control of the system of the Eastern & Midlands Railway, then aggregating 173 miles, which was largely single line. The Eastern & Midlands Railway – incorporated 18th August 1882, to take effect from the 1st January 1883 – was itself an amalgamation of three small undertakings now comprised in the eastern section of the system, to which was added, on the 1st July 1883, the western section, consisting of the lines which were known as the Bourne & Lynn Joint and the Peterborough, Wisbech & Sutton Railways. The new owners, however, did not work the western section.

Before dealing in chronological order with the growth of the system, a brief summary written by GNR employee H.L. Hopwood, which was published in the August 1908 *Railway Magazine*, may be useful in understanding the importance of the various lines that comprised the M&GN. Note the old spellings of Wisbech and Sheringham which were abandoned in the 1890s.

Before touching on these early lines we will describe the situation of the railway as it is today. The Midland and Great Northern Joint main line starts at a junction with the Great Northern Railway 60 chains north of Peterborough and runs via Wisbeach (the centre of a large fruit-growing district), South Lynn, Fakenham, and Melton Constable to Yarmouth (Beach Station) a total distance of 108 miles 72 chains. There is a branch westward from Sutton Bridge through Bourne to Little Bytham where there is a junction with the Midland Railway to Saxby. From South Lynn a short connection enables the Midland and Great Northern Joint Railway to gain access to the Great Eastern Railway station at King's Lynn. At Melton Constable there are branches north eastwards to Sherringham and Cromer and southwards to Norwich. In recent years lines have been constructed, (1) from North Walsham to Mundesley,

Plate 1
Corpusty & Saxthorpe station was 4 miles 64 chains east of Melton Constable on the line to Yarmouth. The station was opened on the 5th April 1883 and closed on the 2nd March 1959. The east end of the station marked the end of the double track from Melton and the start of the single line to Honing, although there were passing loops at Aylsham and North Walsham. No doubt this picture was taken to record some event and it shows the staff employed at the time. It is unfortunate that not all of the station nameboard is in the picture; the board and posts were made of wood but the letters were metal. Finally, note the station name to the left of the building, which has been made by using pebbles that have been whitewashed. R.J. ESSERY COLLECTION.

(2) coast line from Yarmouth to Lowestoft, (3) coast line from Cromer to Mundesley. These undertakings have been carried out jointly with the Great Eastern Railway, and the lines are known as those of the Norfolk and Suffolk Joint Committee.

Beginning with the lines west of Lynn, the oldest part was authorised on the 4th August 1853 – under the Norwich & Spalding Railway Act – being opened from Spalding (South Junction) to Holbeach, 7½ miles, on the 15th November 1858, and from Holbeach to Sutton (old station) on the 3rd July 1862, making a total of 15¾ miles. When opened, the Great Northern Company worked this line. The original company never reached beyond Sutton Bridge in the direction of Norwich, and it was left to others to complete the original scheme and twenty-nine years elapsed before the lines reached Norwich.

The Lynn & Sutton Bridge Railway was authorised on the 6th August 1861, opened for goods in November 1864 and for passengers on the 1st March 1866. It consisted of a line from Sutton Bridge to a junction with the Great Eastern Railway just south of Lynn Harbour Junction, 11 miles from Lynn station; the line was 9½ miles in length. The railway obtained powers to carry its line over the road swing bridge across the River Nene at Sutton Bridge. This bridge was built to the design of Robert Stephenson, and for over thirty years carried both the railway and road traffic. The old bridge was replaced in 1897 by a new bridge which was built further to the south. This fine structure was a steel girder bridge; the swing span, which was at the west end, was 176 feet long – the landward part of it being 76 feet, and the portion over the fairway a span of 100 feet; the remaining part to the east composed of two shorter fixed spans. Three main girders formed the swing span, which was arranged to carry the road traffic through the north side and a single line of railway through the south; it was operated hydraulically, there being a steam plant to supply the

necessary power. The bridge was designed and constructed under the direction of Mr McDonald, the chief engineer of the Midland Railway at that time. On the completion of the new bridge it was necessary to divert the approaches of the railway at either end and Sutton Bridge station was considerably altered.

On this line there was also the West Lynn (railway) Bridge over the Great Ouse River. It was built in 1866 by Waring & Eckersley and had five lattice girder spans – three central ones of 117 feet and two end ones of 70 feet each. It was always rather inadequate; the M&GN had to strengthen it and it was put forward as one of the reasons for closure.

The Spalding & Bourne Railway was authorised on the 29th July 1862, running from Bourne – on the Essendine to Sleaford branch of the Great Northern – to Spalding (South Junction), and using the Great Northern station at Spalding. The line was 9½ miles long and was opened in August 1866. The Lynn & Sutton Bridge and Spalding & Bourne railways were amalgamated, and the Norwich & Spalding leased, as of the 23rd July 1866, and became the Midland & Eastern Railway with a total mileage of 34 miles, all being worked by the Great Northern Company. On the 1st July 1877, the leased Norwich & Spalding line was amalgamated with the Midland & Eastern Railway.

In 1866 the Midland & Eastern tried to obtain powers to extend their system westwards from Bourne to join the Midland Railway near Saxby, but the project was opposed by the Great Northern Company as against their interests. As a compromise to the Midland Railway, which supported the Bill, running powers were given to them over the Great Northern line from Stamford to Bourne via Essendine, and it was agreed for the Midland & Eastern to be worked jointly. The two Companies guaranteed a minimum annual rental of £15,000 to the Midland & Eastern, and from this time onward the

Plate 2
Corton station was on the Norfolk & Suffolk Joint Line, one mile 34 chains north of Lowestoft North station. When this picture was taken the photographer was looking towards Great Yarmouth. Note the rather impressive station master's house to the right of the picture. Corton was opened for passenger traffic on the 13th July 1903 and closed on the 4th May 1970. Although not dated, it is believed this picture was taken shortly after the line was opened. R.J. Essery collection.

Plate 3
Two pictures of Cromer Beach station have been included here. This view was taken circa 1902 and is facing the 'stop blocks', to use a railway expression. There is an unidentified Beyer Peacock 4-4-0 in the platform with a train made up of GNR coaches, this is the only locomotive that can be seen. To the left are a number of sidings – but the only activity is a man with a horse-drawn wagon backed up to an open wagon, which is being loaded or unloaded. The bracket carrying the starting signals from the platform are the original Saxby & Farmer signals, installed when the line was opened. R.J. Essery collection.

BELOW: Plate 4
This photograph was taken in 1914 from the buffer stops and is looking towards Runton East Junction. There is no sign of any activity on this picture but it does provide a good view of the main platform with the locomotive run round. To the right there is a part view of M&GN cattle wagon No. 75 and what appears to be a train of GNR carriages. Note the lightweight flatbottom rail remaining on the siding where the cattle wagon is standing. Cromer Beach station was opened for passenger traffic by the Eastern & Midlands Railway on the 16th June 1887 and renamed Cromer on the 30th October 1969. R.J. Essery collection.

ABOVE: **Plate 5**
It was not uncommon for railway companies to open stations in what could be considered as being unlikely places. Usually they took the form of an unmanned halt with minimum facilities and they could be in the country for those who enjoyed walking, or close to a rifle range for marksmen, or to a holiday camp. Another source of traffic was golfers, and this is an example of an unmanned halt to cater for that class of traffic. Cromer Golf Links halt was opened on the 9th July 1923 and closed on the 7th April 1953. As can be seen it was a simple affair with no facilities other than two wooden seats. **R.J.** ESSERY COLLECTION.

Plate 6
Gedney was on the line between Spalding and Sutton Bridge, which included the long section, 8 mile 63 chains of single line, between Cunningham's Drove signal box and Sutton Bridge Dock Junction. There were, however, passing places at Moulton, Holbeach and Gedney. The station was opened on the 1st July 1862 and closed on the 2nd March 1959. This picture was taken circa 1910 and shows the station crossing with the small gate cabin clearly visible; the signal box was at the other end of the station until it was moved here in 1926. **R.J.** ESSERY COLLECTION.

Plate 7
Gorleston on Sea was between Yarmouth and Lowestoft on the Norfolk & Suffolk Joint Line. This station was opened on the 13th July 1903 and closed on the 4th May 1970. The goods station, not visible in this picture, was close to the passenger station and was able to handle a wide variety of traffic. Although undated, it is probable that this picture, which shows a M&GN train for Lowestoft, was taken in the 1920s. NEIL PARKHOUSE COLLECTION.

line became known as the Bourne & Lynn Joint Line. The Midland Railway running powers between Stamford and Bourne were only exercised once a year when a special Midland excursion from Lynn to Matlock and Buxton was run through. The Leicester cattle train from Lynn on Tuesdays was worked via Essendine, but by Great Northern engines from Bourne to Stamford.

The other independent line was the Peterborough, Wisbech & Sutton Railway, incorporated on the 28th July 1863 and opened on the 1st August 1866, from Peterborough (Wisbech Junction, Midland) – ¾ mile north of the Great Northern station – to Sutton Bridge Junction, a distance of 26 miles, where it joined the Norwich & Spalding Railway (then leased to the Midland & Eastern). The line crossed the Great Northern & Great Eastern Joint Line on the level at Murrow, and there was a branch at Wisbech to the riverside. The Peterborough, Wisbech & Sutton Railway was worked by the Midland Railway using Midland rolling stock, payment being 50 per cent of the gross receipts. The trains used the Great Eastern stations at both Peterborough and Lynn. This line, together with the Midland & Eastern (Bourne & Lynn Joint), formed the western section of the Eastern & Midlands Railway from 1st July 1883, but as mentioned previously the Eastern & Midlands company did not work them. None of these railways passed any locomotives to the M&GN, the system being worked by the motive power of the Midland or Great Northern Railways from inception.

The three railways forming the section east of Lynn were the Lynn & Fakenham, and the Yarmouth & North Norfolk with its affiliated line the Yarmouth Union Railway; the two former each having their own locomotives and rolling stock, but the latter being worked by the Yarmouth & North Norfolk Company. Prior to the establishment of these railways there was practically no direct cross-country communication between the important towns of Lynn, Fakenham, Aylsham, North Walsham and Yarmouth. The Lynn &

Fakenham Railway, authorised on the 13th July 1876, was built from a junction with the Great Eastern's Hunstanton line at Gaywood, 1¼ miles from Lynn (Great Eastern Railway) station. Opening first as far as Massingham (11¾ miles from Gaywood Junction) on the 16th August 1879, then to Fakenham (8¾ miles further) on the 6th August 1880, extended through Melton Constable to Guestwick (14¼ miles) on the 19th January 1882, and in the same year – the last of its separate existence – the line was completed to Norwich, opening from Guestwick to Lenwade (6¼ miles) on the 1st July, and from Lenwade to Norwich City (10½ miles) on the 2nd December 1882, when a special express from King's Cross was run through for the opening. The total distance from Gaywood Junction to Norwich was 51½ miles. The Great Eastern Railway terminus was used at Lynn. It had been intended to construct a line from Melton Constable to Cromer and Blakeney, but this project was dropped, although the Eastern & Midlands Railway made the line to Cromer some years later. Prior to being worked by the Lynn & Fakenham Railway proper, the earlier sections were worked by the contractors as opened.

The Great Yarmouth & Stalham Light Railway was authorised on the 27th June 1876, and its name changed to Yarmouth & North Norfolk Railway by Act of 27th May 1878. It was opened from Yarmouth Beach to Great Ormsby (5½ miles) on the 7th August 1877, to Hemsby (1¾ miles) on the 16th May 1878, to Martham (2¾ miles) on the 15th July 1878, to Catfield (5½ miles) on the 17th January 1880, to Stalham (2¼ miles) on the 3rd July 1880, and from Stalham to North Walsham (6¾ miles) on the 13th June 1881, a total mileage of 24½.

To this must be added the Yarmouth Union Railway, authorised on the 26th August 1880, 1¼ miles in length. Extending from the Yard Junction at Yarmouth Beach station to the North Quay on the River Yare, where it joined the Great Eastern Railway Quay Tramway near Vauxhall station, it opened on the 15th May 1882. At 2½ miles north

ABOVE: **Plate 8**
Hemsby station as seen circa 1900. Hemsby was on the line between Melton Constable and Yarmouth Beach, the final section being single line from Honing to the terminus at Yarmouth Beach. Although there were crossing loops at four stations, Hemsby was not one of them, nor was it ever a block post. The small signal box on the platform controlled only the siding points and their protecting signals. Later the box was removed and a new cabin was built adjacent to the station crossing. There was a goods siding with dock behind the platform and two sidings adjacent to the running line, to the left behind the photographer. Opened by the Great Yarmouth and Stalham Light Railway on the 16th May 1878, the station was closed on the 2nd March 1959. BERNARD MATTHEWS COLLECTION.

Plate 9
In this 1936 picture we can see that the station nameboard states Hillington for Sandringham, although the Great Eastern station at Wolferton on that company's Hunstanton and West Norfolk line was much closer to the royal residence. On the M&GN the double track line from South Lynn to Melton Constable ended at Grimston Road, then it was single line to Fakenham and the first passing loop, some 18 chains long, was at Hillington. Opened on the 16th August 1879 by the Lynn & Fakenham, the station was closed on the 2nd March 1959. The first signal box was at the west end of the station, but in 1927 the position was changed and it was placed by the station crossing as seen in the picture, which is facing Melton Constable. The small goods yard was to the right of the picture. BERNARD MATTHEWS COLLECTION.

of Martham, before reaching Potter Heigham, the railway crossed the river Thurne by a bridge of three spans of 79 feet; the main girders were of the through Pratt truss type, each divided into five equal bays.

After the formation of the Eastern & Midlands Railway by Act of the 18th August 1882, amalgamating all the lines on 1st January 1883, the connecting link between the Lynn & Fakenham Railway at Melton Constable and the Yarmouth & North Norfolk Railway at North Walsham (17 miles) was opened on the 5th April 1883, thus forming a continuous line of railway from Bourne and Peterborough on the west, to Norwich and Yarmouth on the east, except that all traffic had still to be worked over the Great Eastern Railway at Lynn and to use their station there; trains from the west coming on to the Great Eastern Ely–Lynn line near Lynn Harbour Junction, and the Hunstanton branch being used as far as Gaywood Junction in the easterly direction. At the Great Eastern terminus at Lynn a new platform bay and booking office had been added for the Lynn & Fakenham Railway traffic on the north side of the station.

The Eastern & Midlands Railway at first intended having their own terminus at Lynn in Austin Street, and land for the line was bought and fenced in, but the project was abandoned, although the general offices of the Railway occupied part of the site. Instead they constructed a through loop line between the east end of the bridge over the river Ouse at West Lynn, and Bawsey, 3 miles from Gaywood Junction, on the former Lynn & Fakenham line. This line, 4½ miles long, was authorised in 1884 and opened 1st January 1886, when the old section between Gaywood Junction and Bawsey (3 miles) was closed. At Bawsey sidings signal box a part of the old line remained as a siding for many years. The opening of the South Lynn–Bawsey direct line placed the eastern and western sections in direct communication and avoided the necessity of using the Great Eastern

system for through traffic. Running powers into Lynn (GE) were, however, retained and a shuttle service was provided by the E&MR (and later by the M&GN) between South Lynn M&GN station and King's Lynn Great Eastern to give connection for the principal trains of the two lines. When the new line was made, South Lynn station was erected, and the old West Lynn station, which was a single platform just west of the bridge over the Ouse, was therefore closed as from 1st July 1886 and removed.

The line from Melton Constable to Holt and Blakeney was authorised by the Lynn & Fakenham Railway Act of 12th August 1880, and a branch diverging from this line at Kelling to Cromer was authorised by the same company's Act of 11th August 1881. It was opened from Melton Constable West Junction to Holt (5 miles) on the 1st October 1884, and thence to Sheringham and Cromer Beach (10 miles) on the 16th June 1887, but the section between Kelling and Blakeney was never made. The section from Melton Constable to Cromer was constituted a separate undertaking by the Eastern & Midlands Railway Act of 28th April 1885. There was no station between Holt and Sheringham until 1901, when Weybourne station was opened.

During its ten years' existence as the Eastern & Midlands Railway, from 1st July 1883 to 1st July 1893, the company occupied a somewhat anomalous position, as although the owners worked the eastern section quite as an independent concern with its own locomotives and rolling stock, the western sections, that is, the old Peterborough, Wisbech & Sutton and the old Midland & Eastern (Bourne & Lynn Joint) lines, were worked for it respectively by the Midland and Great Northern companies. For a brief period, however, the Eastern & Midlands Railway worked their Cromer express trains to and from Peterborough during the summer months and from 1891, all year. In March 1888, the Eastern & Midlands company made an arrangement for the Midland to purchase its entire western section,

Plate 10
This exterior picture shows the Great Eastern station at King's Lynn, opened on the 28th August 1871 and known as Lynn until it was renamed on the 1st January 1911. The original E&M line from Bawsey Junction was closed following the opening of the line through South Lynn. The M&GN ran a passenger service between King's Lynn and South Lynn; as shown in the plan on page 173, the section from Harbour Junction to the station was over Great Eastern lines, the M&GN exercising running powers. R.J. ESSERY COLLECTION.

Plate 11
Massingham station was between South Lynn and Melton Constable. The double line section from South Lynn ceased at Grimston Road and it was single until Raynham Park; there were, however, three passing places, one being Massingham. The station was opened on the 16th August 1879 and was closed on the 3rd March 1959. This undated picture was taken looking west towards South Lynn. R.J. ESSERY COLLECTION.

to take effect from the 1st January 1889; in addition it had in the same year obtained the powers, which the Midland & Eastern had sought, for a direct line from Bourne to join the Midland's Leicester–Peterborough line at Saxby.

These facts comprised a serious menace to the interests of the Great Northern Railway, and soon after the passing of the Bourne and Saxby Railway Bill the Midland and the Eastern & Midlands authorities allowed the powers which the Great Northern already possessed as joint lessee of the Bourne & Lynn Joint to be converted into joint equal ownership. The agreement with the Midland Railway also provided that Parliamentary sanction should be sought for the joint ownership of the Bourne & Lynn Joint and also the Peterborough, Wisbech & Sutton Railways, and this was obtained by the Midland Company's Act of 24th June 1889. In 1893 the joint ownership was extended to include the whole of both sections of the Eastern & Midlands system under the title of the Midland and Great Northern Railways Joint Committee as from the 1st July of that year, from which time it worked all its own lines; although there were still certain Midland locomotive workings which will be referred to later.

After the formation of the joint railway the following sections were added to the system:

- Bourne to Little Bytham Junction (5 miles) opened for goods on the 15th May 1893 and for passengers on the 1st May 1894. In addition there was the Midland branch from Saxby to Little Bytham where it crossed the GN main line, to an end-on junction with the Joint line, which was opened on the 1st May 1894, giving a direct route from the greater part of the Midlands and the North;
- Welland Bank Junction to Cuckoo Junction (1¼ miles) opened on the 15th May 1893 (Spalding avoiding line);
- North Walsham to Antingham Road Junction (½ mile) opened on the 1st July 1898;
- Caister Road Junction to North Gorleston Junction (2¼ miles)

opened on the 13th July 1903. Caister Road Junction was the junction with the old Yarmouth Union Railway and this section had its gradients considerably modified in order to avoid crossing the Caister Road on the level;
- Runton East Junction to Newstead Lane Junction (½ mile) opened on the 3rd August 1906.

Further acts permitted the construction of the already mentioned Norfolk and Suffolk Joint Committee (M&GN and GER). These Norfolk and Suffolk Joint lines were as follows:
- Antingham Road Junction (North Walsham) to Mundesley (4¾ miles) opened 1st July 1898;
- North Gorleston Junction to Coke Ovens Junction (Lowestoft) (8¾ miles) opened 13th July 1903;
- Runton West Junction to Roughton Road Junction (Cromer) (2¼ miles) opened 23rd July 1906;
- Roughton Road Junction to Mundesley (6½ miles) opened 3rd August 1906.

This mileage was worked jointly with the Great Eastern Railway, although after 1923 the arrangements were slightly different.

The old Eastern & Midlands line, that is, the portion east of Lynn, had its own design of signal box, used lower quadrant signals of Saxby & Farmer design, and was laid with flat bottomed rails of the Vignoles pattern weighing 70 pounds per yard, spiked directly to the sleepers. Standard 85 pound bull-headed rails, with chairs, only replaced these after the line became M&GN Joint. Some parts of the main line were still composed of the flat-bottomed pattern until replacement in 1905, however this rail section remained in sidings for many years, and in the case of bufferstops, until closure. The years 1896–1901 also saw several sections of line being doubled.

The signals on the old Peterborough, Sutton Bridge and Lynn section were originally of Midland pattern, except where new ones had been provided; whilst east of Lynn, and between Bourne and Sutton Bridge, they were of the Great Northern 'somersault' pattern. Following the formation of the M&GN Joint line, all new signals,

ABOVE: Plate 12
This interior view of Melton Constable carriage & wagon shop, taken between 1932 and 1936 judging by the lettering style on carriage No. 61, underlines the fact that the Joint line was self supporting as far as repairs and maintenance of rolling stock was concerned. There were two roads in the carriage & wagon shop and two in the adjacent paint shop, whilst the fitting shop had three roads. W.A. CAMWELL.

Plate 13
Melton Constable was an important junction where, from the west, the lines from Lynn and Cromer converged and, from the east, the lines from Yarmouth and Norwich. It was built by the Lynn & Fakenham Railway and opened on the 19th January 1882. This view is from the west end of the station, where the photographer was overlooking the engine turntable that was installed in 1953. To the left is the island platform, while part of the engine shed can be seen to the right. The picture was taken in September 1958 when the 'Ivatt' Class '4MT' were the mainstay as far as steam locomotives were concerned during the final years of the line, three being visible in this picture. R.J. ESSERY COLLECTION.

Plate 14 (ABOVE) **& Plate 15** (BELOW)
Both of theses pictures were taken from a similar standpoint at Melton Constable when the photographer was facing west, but many years separate them. In Plate 14, photographed in 1936, the buildings to the left are the offices and stores, while the water tank dominates the centre of the picture where we can also see the works shunter, No. 16A. The presence of the stands or trestles suggests that work is taking place in the open. In Plate 15, photographed in 1959, we can see more of the station and the locomotive shed with two 'Ivatt' Class '4MT's in the yard. Also prominent in this picture is the coaling stage, while at the platform to the right is a two-coach DMU. V. FORSTER AND R.J. ESSERY COLLECTION.

wherever placed, were of the standard Great Northern pattern. Although some Great Northern and Midland signal boxes were installed in the first few years, particularly on the western section, Melton Constable designed its own standard M&GN signal box, which was used extensively. Other items such as level crossing gates, while having a familiar link with GN equipment, also had their own uniquely M&GN appearance.

The locomotive running sheds of the Midland and Great Northern Joint Railway were as follows:

- Eastern section: South Lynn, Melton Constable, Norwich, Cromer and Yarmouth (all owned by the Joint line), also Mundesley (Norfolk & Suffolk Joint);
- Western section: Peterborough (Midland shed), Bourne (jointly with Midland) and Spalding (jointly with GN until 1895).

In addition to the chief works at Melton Constable, there was a small repairing shop and shear-legs at South Lynn, and shear-legs and other facilities at Norwich. Details are given in Appendix D.

On the M&GN section from Caister Road Junction, Yarmouth, to North Gorleston Junction there was the most important engineering work of the whole system, that is, Breydon Viaduct – known locally with typical Norfolk understatement as 'Breydon Bridge'. This viaduct crossed the large sheet of tidal water called Breydon Water, where it commences to narrow before joining the river Bure above Yarmouth Bridge; the ebb and flow of the tide is considerable and there was a large amount of river traffic, mostly sailing craft. The viaduct was 800 feet long and consisted of four fixed spans and a double swing span on a central pier – three fixed spans were to the

north-east end and each was 168 feet long, then followed the swing span giving 60 feet clear waterway in each opening, and finally the remaining fixed span of 108 feet reached to the Suffolk side of the river. The power for operating the opening span was provided by a gas engine, supplemented by hydraulic adjusting gear, the whole being self-contained on the central pier and operated from a cabin above the centre of the span. The bridge was nominally designed by Mr A. Ross, then chief engineer of the Great Northern Railway, but all the calculations and drawings were done at Melton Constable. It was erected under the supervision of Mr Marriott. The viaduct was tested on the 8th July 1903, five days before the opening of the line, by running six heavy locomotives coupled together over it.

This more or less completed the system, but it is worth pointing out that modern King's Lynn was, as far as the station was concerned, known simply as Lynn until 1911, and we have used the appropriate term in an historical sense. As previously mentioned, due to a shortage of motive power the lines west of Lynn were until 1895 worked by both the Midland and Great Northern railways. After 1893, given the Midland Railway's responsibility for the locomotives, future construction was by and large to be to Midland designs but, as will be seen, this 'Derby influence' was not 100 per cent. Until 1937 the Joint line possessed its own workshops at Melton Constable where all the re-buildings and repairs were carried out, and this works, together with the Joint line partners, provided the 'motive power design input'.

The M&GN on its formation was a self-contained system with headquarters at Lynn, and the organisation is considered further at

Plate 16
Norwich City station was the terminus of the Lynn and Fakenham line from Melton Constable. Opened on the 2nd December 1882, the station was closed on the 2nd March 1959 for passengers, and to goods on the 31st October 1962. Considering the size of the station it is perhaps surprising to realise that it was at the end of a long section of single track some 21 miles 7 chains, with only two passing loops at Whitwell & Reepham and Drayton, although there were block posts at Guestwick and Lenwade. There were two inner bay lines, largely used for holding stock (note the open and covered carriage trucks), and two outside platform lines for passenger traffic, while goods traffic was dealt with at the City Goods station, a 27 chain branch from North signal box. To the left, although not visible in this 1914 picture, was the locomotive depot. R.J. ESSERY COLLECTION.

the beginning of Chapter 3. The locomotive headquarters and works were both situated at Melton Constable and for many years were in charge of William Marriott who, while nominally answerable to Derby, enjoyed much local autonomy. This had the consequence (as was also the case with the S&DJR) of giving the M&GN engines (even those built by the MR after 1893) their own characteristic forms that were never 'pure' Derby in outline. They also had their own livery too, which it will be easier to comprehend in detail (see Chapter 11) after considering the engines themselves.

Locomotives of MR or GNR ownership had always worked the lines west of Lynn, and this remained the case even after they were added to the E&MR in 1883. In consequence, when the M&GN was formed ten years later, the locomotive situation already had something of a dual personality. On the western section, MR and GNR lineaments prevailed, while the eastern section was 'home' to the miscellaneous assortment of engines which had been acquired over the years for the several different companies which went to form that part of the E&MR in 1883 and to which had been added a few more in the company's brief ten-year life. Our concern, of course, is primarily with the locomotive history of the Joint line itself from 1893 onwards, but, as will now be apparent, the story started much earlier and in fact dates from the Midland's first direct involvement in 1866 when, together with the GNR, it formed a joint committee with an interest in the lines 'west of Lynn'.

At the grouping in 1922, the M&GN formed part of a through route from many of the East Coast resorts and fishing ports of Norfolk to the Midlands and North – and to a lesser extent to London. It consisted of 194 miles of first track, 79 miles 57 chains of second track, 2 miles 50 chains of third track and 66 chains of fourth track. The length of the sidings reduced to single track came to 61 miles

5 chains, the total being expressed as 388 miles 65 chains of single track (source *Railway Returns 1922*). In addition, the same source describes two sections of the Norfolk & Suffolk Joint Railways (between Gorleston North Jct and Lowestoft, and between Runton East Junction and Antingham Road Junction via Mundesley-on-Sea) as 22 miles 22 chains of first track, 10 miles 64 chains of second track, 19 chains of third track and 8 chains of fourth track. When reduced to single track the total was 33 miles 33 chains. In addition there were 5 miles 12 chains of sidings. Prior to the grouping there were various running powers over the GNR and GER at some of the more important centres like Peterborough, Spalding, King's Lynn and Lowestoft.

The first major change came in 1923 when the Midland Railway became part of the LM&SR and the Great Northern Railway was to go into the 'East Coast' group to be known as the L&NER. Life on the Joint railway continued much as before, but on the 1st October 1936 the L&NER took over the operation of the Joint lines and in 1948 the system became part of British Railways (Eastern Region). Eleven years later in 1959 the end came. The last trains ran on Saturday the 28th February and on the 2nd March most of the M&GN was closed, in all some 161½ miles of track was no longer served by passenger trains with some 79½ miles being closed entirely.

Before concluding this general outline of the M&GN, the predominantly single-track nature of the whole system should be re-emphasised. The single line sections were controlled by Tyer's electric tablet system, and between 1906 and 1908 the 'Whitaker' tablet exchanging apparatus was installed on the engines and at the stations, by means of which tablet changing was greatly improved – it then being possible to carry out this operation at speeds up to forty miles per hour without risk to either enginemen or signalmen, and

Plate 17
Potter Heigham Bridge halt was opened on the 17th July 1933 to cater for the holiday traffic that was generated following the opening of Caister holiday camp. Following the outbreak of the Second World War it was closed in September 1939, reopened in June 1948 before finally closing on the 2nd March 1959. R.J. Essery COLLECTION.

J&S 682Y RAYNHAM PARK STATION.

Plate 18
Raynham Park station was on the line from South Lynn to Melton Constable and marked the end of the single line section from Grimston Road and the start of the double line section to Melton Constable. Opened on the 16th August 1880 by the Lynn & Fakenham Railway, this picture is facing west, the up direction, towards South Lynn. To the left of the picture behind the fence is the goods siding with loading dock, while beyond is the station crossing and signal box. Five chains further west there is the junction where, for up trains, the double line becomes single. R.J. ESSERY COLLECTION.

Plate 19
This picture shows the first station at South Lynn. Opened on the 1st January 1886, it was of wooden construction with a platform-mounted Midland signal box as shown in this picture (taken before the new station opened in 1901 on the other side of the road bridge), which was itself demolished and replaced. BERNARD MATTHEWS COLLECTION.

Plate 20
This shows the second South Lynn station, and when the picture was taken the photographer was facing west, or in the up direction, towards Peterborough. Just visible on the left of the picture is the wall of the engine shed while behind and to the left of the photographer are the locomotive shed yard and East Yard sidings. The down line to Melton Constable and King's Lynn is to the right of the platform. R.J. ESSERY COLLECTION.

Plate 21
This picture of South Lynn was taken in 1950, looking west from the bridge. The mainline platform still has the wartime painted edging, while the small platform was used for local traffic. Note the colour light signals installed in 1931, which seem rather out of place on the Joint line! R.J. ESSERY COLLECTION.

this is no doubt partly the reason that the Midland & Great Northern Joint made some of the smartest long-distance single line running in the country. The various single and double line sections, as well as the principal features concerned with the locomotive workings, are given in Plate 22. The Whitaker tablet catching apparatus had been specifically developed by Mr Alfred Whitaker for the Somerset and Dorset Joint Railway – yet another point of similarity between the two systems. There was a second Midland influence in that Mr Whitaker, prior to joining the S&DJR, had been a lifelong MR employee. Brief details of the Whitaker system appear in Appendix B.

The following tables summarise the single line and tablet sections accompanied by opening and closings dates together with details of the station accommodation. Information is taken from the 1938 edition of the Railway Clearing House *Official Hand Book of Stations etc.* and R.V.J. Butt, *The Directory of Railway Stations*, both with additions and amendments as necessary. In this work the author quotes only the dates that stations were opened or closed for passenger services. Dates for closure to goods traffic are noted below each section. Private sidings show the actual location of the private sidings either within station limits or close to the passenger/ goods stations noted in the Railway Clearing House tables.

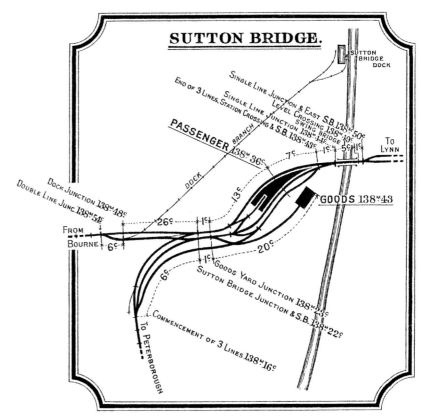

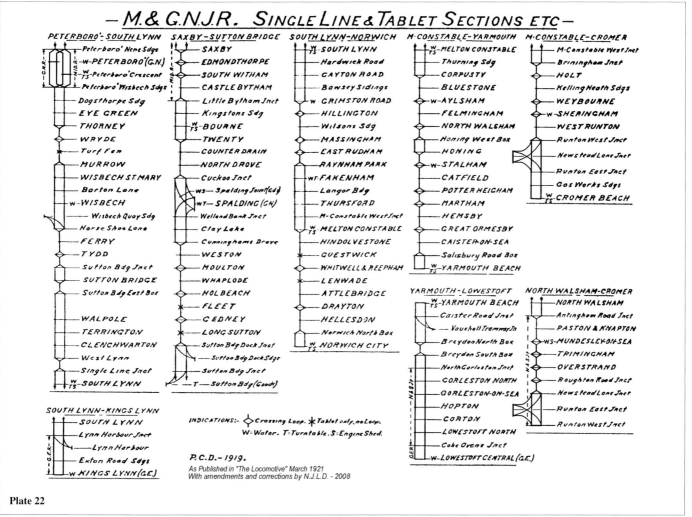

Plate 22

ABOVE: Plate 23
Sutton Bridge was a fascinating place; the junction of the lines from Bourne, Peterborough and South Lynn, with a passenger station, goods station, dock branch and swing bridge over the Nene Outlet. This picture was taken from the bridge looking towards Bourne and shows the island platform with the station, while to the left there was a brick-built goods shed together with a locomotive turntable. Although the Midland Railway supplied the signals and signal boxes between Peterborough and Lynn it is worth pointing out that the signals on the M&GN differed from those on the parent system at this time in not displaying a white circle on the front and a black circle on the spectacle arms. Instead they employed a white strip from at least 1897, about 13 years before this was adopted by the Midland on its own lines. R.J. ESSERY COLLECTION.

Plate 24
A view of the island platform at Sutton Bridge. Although not visible in the picture, there was a short bay at the Bourne end of the station. Note the tight curve of the platform line, which required a continuous checkrail, and the station name board with the various routes served by trains from the station. R.J. ESSERY COLLECTION.

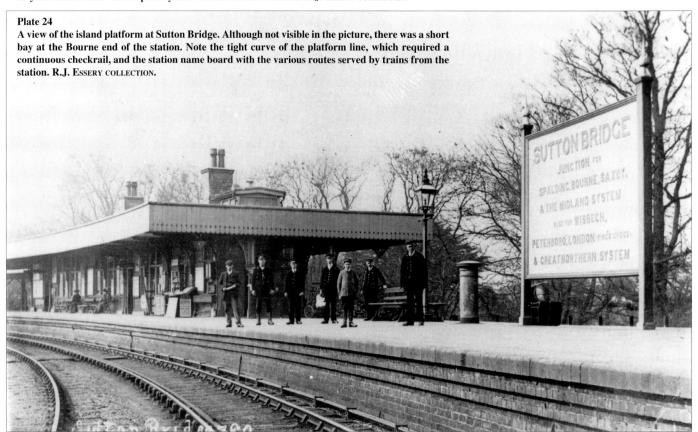

Plate 25

This picture of circa 1910 shows the eastern approach to Sutton Bridge with Cross Keys swing bridge dominating the scene. Note the checkrail for the running line is an extension of the point crossing, and you can see the rear of the Midland signal arms referred to in Plate 23. Apart from the variation of painting the signal arms, all M&GN signal posts were painted white with black bases, regardless of Midland or GNR origin. R.J. ESSERY COLLECTION.

PETERBOROUGH TO SOUTH LYNN

STATION	OPENED	CLOSED TO PASSENGERS	PRIVATE SIDINGS	STATION ACCOMMODATION	CRANE POWER (TONS.CWT)
Peterborough Great Northern station	7/8/1850	(M&GN Running powers from Wisbech Junction)			
Eye Green (for Crowland)	1/8/1866	2/12/1957	2 sidings (1)	G P F L H C	1. 0
Thorney	1/8/1866	2/12/1957		G P F L H C	1.10
Wryde	1/8/1866	2/12/1957		G P F L H C	
Murrow	1/8/1866	2/3/1959		G P L H	
Wisbech St Mary	1/8/1866	2/3/1959		G P L H	
Wisbech Renamed Wisbech North 27/9/1948	1/8/1866	2/3/1959		G P F L H C	7. 0
Ferry	1/8/1866	2/3/1959		G P	
Tydd	1/8/1866	2/3/1959		P+	
Sutton Bridge	3/7/1862	2/3/1959		G P F L H C	5. 0
Walpole	1/3/1866	2/3/1959		G P F L H C	
Terrington	1/3/1866	2/3/1959		G P F L H C	1.10
Clenchwarton	1/3/1866	2/3/1959		G P F L H C	
South Lynn	1/1/1886	2/3/1959	3 sidings (2)	G P F L H C	5. 0

(1) Dogsthorpe Star Brick Co. Ltd siding. Northam Brick Co. siding.
(2) British Sugar Corp. Ltd siding. Unbreakable Pulley & Mill Gearing Co. (Cooper Roller Bearing Co.) siding. West Norfolk Farmer's Manure & Chemical Co-Operative Co. Ltd siding.
NOTE: The section between Murrow and Wisbech remained open for Goods, closed 31st October 1965. The section between Murrow and Dogsthorpe (near Peterborough) remained open for Goods, closed 18th April 1966. See page 39 for key to station accommodation.

Plate 26
Sheringham was on the line between Melton Constable and Cromer. The station was opened by the Eastern & Midlands Railway on the 16th June 1887 as Sherringham, but was renamed Sheringham in 1897. It was closed by British Rail on the 2nd January 1967 and replaced by a new station on the opposite side of the station crossing. This undated picture was taken when the photographer was facing west. The siding where he was standing leads to a loading dock and the trap points are behind him. R.J. ESSERY COLLECTION.

ABOVE: Plate 27
West Runton was on the line from Melton Constable to Cromer and the station was opened for passenger traffic by the Eastern & Midlands Railway in September 1887. The line was single track and the station was not a block post. Whilst showing the very rural nature of the area, this undated, but probably circa 1920, picture provides a clue to the traffic dealt with at the station. The family waiting for a train have a considerable amount of luggage and have probably been on holiday at the nearby West Runton Links Hotel. R.J. ESSERY COLLECTION.

BELOW: Plate 28
West Runton was less than one mile from the beach and no doubt the Links Hotel attracted a large number of visitors during the year, most travelling by train. This picture shows the station buildings which include a grounded van body. Note the limited number of oil lamps for lighting the platform. R.J. ESSERY COLLECTION.

ABOVE: **Plate 29**
Walpole was opened on the 1st March 1866 by the Lynn & Sutton Bridge Railway and closed on the 2nd March 1959. The line between Sutton Bridge East signal box and West Lynn signal box was double track, and the signal box, of Midland design, was at the west end of the station. Note the Midland design Down home and Up starting signals in this undated but probably pre-First World War picture. BERNARD MATTHEWS COLLECTION.

Plate 30
South Witham was 6 miles 13 chains from the end-on junction of the Midland Railway with the M&GN at Little Bytham. The station was opened on the 1st May 1894 and closed on the 2nd March 1959. As we can see the passenger facilities were limited and the platforms were of wooden construction, but there was a reasonable goods yard and a quite large goods shed. The Midland Railway's Saxby & Bourne line provided the western outlet for Midland traffic to and from the Joint line. R.J. ESSERY COLLECTION.

NOTICE

THE TURNTABLE MUST ALWAYS
BE KEPT IN THIS POSITION

NO ENGINE TO TURN WHEN
A TRAIN IS RUNNING BY
OR STANDING AT PLATFORM
BY ORDER

Plate 31

This is a very atmospheric view of Melton Constable, taken from inside the turntable pit. The date is probably 1894 and it was taken by the Midland Railway photographer. The view is looking north from the loco area to the island platform, revealing the boarded ceiling of the platform canopy and the Central Norfolk Railway spandrels. The flat bottom rail is in evidence, replaced here by bullhead in 1896. The attractive platform seats supplied by the contractor can be seen. The First Class Waiting Room on the right had only been recently built circa 1886 in the 'arts and crafts' style adopted by the Melton drawing office at that time. As stated on the notice, the turntable was meant to be kept in the one position because there was a siding, reached only by shunting across it, where the all breakdown vehicles other than the crane, were kept. R.J. ESSERY COLLECTION.

Plate 32
This picture shows part of the interior of South Lynn station with a Midland Railway 2-4-0 at the head of an Up express passenger train. It was taken sometime between January 1903, when the locomotive headlamp codes were changed and the lamp holder positions were altered, and December 1907, when No. 69A was renumbered and became No. 107. P.C. DEWHURST.

SAXBY TO SUTTON BRIDGE

Saxby to Little Bytham Junction, near Bourne: (M&GN running powers over the Midland Railway)
Bourne L&NER: (M&GN running powers between Bourne East and West Junctions; see map on page 167 for extent)

STATION	OPENED	CLOSED TO PASSENGERS	PRIVATE SIDINGS	STATION ACCOMMODATION	CRANE POWER (TONS.CWT)
Bourne L&NER	16/5/1860	2/3/1959			
Twenty	1/8/1866	2/3/1959		G P L	1. 5
Counter Drain	1/8/1866	2/3/1959		G P L	1. 5
North Drove	1/8/1866	2/3/1959		G P L	1. 5
Spalding GN	17/10/1848	(M&GN running powers over L&NER lines south of the station)			
Weston	15/11/1858	2/3/1959		P	
Moulton	15/11/1858	2/3/1959		G P F L H C	1. 5
Whaplode	15/11/1858	2/3/1959		P	
Holbeach	15/11/1858	2/3/1959		G P F L H C	1.10
Fleet	3/7/1862	2/3/1959		G P L	
Gedney	3/7/1862	2/3/1959		G P F L H C	
Long Sutton	3/7/1862	2/3/1959		G P F L H C	2. 0
Sutton Bridge	3/7/1862	2/3/1959		G P F L H C	5. 0

NOTE: Spalding to Bourne section remained open for Goods, closed 5th April 1965. Spalding to Sutton Bridge section remained open for Goods, closed 1st May 1965.

SOUTH LYNN TO NORWICH

STATION	OPENED	CLOSED TO PASSENGERS	PRIVATE SIDINGS	STATION ACCOMMODATION	CRANE POWER (TONS.CWT)
South Lynn	1/1/1886	2/3/1959	3 sidings (2)	G P F L H C	5. 0
Hardwick Road	1/1/1886	2/3/1959		G L	
Gayton Road	1/1/1886	2/3/1959		G P L	
Grimston Road	16/8/1879	2/3/1959		G P L H	
Hillington (for Sandringham)	16/8/1879	2/3/1959		G P F L H C	
Massingham	16/8/1879	2/3/1959		G P F L H C	
East Rudham	6/8/1880	2/3/1959		G P F L H C	1. 0
Raynham Park	6/8/1880	2/3/1959		G P	
Fakenham Town	6/8/1880	2/3/1959		G P F L H C	3. 0
Langor Bridge	1/7/1898	2/3/1959	(3)	G	
Thursford	1/1/1882	2/3/1959		G P F L H C	
Melton Constable	19/1/1882	6/4/1964		G P F L H C	1. 0
Hindolvestone	19/1/1882	2/3/1959		G P	
Guestwick	19/1/1882	2/3/1959		G P L H C	
Whitwell & Reepham	1/7/1882	2/3/1959		G P F L H C	
Lenwade	1/7/1882	2/3/1959		G P F L H C	
Attlebridge	2/12/1882	2/3/1959		G P F L H C	
Drayton for Costessey	2/12/1882	2/3/1959		G P F L H C	
Hellesdon	2/12/1882	15/9/1952		G P F L	1. 0
Norwich City	2/12/1882	2/3/1959	4 sidings (4)	G P F L H C	10. 0

(2) British Sugar Corp. Ltd siding. Unbreakable Pulley & Mill Gearing Co. (Cooper Roller Bearing Co.) siding. West Norfolk Farmer's Manure & Chemical Co-Operative Co. Ltd siding.
(3) Langor Bridge Siding. Although noted in the 1938 Handbook as private, this was in fact a public siding.
(4) British Gas Light Co. siding. Barker Street Depot. Westwick Depot. Cushion Bros siding.
NOTE: South Lynn to East Rudham section remained open for Goods, closed 6th May 1968.

SOUTH LYNN TO KING'S LYNN

King's Lynn (GER) (M&GN running powers from King's Lynn Junction; see map on page 173 for extent of M&GN route)

MELTON CONSTABLE TO YARMOUTH

STATION	OPENED	CLOSED TO PASSENGERS	PRIVATE SIDINGS	STATION ACCOMMODATION						CRANE POWER (TONS.CWT)
Melton Constable	19/1/1882	6/4/1964		G	P	F	L	H	C	1. 0
Corpusty & Saxthorpe	5/4/1883	2/3/1959		G	P	F	L	H	C	
Bluestone (for Cawston)	5/4/1883	1/3/1916		G	P		L			
Aylsham Town Renamed Aysham North 27/9/1948	5/4/1883	2/3/1959		G	P	F	L	H	C	1. 0
Felmingham	5/4/1883	2/3/1959		G	P		L			
North Walsham Town	13/6/1881	2/3/1959		G	P	F	L	H	C	
Honing (for Worstead)	August 1882	2/3/1959		G	P	F	L	H	C	
Stalham (for Happisburgh & Palling on Sea)	3/7/1880	2/3/1959		G	P	F	L	H	C	
Sutton Staithe Halt	17/7/1933	1933			P+					
Catfield	17/1/1880	2/3/1959		G	P		L			
Potter Heigham & Ludham	17/1/1880	2/3/1959		G	P		L	H		
Potter Heigham Bridge Halt	17/7/1933	2/3/1959			P+					
Martham Renamed Martham for Rollesby 1/11/1887	15/7/1878	2/3/1959		G	P	F	L	H	C	
Hemsby	15/5/1878	2/3/1959		G	P	F	L	H	C	
Little Ormesby Halt	17/7/1933	1933			P+					
Great Ormesby	7/8/1877	2/3/1959		G	P		L	H	C	
Scratby Halt	17/7/1933	2/3/1959			P+					
California Halt	17/7/1933	2/3/1959			P+					
Caister Camp Halt	17/7/1933	2/3/1959			P+					
Caister Renamed Caister on Sea 1/1/1893	7/8/1877	2/3/1959		G	P					
Newtown Halt	17/7/1933	2/3/1959			P+					
Yarmouth Beach	7/8/1877	2/3/1959	5 sidings (5)	G	P	F	L	H	C	5. 0

(5) Co-operative Society siding. Fish Market. Lacon & Co. siding.
Quayside & Wharf sidings. J.S. Sterry siding.
Note that the summer-only halts on this section were closed for the
duration of the 1939–45 war, reopened 1946.

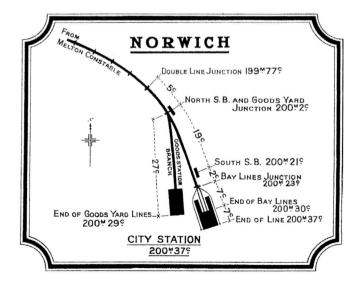

NORWICH

FROM MELTON CONSTABLE

DOUBLE LINE JUNCTION 199ᴹ77ᶜ

5ᶜ

NORTH S.B. AND GOODS YARD JUNCTION 200ᴹ2ᶜ

19ᶜ

SOUTH S.B. 200ᴹ21ᶜ

GOODS STATION BRANCH

27ᶜ

BAY LINES JUNCTION 200ᴹ23ᶜ

2ᶜ

END OF BAY LINES 200ᴹ30ᶜ

END OF GOODS YARD LINES 200ᴹ29ᶜ

END OF LINE 200ᴹ37ᶜ

CITY STATION 200ᴹ37ᶜ

Plate 33
Following the formation of the M&GN Joint Railway on the 1st July 1893, the Midland Railway Photographer was sent to take photographs of various subjects. The negatives of the items that were photographed are numbered in the 85xx series but they are not recorded in the register held at the NRM. The register was rewritten and so the negative numbers are not always in ascending date order, which makes it difficult to be precise about certain pictures, although it has been suggested that this picture was taken on the 5th October 1894. The photograph shows an ex-E&MR ventilated covered goods wagon that is dual piped for Westinghouse and automatic vacuum brakes. This arrangement allowed it to run over the entire British railway system in trains that were fitted with automatic brakes. This vehicle carries the first lettering style adopted by the M&GN. Points of interest are the safety chains, grease axleboxes and single side brake with the brake lever on one side only. Many years were to pass before all goods rolling stock had a brake lever on each side of the vehicle with the lever to the right of the man when he was facing the vehicle. R.J. ESSERY COLLECTION.

ABOVE: Plate 34
This picture was taken at Melton Constable on the 28th May 1937 and shows a number of low sided wagons in use as service stock with ballast brakes 13 and 103. H.C. CASSERLEY.

BELOW: Plate 35
Reference to the Derby Photograph Register shows that three pictures were taken 21st June 1920 showing a traction engine loaded on 10 ton machinery wagon No. 164. The Diagram book notes that four of these wagons were in stock in 1919; in 1928 they were divided between the LM&S and L&NER, two going to each company. This example is fitted with grease axleboxes and retains the original arrangement of a hand brake lever on one side of the wagon. R.J. ESSERY COLLECTION.

YARMOUTH TO LOWESTOFT

STATION	OPENED	CLOSED TO PASSENGERS	PRIVATE SIDINGS	STATION ACCOMMODATION	CRANE POWER (TONS.CWT)
Yarmouth Beach	7/8/1877	2/3/1959	5 sidings (5)	G P F L H C	5. 0
Gorleston North	13/7/1903	5/10/1942		G P	
Gorleston on Sea	13/7/1903	2/5/1970		G P F L H C	
Hopton Renamed Hopton on Sea 8/7/32	13/7/1903	2/5/1970		G P	
Corton	13/7/1903	2/5/1970		G P F L H C	
Lowestoft North	13/7/1903	2/5/1970		G P F L H C	
Lowestoft Central G E R	1/7/1847	(M&GN running powers from Coke Ovens Junction)			

(5) Co-operative Society siding. Fish Market. Lacon & Co. siding. Quayside & Wharf sidings. J.S. Sterry siding.

MELTON CONSTABLE TO CROMER

STATION	OPENED	CLOSED TO PASSENGERS	PRIVATE SIDINGS	STATION ACCOMMODATION	CRANE POWER (TONS.CWT)
Holt	1/10/1884	6/4/1964		G P F L H C	
Weybourne	1/7/1901	6/4/1964		G P F L H C	
Sheringham Sherringham until 1897	16/6/1887	2/1/1967 Replaced by new station		G P F L H C	
West Runton	9/1887			P	
Cromer Beach Renamed Cromer 30/10/69	16/6/1887		2 sidings (6)	G P F L H C	

(6) Cromer Gasworks siding, Cromer UDC siding

NORTH WALSHAM TO CROMER

STATION	OPENED	CLOSED TO PASSENGERS	PRIVATE SIDINGS	STATION ACCOMMODATION	CRANE POWER (TONS.CWT)
North Walsham Town	13/6/1881	2/3/1959		G P F L H C	
Paston & Knapton	1/7/1898	5/10/1964		G P L	
Mundesley on Sea	1/7/1898	5/19/1964		G P F L H C	
Trimingham	3/8/1906	7/4/1953		G P F L	
Sidestrand Halt	25/5/1936	7/4/1953		P+	
Overstrand	3/8/1906	7/4/1953		G P F L	
Cromer Links Halt	16/7/1923	7/4/1953		P+	

KEY TO STATION ACCOMMODATION

G   Goods Station
P   Passenger and Parcels Station
P+ Passenger, but not Parcels or Miscellaneous Traffic
F   Furniture Vans, Carriages, Motor Cars, Portable Engines and Machines on Wheels
L   Live Stock
H   Horse Boxes and Prize Cattle Vans.
C   Carriages and Motor Cars by Passenger Train
Crane Power. This is the maximum fixed crane power at each station.
Coal. Coal Class traffic (Coal, Coke and Patent Fuel) can be dealt with at most Goods Stations and in many instances Coal Sidings are provided adjacent to Passenger Stations.

ABOVE: **Plate 36**
Open goods wagon No. 674 is similar to No. 107 shown in Plate 38. The photograph shows the style of lettering adopted by the Joint line from circa 1900 and the position of the wagon numberplate, which was between the arms of the 'V' hanger. After 1917, M&GN common user goods stock was painted dark grey. J.P. RICHARDS.

Plate 37
This picture of M&GN Horse Box No. 231 was taken when it was standing on one of the short bay lines at Norwich on the 29th August 1929. The vehicle is straight sided with a compartment for the groom or person accompanying the horse. H.F. WHEELER COLLECTION.

Plate 38
This is a typical British railways late nineteenth century open goods wagon, probably 9 feet wheelbase and 15 feet 6 inches over the headstocks with an 8 ton carrying capacity. It is similar but not identical to the open goods wagon No. 674 shown in Plate 36. The painting date 30/3/93 tells us when it was repainted and the fact that it was one of the subjects taken by the Midland Railway Photographer suggests it was either late 1893 or 1894. It is important in so far as it shows the Eastern & Midlands Railway painting style at the time of the formation of the M&GN, when goods vehicles were painted in brown oxide livery. R.J. ESSERY COLLECTION.

Plate 39
M&GN Cattle wagon No. 366 is an example of a long cattle wagon. During the nineteenth century, cattle wagons were long, medium or short and the farmer paid a rate dependent upon the size of wagon; but later a partition was provided so that the size of the wagon and the rate paid could be varied, meaning that only one size of wagon was required. This example is an 8 ton, 18 feet 8 inches long vehicle fitted with a vacuum through pipe which meant it could be worked in passenger trains. This is the form of cattle wagon shown in the 1919 Diagrams, being rebuilds of the original wagons carried out from 1910 onwards.
R.S. CARPENTER COLLECTION.

BELOW: Plate 40
This photograph provides a close up of an M&GN axlebox. Above the B, the letters E&MR are on the face of the axlebox and they are repeated on the lid, which could be lifted to allow the grease to be placed in the box. This was done by a wagon greaser who carried the grease in a large bucket and used a wooden spatula to transfer the grease from the bucket to the box. This particular axlebox was fitted to mess and tool van No. 100. G.Y. HEMINGWAY.

ABOVE: **Plate 41**
This goods brake van was built in 1899 and rebuilt in 1919. It was withdrawn in 1947 and is now preserved. Note the fixed side light; by using a red shade the guard could change the colour from white to red. White was the colour that the enginemen would see from the locomotive while red would be visible to the rear of the train. The location is not known, but the date of the picture is probably mid 1930s. G.Y. HEMINGWAY.

BELOW: **Plate 42**
This example of a two-plank dropside wagon was photographed at South Lynn in 1936 and shows a rather interesting and untypical wagon. The curved ends and tarpaulin bar appear to be original. It was built as goods stock in 1881 but it is not known how many more, if any, of this type there were. No. 116 was obviously transferred from revenue stock to internal use at some point, and as such carried the 'RAILWAY SERVICE VEHICLE' plate on its lower rail. It was painted red oxide and traces of two previous lettering styles can be seen showing through. The diagrams denote No. 116 as a 'covered packing wagon', the packing (bits of wood) being used to re-rail stock that had come off the road. G.Y. HEMINGWAY.

Plate 43
This ex-L&NWR Third Class carriage was photographed at South Lynn on the 15th April 1947, having been transferred in 1938. It is still carrying M&GN identity, but the stock number is 81041 in the M&GN series devised by the L&NER after 1936. H.C. CASSERLEY.

BELOW: **Plate 44**
This picture shows an ex-Midland Railway Third Class semi-saloon corridor coach, built in 1911 and transferred to the M&GN in 1936. The original Midland Railway number was 59, later becoming LM&SR No. 3082 and then M&GN No. 68. Later still it became No. 81014, as seen here at Melton Constable on the 14th April 1947. It was later renumbered E60107E by British Railways and was scrapped in 1958. H.C. CASSERLEY.

Plate 45
This picture of an ex-L&NWR corridor composite was taken at South Lynn on the 27th May 1937 and shows a carriage that had been transferred from LM&S to M&GN stock. The coach is painted in LM&S Period One livery, although one cannot be sure that the ends are red, and has been renumbered as M&GN 10. H.C. CASSERLEY.

Plate 46
Ex-Midland Railway Third Class corridor carriage photographed at South Lynn on the 27th May 1937 after it had been renumbered as M&GNR No. 99. H.C. CASSERLEY.

Plate 47
This is another picture taken by the Midland Railway Photographer in 1894. This four-wheel five-compartment composite coach No. 15 was built for the L&FR and originally had a clerestory roof. During its ownership by the Eastern & Midland Railway it had the clerestory removed and Mansell wheels fitted to replace the original open-spoke iron wheels. It has oil lamps and one third class compartment is designated for smoking while another is a ladies compartment. The carriage carries the first style of lettering. Although it has been fitted with the vacuum brake by the M&GN, when built it was an unbraked vehicle. R.J. ESSERY COLLECTION.

ABOVE: **Plate 48**
The chapter concludes with some locomotive depot views, beginning with this of Melton Constable which was taken circa 1938 and includes three M&GN 4-4-0 passenger engines. From left to right they are No's 055, L&NER 373, 054 and 038. R.S. CARPENTER COLLECTION.

Plate 49
This picture of No. 43 at Yarmouth Beach was taken circa 1935 and shows a locomotive in steam but the enginemen are not on the footplate. There was nothing unusual about this, the men were probably in 'the cabin', a term often used to describe their mess room or similar place where they had their meal break between duties. Presumably the locomotive has been prepared for its next turn, as there is plenty of coal on the tender. Note the Yarmouth Beach turntable – originally it was 45 feet in length but in 1931 it was replaced by a 60-foot table. ALAN WELLS COLLECTION.

THE M&GN IN 1922

It is appropriate to include some statistics, extracted from the Railway Returns for the year ending 31st December 1922, to show the nature of the M&GN at the time of the Great Amalgamation, which today we call the Grouping.

LOCOMOTIVE STOCK:	
Tender engines	83
Tank engines	14
Total	97
Employed exclusively in departmental services	1

ROLLING STOCK:	
Carriages of uniform class (third class)	131
Composite	42
Other coaching vehicles, luggage/parcels and brake vans	32
Carriage trucks	6
Horse boxes	8
Total	219

FREIGHT TRAFFIC AND SERVICE VEHICLES:	
Merchandise wagons open	151
Covered	51
Cattle trucks	136
Rail & timber trucks	22
Total wagon stock	359
Goods brake vans	29
Railway service vehicles	160
Grand total	548

ROLLING STOCK AND HORSES:	
Horse wagons and carts	91
Miscellaneous	10
Horses, for shunting	7
for road vehicles	41

LAND AND PROPERTY, NOT FORMING PART OF RAILWAY OR STATIONS:	
Land (acres)	159
Houses	140

PASSENGER TRAFFIC:	
Passengers carried, first class	15,125
third class	1,396,169
Season ticket holders, first class	129
third class	801
Number originating on the company's system, first class	9,933
third class	1,151,977
Season ticket holders, first class	18
third class	496

GOODS AND MINERALS CARRIED (TONS):	
General merchandise	573,296
Coal, coke and patent fuel	490,457
Other minerals	217,933
Total	1,281,696

NUMBER OF LIVESTOCK CARRIED:	
Total livestock	212,754
Of this, total originated on the system	158,372
Comprised of, horses	347
cattle	32,612
calves	2,607
sheep	57,663
pigs	64,907
miscellaneous	236

AVERAGE WAGON AND TRAIN LOAD (TONS):	
General merchandise inc. livestock	2.97
Coal, coke and patent fuel	8.40
Other minerals	8.14
Average train load	101.42

AVERAGE LENGTH OF HAUL (MILES):	
General merchandise inc. livestock	37.39
Coal, coke and patent fuel	62.09
Other minerals	33.53

Plate 50
The M&GN enjoyed running powers into the GNR station at Spalding, but the Committee maintained independent, if limited, locomotive facilities, including a small timber hand coaling stage. This picture, taken on the 22nd October 1936, shows a number of Joint line engines, No's 36, 74, 76, 77 and 90, at the M&GN shed. R.J. ESSERY COLLECTION.

CHAPTER 3

TRAFFIC AND TRAIN WORKING

In the previous chapter it was explained that the Midland & Great Northern Joint Railway was a separate self-contained system, supervised by a directorate drawn from each of the joint owning companies. Each main line company formulated its traffic requirements, and the manager of the Joint line, whose headquarters was at King's Lynn, together with a committee of officers from the parent companies, met regularly to arrange details for working the line to the best advantage as a separate undertaking. The Midland Railway officers directed the Locomotive Department, while the Great Northern oversaw the Engineering Department, including permanent way and signals. Mr William Marriott, M.I.C.E., M.I.M.E., had been the resident engineer and locomotive superintendent for many years, with his offices at the works at Melton Constable and, from the 1st January 1919, he became the traffic manager but still retained the immediate control of his old departments. In fact, the parent companies' officers interfered very little with the running of the railway, merely reporting to the Committee what had been done (mostly by Mr Marriott) in their name.

DESCRIPTION OF THE LINE

As we have seen, the Joint system was a combination of several independent railways which were almost entirely local in character and traffic. But in addition to the main lines there were also dock sidings at Wisbech, Sutton Bridge and Yarmouth. Additionally, we must not overlook the Norfolk & Suffolk Joint Railway, originally worked in partnership with the Great Eastern, later the London & North Eastern Railway Company, which added further mileage and traffic to the system. Finally, there were certain running powers over the old Great Northern at Peterborough and Spalding, also over the old Great Eastern lines into King's Lynn station, the Lynn Harbour Branch, and from Coke Ovens Junction (Lowestoft) into Lowestoft Central station, together with certain workings over the 13 miles of Midland line from Little Bytham Junction to Saxby. Except for such towns as Wisbech, Lynn, Norwich, Cromer and Yarmouth, the whole area covered was somewhat sparsely populated, many of the stations serving only small villages or groups of villages.

Taking Peterborough as the most important of its western portals, the M&GN began its separate existence at a point about 50 chains north-east of Peterborough Great Northern Railway station, which became Peterborough North in 1923. The first M&GN station, Eye Green, was in Northamptonshire. The second, Thorney, was in Cambridgeshire. By the time Murrow, 14½ miles, was reached, the border of Lincoln had been touched. The fen district was then traversed virtually on the level, through Wisbech (Cambridgeshire), Ferry (Norfolk) and Tydd (Cambridgeshire), to Sutton Bridge, a small but important Lincolnshire town serving a large fruit-growing area.

Plate 1
According to the note on the reverse of the print, this picture was taken on the 27th September 1920 at Cromer and shows No. 11, a Johnson 4-4-0 with an extended smokebox, at the head of the 2.40pm express to London. It was not unusual for the Cromer portion of an express to run under the ordinary passenger headcode. R.J. ESSERY COLLECTION.

Plate 2
This undated but 1930s picture was taken at the west end of Sutton Bridge station. Johnson 4-4-0 No. 13 is waiting to depart with an express passenger train. Note the tablet exchanger is in the extended position while Beyer Peacock No. 28 is in the short bay coupled to an ex-Great Northern passenger brake van. R.S. CARPENTER.

Another western gateway, further north than Peterborough, was at Bourne – or, to be correct, Little Bytham, five miles west of Bourne – where an end-on junction was made with the above-mentioned branch of the Midland (later LM&SR) from Saxby. Along this route passed most of the Midland (later LM&SR) passenger traffic to the East Coast. The Great Northern station was used at Bourne, having been rebuilt in 1894 to cope with the expected increase in traffic. From Bourne onwards to Sutton Bridge this section was also in the flat fen country. The original alignments led into and out of the Great Northern station at Spalding, into which station the M&GN had running powers, but to the south, the Spalding Avoiding Line had been opened in 1894 for through running. Spalding was the third and last western gateway through which traffic passed to and from the M&GN. Immediately east of Sutton Bridge station, where the lines from Little Bytham and Peterborough converged, the River Nene was crossed by a swing bridge, and the county of Norfolk was entered.

South Lynn was reached nine miles farther on, and a short branch, two miles in length, left the main line just east of the station in order to reach the old Great Eastern Railway station. This was the only way by which Midland & Great Northern trains were able to enter King's Lynn, and to achieve this they had running powers over the GER lines for the short distance from King's Lynn Harbour Junction into the station. South Lynn was an important junction for the M&GN, and had the largest locomotive depot on the system. Extensive sidings were also provided and the bulk of the Joint line goods train marshalling was done here. Beyond South Lynn, and proceeding in the direction of Yarmouth, the fen country gives place to typical Norfolk scenery, consisting of hills, heaths and commons, with the result that the gradients over the remainder of the line are in parts severe. Fakenham, 24 miles from King's Lynn, is the only town between Lynn and Norwich.

At Melton Constable, 34 miles from Lynn, there were the engineering works, permanent way and locomotive headquarters of the system, and here the line branched into three. The Norwich branch ran

immediately east of the station and followed a southeasterly direction to Norwich, 21¼ miles away; it was single throughout. The main line to Yarmouth, double to Corpusty (4¾ miles) and single beyond, was 41½ miles in length. It passed the towns of Aylsham and North Walsham, beyond which it ran through some miles of the famous broadland districts, particularly at Stalham and Potter Heigham. Beyond Yarmouth access was gained to Lowestoft via the system of the Norfolk & Suffolk Joint Railways Committee (jointly owned by the M&GN and the GER, later the L&NER). Yarmouth was a terminus station; through trains for Lowestoft had to reverse – the branch, 12¼ miles in length, left the main line about a third of a mile west of Yarmouth Beach station, crossing Breydon Water by a five-span steel viaduct which included a large swing span.

From Melton Constable, the Cromer branch ran in a north-westerly direction, and through trains from the direction of Lynn had to reverse at Melton. This section was 15 miles in length, and was somewhat steeply graded. The market town of Holt was passed, and also Sheringham, into which the GER (later L&NER) had running powers from Roughton Road Junction, near Cromer. By this means Sheringham was provided with a train service to and from London (Liverpool Street) superior to the best possible by the M&GN route from King's Cross. However, the M&GN service remained successful because many passengers preferred to use King's Cross, rather than travel across London to Liverpool Street and its less salubrious surroundings. Cromer Beach station, 3¾ miles beyond Sheringham, occupied an excellent position within easy access of the promenade and sea. A distinction that was also shared by Yarmouth Beach station. Another short line, owned by the Norfolk & Suffolk Joint Committee, ran for 14½ miles round from Cromer (leaving the main line at Runton East and Runton West junctions) via Overstrand and Mundesley to North Walsham, where access was gained to both M&GN and L&NER stations. At first operated concurrently, after 1923 the L&NER worked the goods traffic over this branch, while the passenger traffic was worked by the M&GN and the L&NER alternately on a three-year basis.

ABOVE: **Plate 3**
For the author, this picture, which has been published in previous books about the M&GN, typifies the Joint line probably more than any other. It give an impression of the rural nature of the scene and the Victorian feel: note the flatbottom rails, ash ballast over the sleepers, and the pile of wicker baskets. The picture was taken at Martham circa 1892 and shows ex-Eastern & Midlands Railway No. 13, which was originally a Cornwall Minerals Railway locomotive. The man in the centre of the group of three on the footplate is Jack Loynes who was to become Locomotive Foreman at Melton Constable. ALAN WELLS COLLECTION.

BELOW AND ON FOLLOWING PAGES: **Plate 4**
These gradient sections were published by the Engineers Department Derby in 1902 and show the entire system at that date. The *Railway Year Book* gives the summit of the line as 312 feet above sea level at Piggs Grave Bank, 1¼ miles west of Melton Constable, and the steepest gradient as 1:56 for a distance of 14 chains at North Walsham, falling towards Melton Constable. It was originally printed on a very wide page.

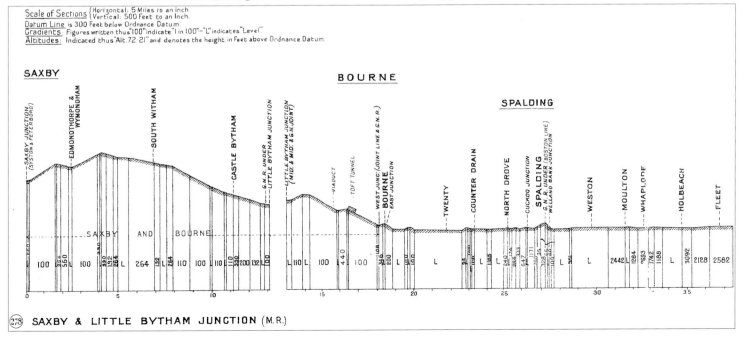

Plate 5
Although the most regular destination for M&GN engines on the Midland and LM&S was Leicester, from 1923 M&GN locomotives were frequent visitors to the Midland station at Nottingham, on the local services to and from Spalding and also on the Liverpool and Manchester express services to and from Yarmouth Beach and Cromer Beach. This 1930s picture shows Class C 4-4-0 No. 12 at Platform 3 of Nottingham Midland station carrying ordinary passenger train headlamps. R.J. ESSERY COLLECTION.

The principal gradients of the M&GN were several stretches of two or three miles at 1 in 100 – the most severe, on account of location, being between Little Bytham and Bourne, against up trains; between Grimston and Massingham, against down trains; and against down trains from a point three miles beyond Fakenham to beyond Thursford, a distance of almost four miles. The steepest gradient on the Cromer branch, between Holt and Sheringham, against up trains, was for a mile on each side of Weybourne station, at 1 in 80, much of which was also on severe curves. The summit level of the M&GN,

312 feet above sea level, was about one mile west of Melton Constable on the Lynn line. The number of lengths of single line did not help the operating problems of the M&GN. The two longest double-line stretches were between Raynham Park and Corpusty, 18½ miles, and between Sutton Bridge and Grimston, 15½ miles. With the amount of traffic passing over the system at various seasons of the year, having long sections of single track was a serious obstacle, especially on Saturdays during the summer when the excursion traffic from the Midlands was particularly heavy.

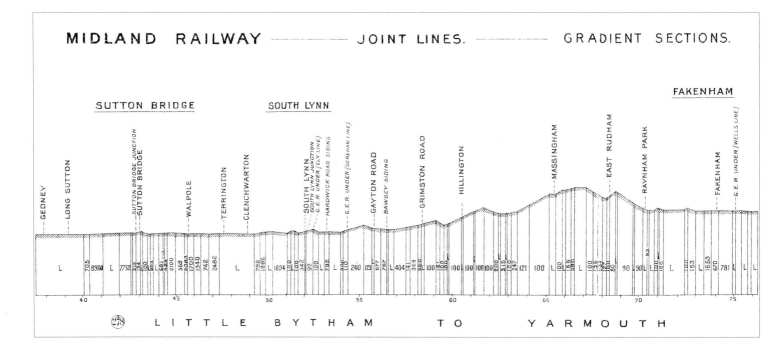

Plate 6
Melton Constable was the headquarters of the M&GN system and here we see Johnson 4-4-0 No. 79 at the head of an afternoon ordinary passenger train heading for Lynn passing the West signal box. The entire train is made up of Great Northern stock. ALAN WELLS COLLECTION.

A SURVEY OF TRAFFIC

Goods traffic on the M&GN system was of major importance. By far the largest proportion of freight traffic originated on the western section, that is, those lines west of King's Lynn. The exceptionally fertile fen country, through which the M&GN passed for about 50 miles, produced a wide variety of crops. Before the loss of traffic from rail to road and the closure of the line, the variety of fruit and vegetables were of great value to the railway, especially as

they were a source of revenue over the whole twelve months. Owing to the perishable nature of the bulk of this traffic, special attention had to be paid to its transit, and a service of trains was provided throughout the year from various stations to points of exchange with the parent companies, which were at Peterborough, Spalding and King's Lynn with the L&NER, and Peterborough and Bourne with the LM&SR. The flower traffic began very soon after Christmas, and for the next four months this traffic grew unceasingly. Quite early in the year, special vans of the steam-heated vacuum-fitted

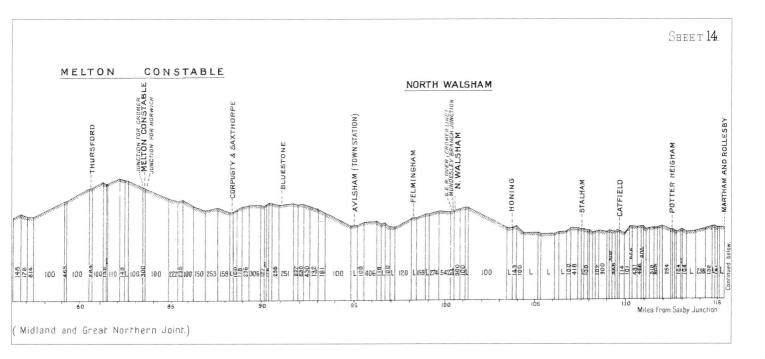

Plate 7
Photographed at Spalding in 1926, this picture shows Class 'DA' 0-6-0 No. 86 engaged in shunting duties at the north end of the station yard. The presence of LM&S brake No. 1534 indicates that this train is probably destined eventually to reach London Somers Town *via* Saxby. H.C. CASSERLEY.

stock were provided, particularly between Lynn and Spalding, and Bourne. Some hundreds of thousands of consignments, consisting of daffodils, narcissi, hyacinths, tulips and so on, were conveyed to hundreds of destinations during the season. In the early spring the fenland farmer had enormous quantities of cabbage, broccoli, and lettuces ready for the various London and provincial markets. This traffic was considerable, even though road transport began to take an increasing proportion from the railway.

But the real peak for the fruit and vegetable traffic on the M&GN was from about the third week in June to the first or second week in August, when the soft fruit ripened. This traffic, consisting principally of gooseberries, red and black currants (especially from stations on the Yarmouth line), strawberries and raspberries, was conveyed practically all over Britain and even to destinations in Ireland. During the latter part of the nineteenth century the cultivation of fruit extended greatly in the Wisbech district so that it became one of the largest fruit growing areas in England, covering parts of the counties of Cambridge, Lincoln and Norfolk. About one half was orchard, the remainder being devoted to the cultivation of strawberries, raspberries, currants and gooseberries. All classes

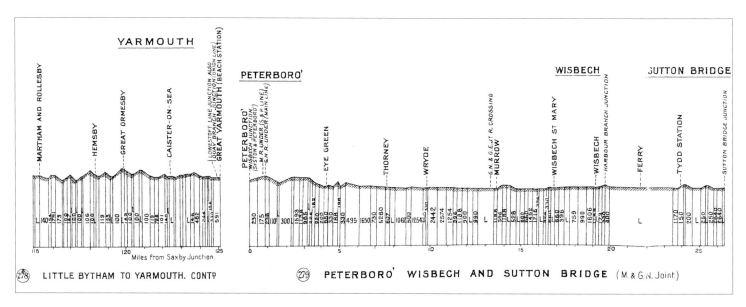

Plate 8
Here we see 4-4-0 No. 1 leaving Sheringham on a Down stopping good train about 1930/31, before it received a second-hand boiler in 1932, but after being painted dark brown circa 1929. Note the absence of 'No.' on the left hand section of the buffer beam. R.J. ESSERY COLLECTION.

of fruit demanded special measures on the part of the railway companies concerned, but the strawberry traffic was one of the most difficult to conduct owing to the large volume of the traffic confined within a short period and the perishable nature of the fruit. The task of transporting the fruit to the market, generally to the industrial centres of the Midlands, the northern counties and Scotland, was shared between the Midland & Great Northern Joint and the Great Eastern (later the L&NER). The former served the larger portion of the district, nineteen stations being concerned and the needs of some 2,000 growers being met. During the peak of the season, the

daily average number of loaded wagons required, both open and covered, was between 350 and 500; for the remainder of the season the demand was also heavy, though not to the same extent.

On the M&GN, fruit was conveyed exclusively by special trains during the season, these trains being despatched to the junctions in quick succession. The baskets containing the fruit were placed in tiers, fitting together so that they rode firmly without damage to their contents. About five tiers were usual, but at times eight and even ten travelled without harmful effects, while road vehicles carrying supplies to or from the rail sometimes built up as many as twelve

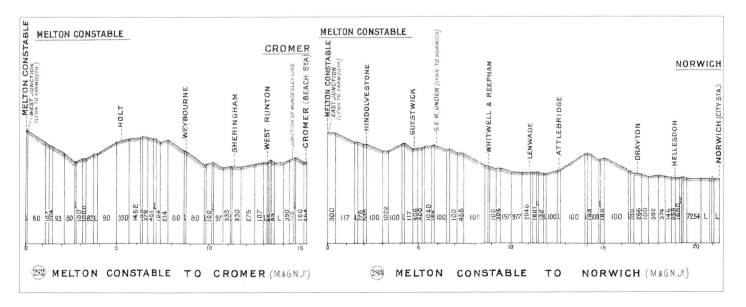

②⑧② MELTON CONSTABLE TO CROMER (M&G.N.J⁼)   ②⑧③ MELTON CONSTABLE TO NORWICH (M&G.N.J⁼)

tiers. Experiments were made with railway vans having shelves to avoid placing one 'chip' on another, but generally the practice was to use the four-pound chip. As only two chips could be handled at a time when transferring from road vehicle to railway wagon, or vice versa, the use of four-pound chips reduced handling when compared with the three-pound chip. This was an important advantage in favour of the larger type of container as labour time was reduced – to the advantage of growers in getting later acceptance times for loading at stations, whilst labour costs to the railway were also kept down. Both producer and consumer benefited further because the railway rates were regulated by the costs involved.

One of the difficulties encountered was that during a comparatively short period of time a small station had to accommodate a large number of road vehicles, ranging from perambulators to motor lorries, all carrying traffic to be loaded into specified vans. Avoiding congestion in the yard was not easy, as the road vehicles had to move from one railway wagon to another to discharge their loads, it being by no means uncommon for one grower to consign traffic to as many as twenty different destinations. The extremely perishable nature of the fruit and vegetables required special handling, and the growers were promised early morning delivery at the various markets; to ensure this, much of the traffic was passenger rated. A number of stations, particularly Terrington, Walpole, Sutton Bridge, Wisbech, Wisbech St Mary, Murrow, Long Sutton, Gedney and Holbeach, had a train to themselves each day. When it is remembered that each train could load to sixty wagons (and more by special permission), a better idea is given of the extent of this traffic.

About this period of the year, too, the conveyance of green peas formed a considerable item and, beginning in August, plums and apples were conveyed in increasing quantities for several weeks. In fact the apple traffic, due to the many and varied kinds of that fruit cultivated, lasted well into the autumn.

Owing to the properties of the black soil, potato cultivation was also very successful and the grower was able to get his supplies in the market very early. This traffic lasted the whole year round, and during autumn and winter was particularly heavy. Later the cultivation of subsidised sugar beet found more favour with the farmer, so that the acreage under potatoes decreased; however, both crops were carried by rail until road transport took over.

During the period between the grouping and the late 1930s, the conveyance of agricultural traffic represented 90 per cent, of the outwards goods traffic on the M&GN western section, but two other traffics have to be mentioned. The London Brick Co. Ltd had extensive activities in various parts of the county, particularly around Peterborough, with brick yards at Eye Green and Dogsthorpe, from

which one brick train ran daily, and at times more than one. Another traffic was timber: for several months of the year, timber boats, engaged in the Russian and Swedish timber trade, could be seen on the river Nene at Wisbech and also at Sutton Bridge; and at times it was necessary to run special timber trains.

Although it did not produce the same quantity or class of goods traffic, the eastern section, namely all lines east of King's Lynn, was able to make an appreciable contribution to M&GN revenue. Yarmouth and Lowestoft were centres of a seasonal fishing traffic, which required the provision of special fish trains from October to December. The fertile pasturelands around Norwich and throughout the eastern section were prime acres for the fattening of cattle and sheep, and special cattle trains were run, particularly on Tuesdays, Thursdays and Saturdays. Other substantial traffic was in grain and sugar beet, and a fair amount of manufactured goods was handled from Norwich. A summary of the tonnage carried in 1922 is given at the end of Chapter 2.

Passenger traffic on the M&GN, owing to the nature of the district served, was not relatively so important as the goods traffic. Nevertheless, before the increasing use of motor transport it was quite appreciable. Local services were provided throughout the whole of the system in both directions. Thus trains would leave Peterborough for Yarmouth with through connections to Cromer, Norwich and Lowestoft; other local services left Peterborough for King's Lynn; and similarly in the opposite direction. These trains served all or most of the stations and ran daily all the year round. Local services on the Sutton Bridge to Spalding and Bourne section were similar to those between Peterborough and Lynn, and ran in conjunction. At the peak, the passenger services on the Norwich and Cromer branches numbered about six and nine respectively in each direction, with two extra each way between Cromer and Sheringham. An additional service was also run on Saturdays from Fakenham and Melton Constable to meet the requirements of people attending Norwich market; additional trains also ran on the Melton Constable–Yarmouth section between Yarmouth and Stalham, and North Walsham, including a late train from Yarmouth to North Walsham on Wednesdays and Saturdays.

A good express service was also maintained daily throughout the year between the M&GN and the LM&SR; the M&GN supplied the motive power to and from Leicester, and the LM&SR the stock. The timing of a typical service was to depart from Lowestoft in the morning at 8.18am, Yarmouth at 9.0am, Norwich at 9.35am, and Cromer at 9.40am. The three trains were combined at Melton Constable and ran through to Leicester (arriving at 1.48pm), stopping only at Fakenham, South Lynn, Bourne and Melton Mowbray; the

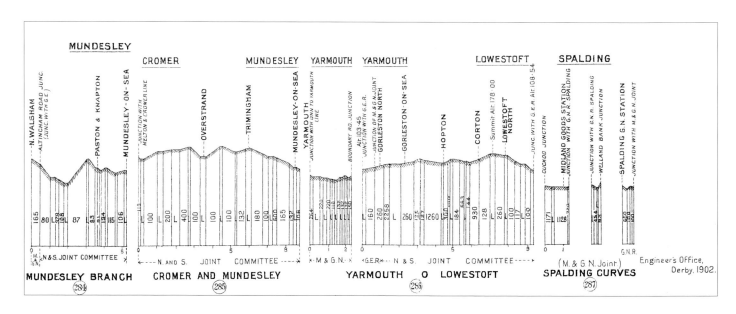

Plate 9
Photographed at Sheringham in August 1937, we see Johnson 4-4-0 No. 17 with an extended smokebox, Melton chimney and Deeley smokebox door, running with a two-coach Cromer train. A.W.V. Mace.

coaches forming this train ran through to Gloucester. In the opposite direction a typical service started from Leicester at 3.22pm, and arrived at Melton Constable 6.28pm, where the train was divided into three sections, one each for Cromer and Norwich, the third for Yarmouth and Lowestoft. An all the year round express service was also maintained between Cromer and London (King's Cross). A typical train would leave Cromer at about midday and arrive at King's Cross a little more than four hours later. Good north-country connections were made at Peterborough for trains originating at various stations on the M&GN.

On Saturdays during the summer a through restaurant car service was run from Manchester (London Road). This through express then went from Uttoxeter via Trent to Nottingham, then on through Saxby, passing onto the M&GN at Little Bytham, with carriages for Cromer, Norwich and Yarmouth; with a return service from Cromer, Norwich and Yarmouth for Manchester. Another important through Saturday service that ran during the summer departed from Manchester (Victoria) on Friday nights and arrived at Yarmouth at about 7.0am, having also conveyed carriages for Norwich and Cromer. Through trains, some with restaurant cars attached, were also run at weekends from Nottingham,

Derby, Sheffield, Halifax, Birmingham and elsewhere, and the problem of handling this heavy traffic called for much thought and efficient management. The M&GN, in common with other mainline railways, recognised the growth of cheap travel, and various day and half-day excursion facilities were provided. An example was a train that ran from Lynn and Wisbech to King's Cross; usually departing late morning and arriving back about 3.0am the next morning. The L&NER provided bogie stock for this service. Similar excursions were run to Leicester and Nottingham, in which case the LM&SR provided the stock.

In the years before the outbreak of the Second World War the M&GN worked practically all of the traffic using engines built prior to 1902, although, as we will see later, rebuilding them meant they were not in their original condition. The parent companies provided the coaching stock for through services, and occasionally for some of the local excursion duties. The original M&GN coaching stock was chiefly of the six-wheeled variety and was not often seen off the system, but later bogie coaches of London & North Western, Midland, North Eastern and even Great Eastern origin were transferred for use in local services.

Other than those joint companies where the pre-1923 owners all became part of the same 'Big Four', the grouping under the Railways Act of 1921 left the position of the joint railways unchanged. The three major joint systems which retained their separate management were the Cheshire Lines, the Somerset & Dorset, and the M&GN. The first to be subjected to any change was the Somerset & Dorset, which ceased to be worked as a separate concern on the 1st June 1930, when the operating and commercial duties were taken over

Plate 10
Johnson 4-4-0 No. 055, running with a G7 boiler with extended smokebox and Nash stovepipe chimney at Melton Constable. The locomotive is in the Up sidings and is carrying fitted freight train headlamp code, meaning that at least one third of the vehicles are fitted with automatic brakes that can be operated from the locomotive. P.C. DEWHURST.

by the LM&SR, while the Southern Railway assumed responsibility for maintenance of way and works. The Cheshire Lines Committee, which owned some rolling stock but no locomotives, was worked by mainline companies, while the changes on the M&GN came following the official announcement that, from the 1st October 1936, the LM&SR and the L&NER had decided to modify the arrangements for working the Joint line. Hitherto, a traffic manager had controlled

the working of passenger and goods traffic with headquarters at King's Lynn, but now the responsibility for working the line would be taken over by the officers of the L&NER. The revised arrangements also included the Norfolk & Suffolk Joint Railways, owned by the M&GN and the L&NER. Therefore, it could be argued that at this point the M&GN became part of the L&NER, although as a legal entity it survived until nationalisation.

ABOVE: Plate 11
When this picture was taken at Melton Constable, sometime during the 1930s, No. 20 was engaged in shunting duties. Both the vans are automatic vacuum brake vehicles. ROGER CARPENTER COLLECTION.

Plate 12
During the final years of the Joint line the LM&S-designed Ivatt 2-6-0s were to be found working many trains. This picture was taken when No. 43104 was crossing the Great Ouse at South Lynn circa 1952 while working a Peterborough train. P. RANSOME-WALLIS.

Plate 13
Norwich City was the largest station on the Joint line and in this picture, taken on the 7th June 1952, we can see the 4.50pm Norwich City to Melton Constable ordinary passenger train headed by an ex-Great Eastern Class 'D15' 4-4-0 No. 62519. The note on the reverse of the print states five coaches, although there appears to be about eleven vehicles at the platform. R.J. ESSERY COLLECTION.

ABOVE: **Plate 14**
The Midland and LM&S Standard Class '4F's were regularly employed on excursion trains over the M&GN lines, and this 1957 picture shows No. 44420 from 17A Derby at South Lynn West signal box at the head of what the photographer describes as a Yarmouth Beach to Nottingham and Derby train, which is running under express passenger train headlamp code. V. FORSTER.

Plate 15
Here we see 4-4-2T No. 20 at Cromer Beach with an ordinary passenger train in August 1929. It is difficult to be sure, but all the carriages on the train appear to be ex-GN stock. The luggage brake to the right was built at Melton Constable, and in the main platform are two LM&S coaches, one of which is ex-L&NWR. R.J. ESSERY COLLECTION.

Plate 16
This picture of Johnson 4-4-0 No. 12 taken at Norwich circa 1896 has been included in order to show the positions of the lamp holders during the period pre 1903. Note there is one holder on the top of the smokebox in front of the chimney and another in the centre of the top half of the door. There were three lamp holders on the front of the platform: one over the right hand buffer (when looking forward) and two over the left hand buffer. Unlike the post-1903 positions there was no lamp holder in the centre over the coupling. ALAN WELLS COLLECTION.

CHAPTER 4

LOCOMOTIVES INHERITED BY THE EASTERN & MIDLANDS RAILWAY

The locomotive history of the M&GN proper begins with the E&MR engines, but as we have seen, the E&MR was itself only ten years old when the M&GN was formed. Within this chapter we shall confine attention to the locomotives which came within the framework of companies which formed the E&MR in 1883, followed in the next chapter by those obtained by the E&MR in its own short lifespan. All told, there were twenty-two locomotives of pre-E&MR origin left by the time the M&GN was formed in 1893 (there had been twenty-six in 1883) and these survivors are given in the table at the end of this chapter. There were two pre-1883 companies involved, the Yarmouth & North Norfolk and the Lynn & Fakenham railways. However, it would be a mistake to separate out the locomotives from the two companies as, although they were different in name and legal standing, from a practical point of view they were one railway, separated by a few miles of open country, soon to be crossed. Even the Working Timetables were published together, referring to the 'Lynn & Fakenham Section' and the 'Yarmouth & North Norfolk Section'. The contractor, Wilkinson & Jarvis of Victoria Street, Westminster, not only built the lines but also operated them, and ordered all the locomotives and rolling stock on behalf of the nominal companies. It was not until the Amalgamation Act was deposited in late 1881 that Wilkinson & Jarvis handed control to the railway, and some of its staff, Mr Marriott for example, remained as the first officers of the railway.

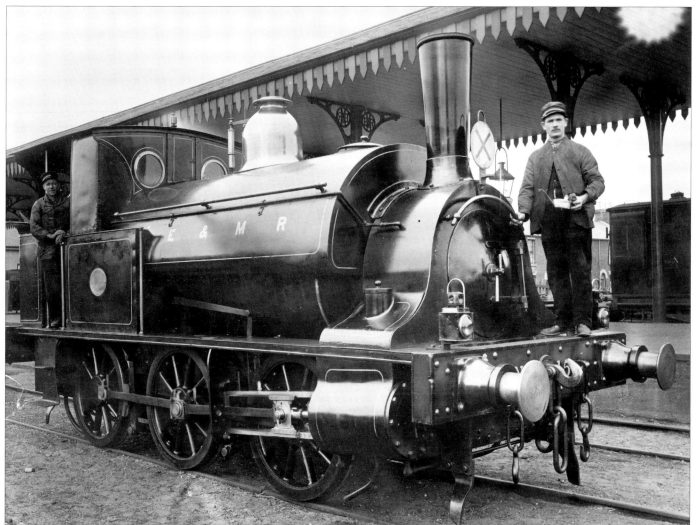

Plate 1
By the time this picture was taken, *Ormesby* was no longer an engine with a name; this had been removed and it had been given a number by the Eastern & Midlands Railway, No. 15. This was one of a pair built by Fox Walker in 1876 for the Great Yarmouth & Stalham Light Railway, which was absorbed into the Yarmouth & North Norfolk Railway, which in its turn became part of the E&MR in 1883. This picture was taken at Yarmouth circa 1888 and displays some changes since the engine was built; the feed pump has been removed from the right hand crosshead (note the holes where it had been connected) and the cab has been altered. Driver Johnson, standing on the front of the locomotive, became the first cinema operator in Yarmouth, but whether he left the railway to take up this work or if this happened when he retired was not recorded. ALAN WELLS COLLECTION.

Plate 2
This picture of No. 16, formerly *Stalham*, was taken in 1894 by the Midland Railway Photographer shortly after the formation of the M&GNJR. It was built by Fox Walker in 1876. Note the impressive works plate, which was replaced by the stock number when this was removed from the saddle tank and the letters M&GN were applied. R.J. ESSERY COLLECTION.

Plate 3
This picture of No. 16A was taken at Melton Constable during the early 1930s when the locomotive was employed as works shunter. Built for the Great Yarmouth & Stalham Light Railway and named *Stalham*, when it became E&MR stock the name was removed and it was numbered 16. In 1905 it was put on the duplicate list and numbered 16A. It is worth drawing attention to the fact that the dome cover, originally brass, has by this time been painted over. The engineman in the cab is Driver Reeve. R.J. Essery collection.

THE SADDLETANKS

These engines consisted of two Fox Walker 0-6-0STs built in 1876 (*Ormesby* and *Stalham*), and three from Black, Hawthorn & Co. in 1877 (*Ida*), 1879 (*Holt*) and 1881 (*Aylsham*). There were also two small 0-4-0STs built by Hudswell, Clarke & Rodgers that were used by the contractor and acquired by the E&MR for construction work thereafter.

Ormesby (makers No. 333 of 1876) and *Stalham* (makers No. 338 of 1876) were supplied to the Great Yarmouth and Stalham Light Railway (later Yarmouth and North Norfolk Light Railway) and pulled through the streets of Yarmouth upon delivery. They were similar to some engines supplied by the same firm to the Midland Railway and had outside cylinders 13 inches × 20 inches which drove 3 feet 6½ inch (later 3 feet 7½ inch) wheels and had a boiler pressure of 140 psi (later reduced to 120 psi). The wheelbase was 9 feet 8½ inches long, equally divided. The boiler was 8 feet long, 3 feet 4⁷/₈ inches mean diameter and had 108 tubes of 1¾ inches outside diameter – which gave a heating surface of 410 square feet, and the firebox added a further 48.5 square feet. The grate area was 7.5 square feet. With 550 gallons of water and 1 ton 5 hundredweight of coal, they weighed 24 tons 10 hundredweight. A second injector soon replaced a crosshead pump that was originally fitted on the right side. The cab was also altered to give more protection and from early photographs it would appear they had back plates to the cab. Neither the GY&S nor the Y&NN engines were numbered, all their engines being named. On coming into the Eastern & Midlands Railway they had the names removed and were numbered 15 and 16.

They were used at Yarmouth for shunting and also running trains in the early years. No. 15 was sold to a colliery in the north of England

in 1900, and No. 16 became works shunter in 1901 and was placed in the duplicate list as No. 16A in 1905 where it remained until 1937 when the locomotive was sold for scrapping. Braking was by hand; blocks were only fitted to driving and trailing wheels. For most of its life No. 16A retained a polished brass dome cover.

Ida (makers No. 416 of 1877) was delivered to the GY&S and was a standard design of Black, Hawthorn & Co. It had outside cylinders 14 inches × 20 inches, coupled wheels of 3 feet 4½ inches (later 3 feet 6 inches) diameter. The boiler pressure was 140psi (later 120psi) and the wheelbase 10 feet 9 inches. The tubes contributed 556.5 square feet and the firebox a further 49.5 square feet of heating surface. With 665 gallons of water and 1 ton of coal the weight was 26 tons. The hand brake operated blocks on driving and trailing wheels only. Like *Ormesby* and *Stalham*, there were no cylinder drain cocks, just a single cock to each steam chest. *Ida* was named after the GY&S Chairman's daughter and, like all former GY&S engines, was never identified by number until it was sold to the Lynn & Fakenham Railway some time before amalgamation; it was numbered 7 both on that line and on the Eastern & Midlands Railway. Placed on the duplicate list in 1894, No. 7A was sold to the Ibstock Brick and Tile Co. via T.W. Ward in the same year. It was given No. 2 in their stock list and scrapped in 1928.

Ida was to all intents and purposes identical to a further pair of Black, Hawthorn 0-6-0STs, one each of which went direct to the Y&NN and the L&F in 1881 (below). They appeared to be domeless, but this was not so. The safety valves were mounted on top of the dome, which was set rather low. They were fitted with dumb buffers and during M&GN days (when they were often collectively referred to as the 'Black, Hawthorns') one of them was usually to be found at South Lynn engaged upon shunting work.

Holt, later *Chairman* (works No. 503 of 1881), the second of the three to enter service, was delivered to the L&FR in 1881 and became No 6. Used for shunting, it was placed on the duplicate list in 1894. No. 6A was then sold to the Ibstock Brick and Tile Co. via T.W. Ward along with No. 7A in the same year and became No. 1 of the Ibstock Company stock. It was scrapped in 1940.

Aylsham (makers No. 516 of 1881) was like the above-mentioned *Ida* in all respects. It was delivered to the Y&NNR and again pulled through the Yarmouth streets to the Beach station. It was used mainly for shunting, although it was sometimes also recorded working passenger trains between Yarmouth and Stalham, and on one occasion even to Melton Constable. It became No. 17 in the

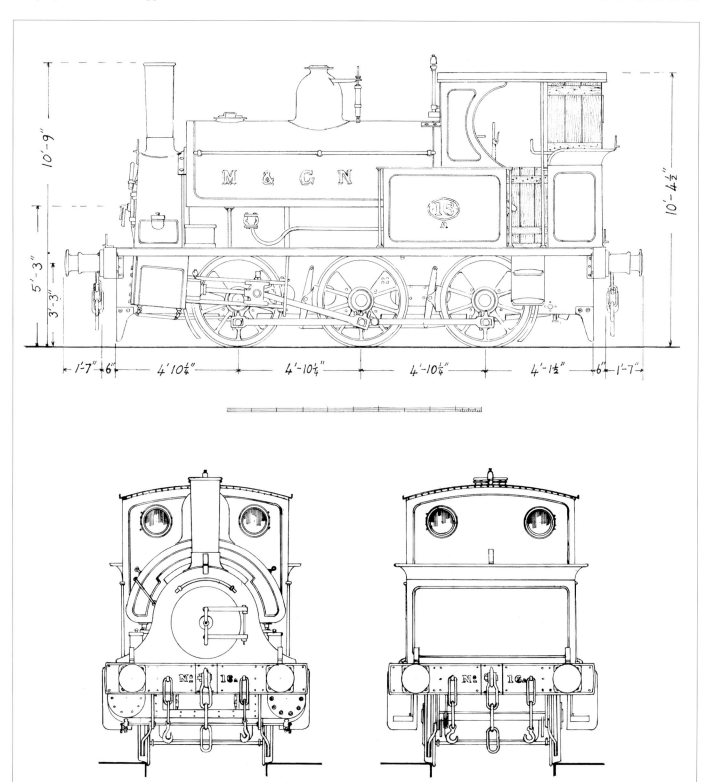

Plate 4
This drawing shows Fox Walker Class 'No. 16A', which was used at Melton Constable as works engine. The front and rear views show the strange arrangement of the safety chains on the buffer beams. For a long time the only lamp bracket was in the top position and, as far as is known, no bracket was ever fitted to the mid buffer beam position.

Plate 5
This interesting picture shows the front of 4-4-0T No. 19, originally Y&NNR *Great Yarmouth*, when it was photographed by the Midland Railway Photographer in 1894. The picture may have been taken to show the new blastpipe and blower ring, but it also shows the screw coupling without a coupling hook and the safety chains that were generally used with coaches at this time. The disc on the chimney was the standard E&M headcode for light engine or ordinary passenger. The engine number was in white on a green disc with a white edge. R.J. ESSERY COLLECTION.

Plate 6
Photographed at Melton Constable, No. 17A was built by Black, Hawthorn in 1881 and named *Aylsham* when it was owned by the Yarmouth & North Norfolk Railway. Following the formation of the Eastern & Midlands Railway in 1883 the name was removed and it became No. 17. Within a year of the formation of the M&GN the locomotive was placed on the duplicate list as No. 17A and it was employed as the works shunter until 1901, being scrapped the following year. R.J. ESSERY COLLECTION.

Plate 7
This locomotive was built by Hudswell, Clarke & Rogers in 1878 for Wilkinson & Jarvis, the contractors for the Lynn & Fakenham Railway, and became L&FR stock in 1881. In 1893 it became M&GN No. 4, being renumbered 4A the following year. In 1917 the locomotive was sold to J. & J. Colman for use on their private sidings and was scrapped in 1928. ALAN WELLS COLLECTION.

E&MR lists, was put on to the duplicate list in 1894 and became the Melton works shunter until replaced by No. 16 (pp. 65–6) in 1901. It was scrapped the following year.

Alpha (Hudswell, Clarke works No. 183 of 1878) was delivered to Wilkinson & Jarvis, the contractors of the L&FR, in 1879, and *Vici* (works No. 192 of 1880) followed in 1880. They were used for traffic purposes as the line progressed. When taken into L&FR stock in 1881 they were numbered 4 and 5 and were the only engines to retain their names. In 1894 they were transferred to the engineers' department of the M&GN and used on the building of the South Lynn direct line and Norfolk & Suffolk line through Mundesley. Apart from the joining of the cab roof plates they were identical. Outside cylinders 8 inch × 15 inch drove 2 feet 6 inch diameter wheels set at a wheelbase of 5 feet. An eccentric-driven feed pump and an injector supplied the boilers, but another injector soon replaced the pump. The boiler had a mean diameter of 2 feet 3 inches, a length of 7 feet 1½ inches and had 39 tubes of 2 inch outside diameter, giving a heating surface of 150 square feet. The firebox had a further 22 square feet, the grate area was 3.4 square feet and the boiler pressure was 140 psi (later reduced to 120 psi). Water capacity was 260 gallons and coal 7 hundredweight, giving a weight of 11 tons 10 hundredweight. Wooden brake blocks were applied to all wheels by hand. Being too small for mainline duty, they were always used for shunting work. In 1894 they were given the suffix A in the duplicate list. No. 4A was renovated and sold to J. & J. Colman (the mustard people) in 1917

and scrapped in 1928. This is despite the fact that the minutes record the sale of both engines to T.W. Ward in 1894 for £320 each. No. 5A stood for many years in a derelict condition and was photographed as late as 1st August 1932 in the yard at Melton.

THE HUDSWELL, CLARKE & RODGERS 4-4-0 TANKS

We now come to that attractive group of 4-4-0T locomotives which over the years came to symbolise much of what was distinctive about the M&GN. Although all very similar, they were not absolutely identical, there being slightly increased dimensions as delivery went on. The smallest were *North Walsham* (Y&NNR) and *Hillington* (L&FR), followed by *Martham* (Y&NNR) and *Fakenham* (L&FR) with enlarged cylinders and heating surface. The final variant with larger fuel and water capacity was represented by *Norwich* and *King's Lynn* (L&FR), and by *Great Yarmouth* (Y&NNR). From 1894, all the engines were reboilered with Melton pattern boilers with Johnson mountings but a new type chimney, and all were fitted with the standard Midland style steam/vacuum brake in place of the hand brake. The new boilers had slightly increased dimensions – barrel length 8 feet 10 inches, diameter 3 feet 9 inches, 190 tubes of one inch diameter, grate area 11.3 square feet and a total heating surface of 821.7 square feet. When built, the engines had been fitted with Ramsbottom safety valves but this was to be replaced by a lock-up valve housed in polished brass cover with two Salter spring balanced valves on the dome, the original dome

ABOVE: Plate 8
M&GN No. 5, later 5A, was one of a pair of almost identical 0-4-0ST built by Hudswell, Clarke & Rodgers in 1878. They were too small for mainline work and their history is described in this chapter. This picture was taken at Melton Constable in 1931 and shows the locomotive after it had been withdrawn but before it was cut up. R.J. ESSERY COLLECTION.

BELOW: Plate 9
This locomotive was built in 1881 by Black, Hawthorn for the Lynn & Fakenham Railway and became No. 6 in the M&GN stock list, the A suffix being added before it was sold in 1894. The new owners were the Ibstock Brick and Tile Company and it was to remain in that company's service until it was scrapped in 1940. BERNARD MATTHEWS COLLECTION.

2356

cover being retained. The M&GN pattern chimney, tapering slightly to the base, was used as a replacement and No. 9 received a steel band to its chimney – a form of embellishment provided by the driver.

North Walsham (Hudswell, Clark & Rodgers No. 208 of 1878) was delivered to the Y&NN. It arrived, like the saddletanks, at Yarmouth dockside on 9th September 1878 and was once again pulled through the streets to the Beach station. It seems probable that it was originally ordered for the GY&SLR before the latter was absorbed into the Y&NNR.

It was a pretty little engine and the design is attributed to Massey Bromley who became Locomotive Superintendent of the Great Eastern Railway. Outside cylinders were 14 inches × 20 inches, bogie wheels 2 feet 4 inches (later 2 feet 5½ inches) diameter and coupled wheels 4 feet 6 inches (later 4 feet 7½ inches). The bogie wheelbase was 4 feet 10 inches, trailing bogie to driving 5 feet 10½ inches and coupled wheelbase 6 feet 9 inches. The boiler was 9 feet 6½ inches long by 3 feet 7 inches mean diameter and contained 100 tubes of 2 inch outside diameter. These gave 512.6 square feet of heating surface, and to this was added 53.2 square feet for the firebox. The grate area was 9 square feet. The boiler pressure of 140 psi was later reduced to 120 psi. With 750 gallons of water and 17 hundredweight of coal the weight was 32 tons 10 hundredweight. The slide bars were of trough section and were covered by plates that were subsequently removed. Chimney caps, dome covers and safety valve base as well as the frames to the cab side windows were of polished brass. Wooden brake blocks to coupled wheels were operated by handwheel and sand for the leading direction was supplied by sandboxes in the

front of the side-tanks. A lever reversed the Howe link motion on the right side. Like the previous engines, no drain cocks were fitted to the cylinders. It became No. 32 in the E&MR list and the name was removed, but it was renumbered 41 in 1886. The boiler was fed by two injectors which were placed upon the top of the tank inside the cab. Dry sand was, somewhat surprisingly, only available when the engine was running forward. Before the 1883 amalgamation it carried no number and it seems likely that this was true of all the 4-4-0Ts, whether Y&NNR or L&FR. Rebuilt with a Melton boiler in 1894, it was withdrawn for stationary work in 1904.

Hillington (works No. 209 of 1878) was identical with *North Walsham* but, unlike the latter, was fitted with cylinder drain cocks. It became No. 8 in the E&MR numbering, probably the first time it actually carried a number. It was delivered to the L&F section on the 6th November 1878, reboilered with a Melton pattern boiler in 1894 and received the standard brake at the same time. It went on loan to the Midland Railway 1906–12 and some sources say it was rebuilt at Derby in 1908. The author has been unable to find an order for this work, but the surviving Derby Locomotive Works orders are not complete, see Appendix D. Whilst on the Midland it carried the number 2. Withdrawn in 1917, it was sold to the War Department in 1917, to Edinburgh Collieries in 1925, then to Ormiston Coal Co., and scrapped in 1935.

The second 4-4-0T for the Y&NNR, *Martham* (works No. 210 of 1879), was slightly larger than the previous engines. It had 15 inch × 20 inch cylinders and the boiler was 3 feet 9 inches mean diameter with 115 tubes of 2 inches outside diameter, giving a heating surface

Plate 10
When No. 41 was owned by the Y&NNR it carried the name *North Walsham* but it was not numbered in the stock list. Built by Hudswell, Clarke & Rodgers in 1878 it became E&MR No. 32, and later M&GN No. 41 as seen in this picture taken at Yarmouth some time after it had been rebuilt in 1894. Note the absence of cylinder drain cocks. In 1904 the locomotive was withdrawn and used as a stationary boiler. KEN NUNN.

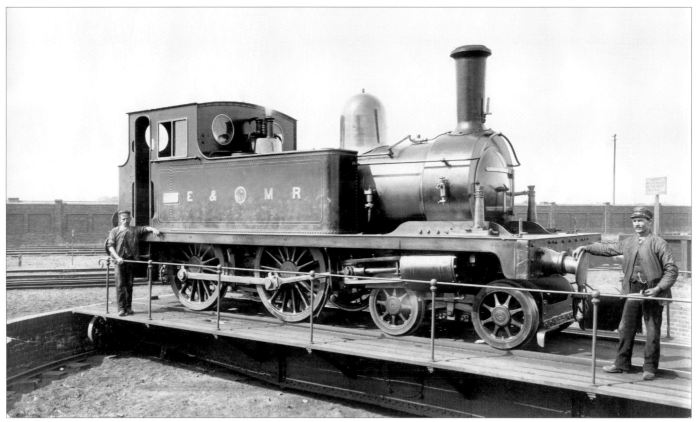

ABOVE: **Plate 11**
This picture of a Hudswell, Clark & Rodgers 4-4-0T illustrates a locomotive that was built in 1879 for the Yarmouth & North Norfolk Railway and carried the name *Martham*. **When the Y&NNR became part of the Eastern & Midlands the name was removed and it was numbered 31 in the E&MR stock list, but it was renumbered and became 40 in 1886. This picture was taken at Yarmouth before the engine was fitted with continuous brake, and shows it with a new chimney and the crosshead guard removed.** ALAN WELLS COLLECTION.

Plate 12
Built by Hudswell, Clarke & Rogers in 1880 and supplied to the Lynn & Fakenham Railway, this locomotive was originally named *Norwich*, **but the E&MR removed the nameplates and renumbered it 10. The picture was taken at Melton Constable; the building in the background is the 'Wicka' or loco office. This engine was one of the four loaned to the Midland Railway for use on motor trains. Note the rather impressive brass dome.** ALAN WELLS COLLECTION.

Plate 13
The 4-4-0Ts epitomised the M&GN. This picture shows Hudswell, Clark & Rodgers engine, works number 211, which became Lynn & Fakenham Railway *Fakenham*, then E&MR No. 9. Until the M&GN adopted the vacuum brake this locomotive was equipped with the Westinghouse brake, note the Westinghouse pump in front of the tank. This was another of the Midland Railway Photographer's pictures that were taken in 1894. R.J. ESSERY COLLECTION.

of 560 square feet. The grate area was 11 square feet and the firebox gave 63 square feet heating surface. With the same water and fuel capacity as the previous engines, the weight was 33 tons. It was numbered 31 by the E&MR and renumbered 40 in 1886. Rebuilt with Melton boiler in 1894, it was one of four of the class to be loaned to the Midland Railway in 1906 and was used to haul a Pullman car. It returned to the M&GN in 1912. Whilst at Derby it was numbered 10 to correspond to the Pullman car it was coupled to. It was rebuilt with Deeley smokebox and chimney at Derby. When it returned it did little work on the M&GN and was sold in 1917 to the Ministry of Munitions, Houston, Georgetown, Renfrewshire, and circa 1919 to National Oil Refineries Ltd, Llandarcy, before being scrapped by E.L. Forester in Swansea in 1934.

Fakenham (works No. 211 of 1879) was delivered on 20th June 1879. It became No. 9 in the Lynn & Fakenham Railway list. It was similar to *Martham* of the Y&NNR, but introduced the Westinghouse brake and was the only one to be fitted with a continuous brake until the M&GN adopted the vacuum brake. The Westinghouse pump was carried on the front of the tank on the right side. *Fakenham* was used on the first train when the Yarmouth and Lynn lines were linked up in April 1883. It was rebuilt with a Melton boiler in 1898 and remained on the M&GN, working on the Mundesley line; but its last job was on the Engineer's saloon where it was a familiar sight. The Melton smokebox and chimney remained to the end. In 1931 it went to Derby and had the cylinders lined up to 12 inches for comparative fuel tests. It was withdrawn in 1933, but stood about Melton yard supplying steam to a pump for some time.

Norwich (works No. 224 of 1880) had the same size cylinders, wheels and boiler as *Martham*, but had larger tanks and bunker (the tanks followed the curve of the boiler). The bunker was 4 inches longer and

3 inches higher and held 25 hundredweight of coal; with 800 gallons of water, it weighed 34 tons and to accommodate these changes, the trailing and frames were increased by 4 inches. It was rebuilt in 1896 with a Melton boiler, while standard brake equipment was fitted and the cylinders increased to 16 inches × 20 inches at the same time. It went to the Midland in 1906 and remained there until 1912. It was rebuilt at Derby with Deeley smokebox and chimney and renumbered 5, but details of this work have not survived, see Appendix A. In 1917 it was sold to the War Department for use at Pirbright and then moved to Woolmer where it was renamed *Kingsley*. It was later used by the Royal Engineers for rerailing practice and finally scrapped in 1953. It had a heavy overhaul at Yorkshire Engine Co. in 1923. It was No. 10 on the L&FR list and this number was retained on both the E&MR and the M&GN.

King's Lynn (works No. 231 of 1881) was delivered to the L&FR on 30th October 1881. Numbered 20, it was put into the duplicate list in 1909. It was identical to *Norwich* and in 1903 was rebuilt in like manner with Melton boiler and the cylinders increased to 16 inches × 20 inches. The engine remained at Melton, but also worked at Lynn and at Bourne on the Saxby branch, also taking turns on the Engineer's saloon. It was withdrawn in 1931 but stood about for some time afterwards.

Great Yarmouth, third of the Y&NNR 4-4-0Ts (works No 232 of 1881), was delivered on the 31st October 1881 to North Walsham GER station before being hauled along the road to the Y&NN station on temporary rails. It was identical to *Norwich* and *King's Lynn*. It was rebuilt in the same way as those two engines in 1903. After service on the Midland Railway it was sold to the War Department, but the scrapping date is not known. It had been No. 19 on both the E&MR and the M&GN.

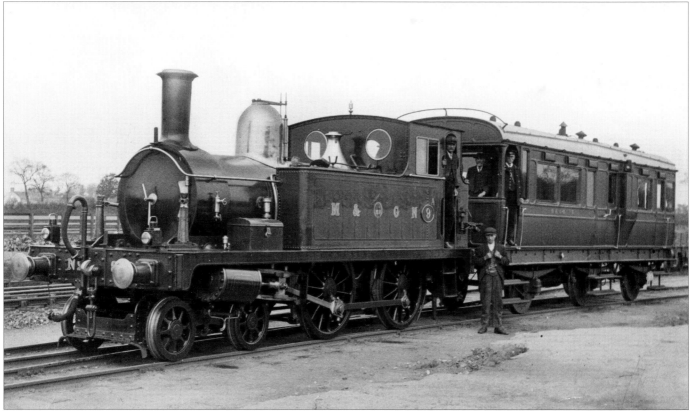

Plate 14
This picture shows Class 'B' 4-4-0T No. 9A. The locomotive entered service as *Fakenham*, but became No. 9 in the M&GN stock list and was later placed on the duplicate list as No. 9A – note the A above and to the right of the number plate. When this picture was taken at Holt the locomotive was coupled to the Engineer's saloon. E.E. Boltz.

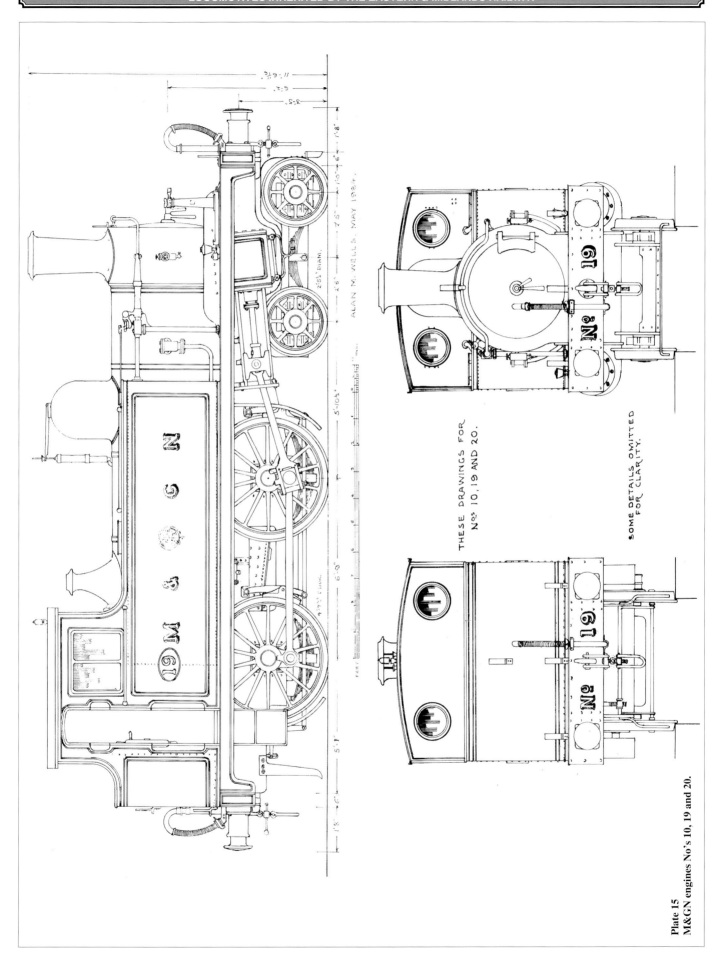

THESE DRAWINGS FOR
Nos 10, 19 AND 20.

SOME DETAILS OMITTED
FOR CLARITY.

ALAN M. WELLS. MAY 1984.

Plate 15
M&GN engines No's 10, 19 and 20.

Plate 16
The Sharp Stewart 0-6-0Ts were originally built for the Cornwall Mineral Railway in 1874 and three, No's
1 *Melton Constable*, 2 *Reepham* and 3 *Blakeney*, came to the L&FR in 1880. A further five were obtained in
1881. This picture shows No. 1A, which was originally named *Melton Constable*, after it had become M&GN
stock. No. 1A was withdrawn in 1898 and was one of the six that
were officially rebuilt as 0-6-0Ts, a class described in Chapter 7.
This picture was taken by the Midland Railway Photographer, but
the date is uncertain. R.J. ESSERY COLLECTION.

Plate 17
This delightful picture was taken at Yarmouth and shows No. 11 running as an 0-6-0 in immaculate
Eastern & Midlands livery coupled to a four wheel tender but retaining the side tanks. A note on the
reverse of the print records Driver Leverick is on the footplate. ALAN WELLS COLLECTION.

Plate 18
Photographed at Norwich about 1900, the note on the reverse of the print states that Driver Williams is in
the cab. No. 12 always ran as an 0-6-0 with side tanks coupled to a four wheel tender; it was the last Cornwall
engine to be withdrawn, beings scrapped in 1902. R.J. ESSERY COLLECTION.

Plate 19
This engine was originally L&FR No. 3 *Blakeney*, but became No. 3A in M&GN stock. This picture shows the locomotive after it had been rebuilt as a 2-4-0 in 1891. It was to remain in service until 1899 when it was scrapped. R.J. ESSERY COLLECTION.

THE CORNWALL MINERALS ENGINES

We conclude the review of the pre-1883 components of the M&GN locomotive stock with a most interesting group of eight engines whose story began in 1874 when they were built by Sharp Stewart & Co. to a design by Mr F.B. Trevithick for the Cornwall Minerals Railway, Originally, eighteen of these engines had been built as 0-6-0Ts with high sided tanks surmounted by a coal space. Their lack of any form of conventional bunkers was because they were designed to work in pairs, coupled footplate to footplate – a sort of quasi-articulation one supposes. In 1877, three of them (CMR No's 15–17) were returned to the makers, it is believed in discharge of some sort of debt, while a further nine (CMR No's 1–9) were taken over by the GWR and in due course (1883–84) rebuilt as conventional saddle tanks with rear bunkers (GWR No's 1392–1400). Meanwhile, Sharp's had given the three 'returnees' more substantial cabs with proper back plates and sold them in 1880 to the L&FR. They were the first engines to be given numbers, becoming No's 1–3 on that system (in reverse order to their original CMR numbers) and were named *Melton Constable*, *Reepham* and *Blakeney* respectively. In 1883 they were fitted with tenders.

These three engines were joined on the L&FR in March 1881 by five of the six remaining CMR engines, which had also been set aside four years earlier and which were eventually disposed of to Messrs Sharp's for similar conversion. On arrival on the L&FR they retained their original CMR numbers (11–14, 18) and had tenders from the outset. Purely for the record, the last of the final six CMR engines (CMR No. 10) went to the Colne Valley and Halstead Railway

(where it bore the name *Haverhill)* and from thence to South Hetton Colliery where it survived until 1948. The engines were promptly called 'side tank' engines and their full history is quite involved; it has been covered by Alan Wells in *The Cornwall Minerals Railway and its Locomotives*, published by the M&GN Circle.

Regularly referred to as the 'Cornwall Minerals' engines, in many respects, in spite of their 'Trevithick' origin, they were still fairly typical mid-Victorian 'Sharpies' and not too dissimilar (save for their outside cylinders) from broadly contemporary examples on, for example, the Cambrian and Furness railways. The new tenders were definitely 'Sharp Stewart' in design and tended to reinforce this 'look'.

The outside cylinders of 16¼ inches × 20 inches drove coupled wheels of 3 feet 6 inches diameter on a wheelbase of 11 feet: leading to driving 5 feet, driving to trailing 6 feet. The boilers, 8 feet 2 inches long by 4 feet in mean diameter contained 195 tubes of 1 inch outside diameter, which gave 753 square feet of heating surface and the firebox contributed a further 70.5 square feet. The grate area was 10.8 square feet and boiler pressure 140 psi. With 780 gallons of water and 15 hundredweight of coal they weighed 30 tons 10 hundredweight. They had Allen straight link motion reversed by a wheel on the right side and the left crank led in forward gear. The fireboxes were raised and, with *Alpha* and *Vici*, these were the only M&GN engines to have that feature. It was, in fact, a quite common Sharp Stewart design feature at the time. The tenders supplied in 1883 were to Sharp Stewart standard four-wheel type, carrying 1150 gallons of water and three tons of coal. The wheels were 3 feet 6 inches diameter and the wheelbase 9 feet 3 inches. The weight of the

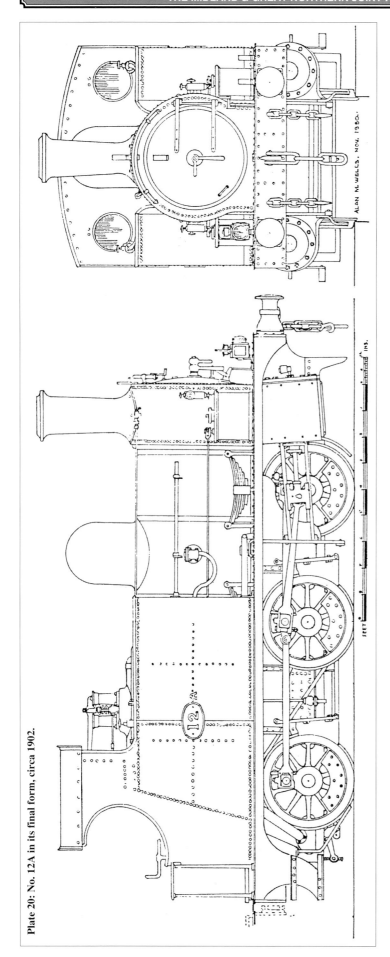

Plate 20: No. 12A in its final form, circa 1902.

tender in full working order was 15 tons 10 hundredweight. The cab back plates were removed when the tenders were supplied and the engine then weighed 29 tons 10 hundredweight. The locomotives carried the numbers on the front of the chimney in cut out brass numerals and the number plates were removed from the tank side. Classed 'C' by the E&MR, they were re-designated Class 'CM' by the M&GN on the arrival of the Johnson 4-4-0s.

Handbrakes were fitted to engines and tenders and the engines were fitted originally with wooden brake blocks, later replaced by iron, acting on the leading and trailing wheels only. Like the 4-4-0Ts already described, in their early days sand was only available for forward running, but later changes saw the addition of sandboxes beneath the cab for use when running in reverse. Cylinders had no drain cocks but the steam chest was so equipped. Gifford type injectors were located on top of the side tanks, control being exercised by the enginemen putting their arms through the forward spectacle plate. New chimneys of the built-up type fairly soon replaced the originals and these in turn gave way to the cast variety.

They were not very successful for goods traffic on long gradients and in 1890 No. 18 was rebuilt as a 2-4-0 with coupled wheels of 4 feet 7 inches diameter. To accommodate the higher wheel centres the whole body was raised 2½ inches. The 3 feet 6 inch leading wheels were kept and deeper hornblocks put on to allow the extra movement. The tender remained at the original height and a wooden footplate was added to come level with the engine footplate. The side tanks were dispensed with and the new cab and splasher provided. On this engine the injector delivery was put on to the boiler backplate. The large sandbox, made integral with the splasher, supplied sand by steam sanding gear. A Melton built-up chimney was used and the engine and tender were equipped with the Westinghouse brake. This complex rebuild was the first to be carried out at Melton Constable.

The work (there were three more) was featured in the engineering press but they were still not very successful engines. No's 3 and 13 were rebuilt to 2-4-0 in 1891, No. 14 in 1892, but the injector clackboxes remained on the boiler barrel and this meant a smaller sandbox was used. A later pattern chimney was also used and careful study indicates that the engines were not raised as No. 18 had been. No. 3 retained its handbrake. All the ex-Cornwall Minerals engines came into joint ownership and were put into the duplicate list in 1894, No. 2A being withdrawn the same year.

Neither as 0-6-0s or 2-4-0s were the engines really popular and no tears were shed when they were finally withdrawn. Six more went between 1897 and 1899, which was no great lifespan for engines built in 1874. In theory, six of them (No's 1A, 2A, 3A, 11A, 12A, 14A) were officially to have been rebuilt as 0-6-0 shunting tanks but all were, in fact, scrapped as they stood. The shunting tanks that took their numbers (Chapter 7) were new engines. No. 12A was the only one to last into the twentieth century, being latterly at Yarmouth in connection with building the new Yarmouth to Lowestoft line of the Norfolk and Suffolk Joint system; it was withdrawn in 1902.

CONCLUSION

The inherited engines of the E&MR in 1883 were an interesting, if not always wholly successful, collection but they undoubtedly gave some character to the system if only because their visual lines were quite different from anything which the MR or the GNR added after 1893. This was further emphasised by the modest additions made to the E&MR stock during 1883–93 and it is to these that we must turn in the next chapter.

EASTERN & MIDLANDS LOCOMOTIVE STOCK TAKEN OVER BY M&GNJR 1893

YARMOUTH & NORTH NORFOLK RAILWAY

M&GN No.	TYPE	NAME	BUILDER	DATE	REMARKS
From Great Yarmouth & Stalham Light Railway					
7	0-6-0ST	*Ida*	Black Hawthorn	1877	Sold 1894
15	0-6-0ST	*Ormesby*	Fox Walker	1876	Sold 1900
16	0-6-0ST	*Stalham*	Fox Walker	1876	To M&GN No. 16A. Sold 1937
Supplied direct to Y&NNR					
17	0-6-0ST	*Aylsham*	Black Hawthorn	1881	To M&GN No. 17A. Scrapped 1902
19	4-4-0T	*Great Yarmouth*	Hudswell, Clark	1881	Sold to War Department circa 1917
40	4-4-0T	*Martham*	Hudswell, Clark	1879	Ex-E&MR No. 31. Sold 1917
41	4-4-0T	*North Walsham*	Hudswell, Clark	1878	Ex-E&MR No. 32. Withdrawn for stationary boiler work 1904

LYNN & FAKENHAM RAILWAY

M&GN No.	TYPE	NAME	BUILDER	DATE	REMARKS
Supplied direct to L&FR					
4	0-4-0ST	*Alpha*	Hudswell, Clark	1878	To M&GN No. 4A. Sold to J. & J. Colman, Norwich, 1917
5	0-4-0ST	*Vici*	Hudswell, Clark	1880	To M&GN No. 5A. Date withdrawn not known
6	0-6-0ST	*Holt /Chairman*	Black Hawthorn	1881	Sold 1894
8	4-4-0T	*Hillington*	Hudswell, Clark	1878	Sold to War Department 1917
9	4-4-0T	*Fakenham*	Hudswell, Clark	1879	To M&GN No. 9A. Withdrawn 1932
10	4-4-0T	*Norwich*	Hudswell, Clark	1880	Sold to War Department 1917
20	4-4-0T	*King's Lynn*	Hudswell, Clark	1881	To M&GN No. 20A. Withdrawn 1931
From Cornwall Minerals Railway					
1	0-6-0	*Melton Constable*	Sharp Stewart	1874	To M&GN No. 1A. Withdrawn 1898
2	0-6-0	*Reepham*	Sharp Stewart	1874	To M&GN No. 2A. Withdrawn 1894
3	2-4-0 (ex-0-6-0)	*Blakeney*	Sharp Stewart	1874	To M&GN No. 3A. Withdrawn 1899
11	0-6-0		Sharp Stewart	1874	To M&GN No. 11A. Withdrawn 1899
12	0-6-0		Sharp Stewart	1874	To M&GN No. 12A. Withdrawn 1902
13	2-4-0 (ex-0-6-0)		Sharp Stewart	1874	To M&GN No. 13A. Withdrawn 1899
14	2-4-0 (ex-0-6-0)		Sharp Stewart	1874	To M&GN No. 14A. Withdrawn 1897
18	2-4-0 (ex-0-6-0)		Sharp Stewart	1874	To M&GN No. 18A. Withdrawn 1895

Plate 21
Here we see one of the ex-Cornwall Minerals Railway engines, Eastern & Midlands Railway No. 13, running as an 0-6-0 tender engine before being rebuilt as a 2-4-0 in 1892. COLLECTION ALAN WELLS.

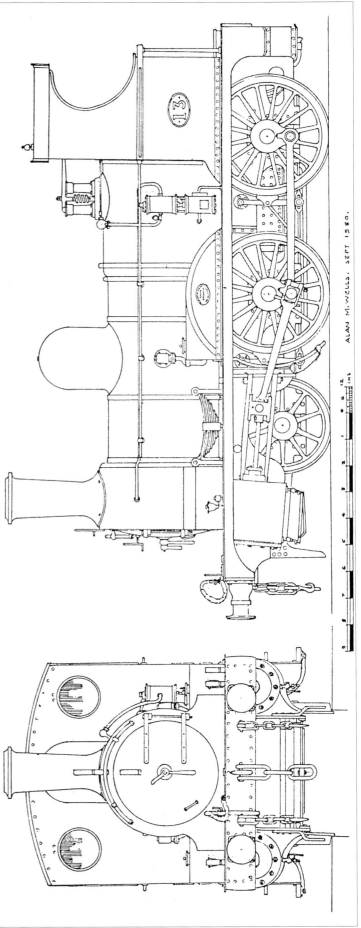

FACING PAGE, TOP: **Plate 22**
In 1881, a second batch of ex-Cornwall Mineral Railway 0-6-0 locomotives was taken into stock by the L&FR. These locomotives were equipped with tenders but retained the side tanks. In about 1891, two, No's 13 and 14, were rebuilt as 2-4-0s and fitted with Westinghouse brakes which would enable them to work fitted trains if required. No. 13A was withdrawn in 1899. This picture was taken at Melton Constable by the Midland Railway Photographer in 1894. Note the experimental lettering almost certainly applied on the E&M livery. R.J. ESSERY COLLECTION.

FACING PAGE, BOTTOM: **Plate 23**
Locomotive E&MR No. 13, as rebuilt in 1891 for use with a tender.

BELOW: **Plate 24**
Sharp Stewart four wheeled tender, measured survey from King's Lynn, 1938.

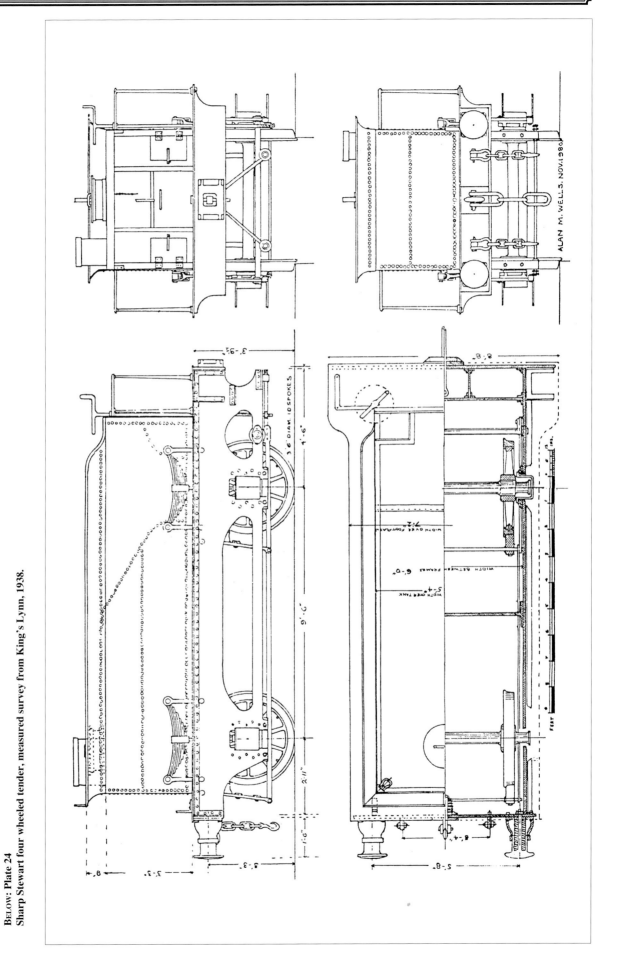

Plate 25

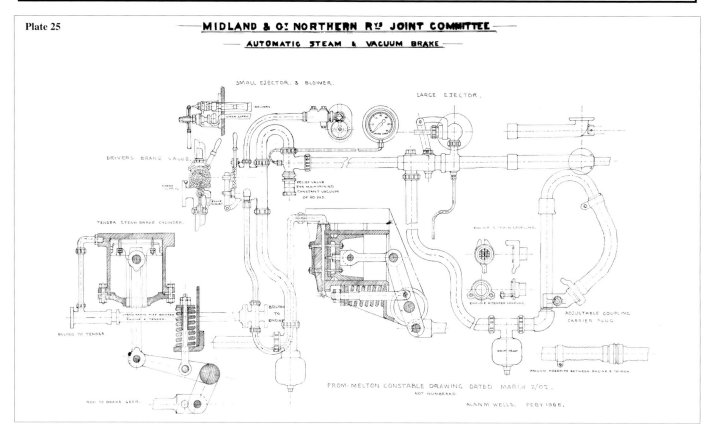

Plate 26
This old tender was originally coupled to a Cornwall Minerals engine, but after the locomotive was scrapped the tender was used to supply water to locations that did not have a water supply. The tenders retained the number of the locomotive to which they had been coupled, in this case No. 1A. They were painted grey and lettered in white, shaded black. J.H.L. ADAMS.

CHAPTER 5

EASTERN & MIDLANDS RAILWAY ACQUISITIONS: 1883–1893

The previous chapter indicated that on the formation of the E&MR in 1883, the newly enlarged railway was not too lavishly endowed with locomotives, even allowing for the fact that the MR and GNR continued to work the 'engine-less' lines of the E&MR lines 'west of Lynn'. It should therefore occasion no surprise that in the brief ten-year existence of the E&MR it added no fewer than seventeen further engines to its stock. In 1893, when the M&GN was formed, these 'extras' represented some 44 per cent of the total E&MR contribution in purely numerical terms, but probably constituted a far higher percentage in terms of actual work done. All but two of these seventeen locomotives were acquired new – the subsequently very celebrated and characteristic Beyer Peacock 4-4-0s. In fact the need for more motive power had been obvious even before the formation of the E&MR and the first order for the 'Peacocks' was actually placed by the Lynn & Fakenham with the first of them just managing to enter service as L&FR engines before the 1883 amalgamations. However, the full class of Beyer Peacock 4-4-0s were essentially put in service as E&MR engines so they are dealt with here. Before that, however, another 'maverick' group must first be considered – a pair of locomotives acquired by purchase from a most unlikely source – the Lancaster and Carlisle section of the old L&NWR.

EX-LONDON & NORTH WESTERN RAILWAY 2-4-0s

There can be little doubt that it was the shortage of main line motive power which prompted the E&MR to purchase two second hand engines in 1883 – presumably as a stop-gap until more of the Beyer Peacock 4-4-0s were in service. The reason why the particular examples (or type) were chosen does not seem to have been recorded – at least no reasons have been put forward in print. Age does not seem to have been a consideration for, unlike the 'Cornwall Minerals' engines (Chapter 4), they were both near-veterans of twenty-six years old when purchased, but they were to a well proven and reliable design and this may have been important in the circumstances. They were both 2-4-0s of the celebrated 'Crewe' type with massive double frames at the front end, fully integrated with the outside cylinders and smokebox wrapper. This idea, conceived principally to eliminate the curse of broken crank axles on inside cylinder engines in earlier days, is often wrongly attributed to Alexander Allan; but it was more

Plate 1
This picture of No. 43A was taken at Yarmouth where the engine was employed on stopping freight trains between Melton Constable and Yarmouth. The locomotive was fitted with hand brakes on both the engine and tender, the driver is recorded as T. Long. ALAN WELLS COLLECTION.

Plate 2
The first of the Beyer Peacock 4-4-0s to enter service were No's 21–24 which were built in 1882 for the L&FR, but the remainder of the class entered service after the L&FR had become part of the Eastern & Midlands Railway. This picture shows No. 24 prior to entering traffic for the L&FR. The photograph was probably taken at Beyer Peacock's works. R.J. ESSERY COLLECTION.

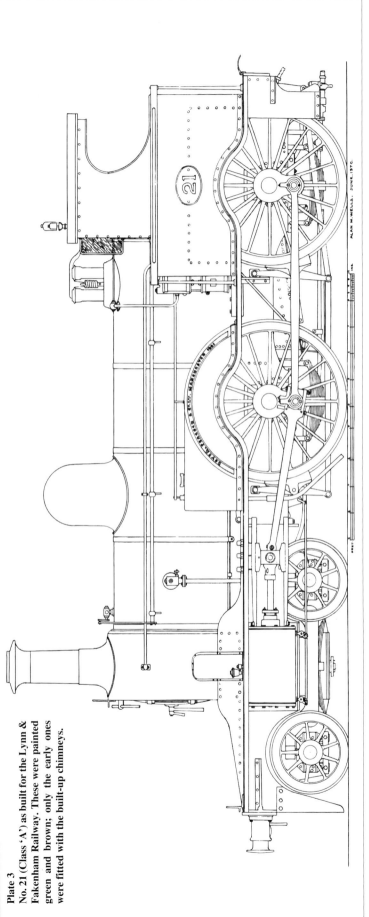

Plate 3
No. 21 (Class 'A') as built for the Lynn & Fakenham Railway. These were painted green and brown; only the early ones were fitted with the built-up chimneys.

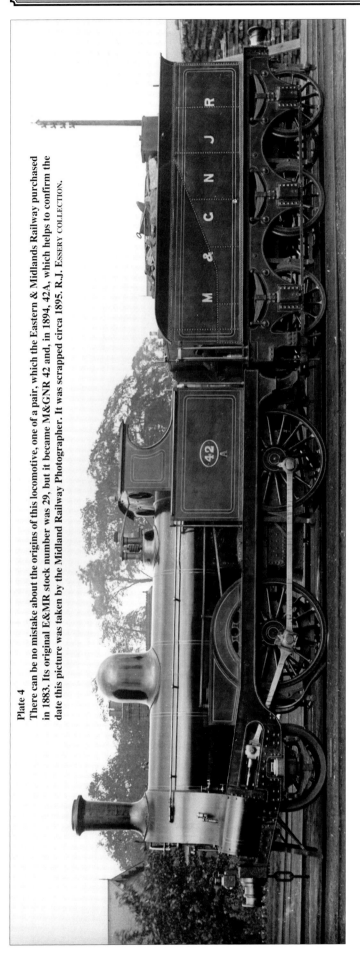

Plate 4
There can be no mistake about the origins of this locomotive, one of a pair, which the Eastern & Midlands Railway purchased in 1883. Its original E&MR stock number was 29, but it became M&GNR 42 and, in 1894, 42A, which helps to confirm the date this picture was taken by the Midland Railway Photographer. It was scrapped circa 1895. R.J. ESSERY COLLECTION.

properly the brainchild of William Barber Buddicom and Francis Trevithick who pioneered its use on the Grand Junction Railway and later exported it to many other parts, including France, where such engines were always known as 'Les Buddicoms'.

The two engines purchased from the L&NWR were both built by Rothwell & Co. of Bolton for the Lancaster and Carlisle Railway. No. 379 *Sedgewick* had been No. 3 on the L&CR and later became No. 1118, 1101 and 1859 on the L&NWR. It was delivered to the E&MR on the 9th April 1883 and became No. 29 (later renumbered 42 and, in 1894, 42A). For many years it was thought that No. 29 was in fact *Rickerby* (No. 377) but that engine is now known to have been scrapped at Crewe. The second 2-4-0, No. 384 *Luck of Edenhall* was, like *Sedgewick*, built in 1857. It was No. 8 of the L&CR and No's 384, 1802, 1112 and 1976 respectively on the L&NWR. It was delivered to the E&MR on the 10th November 1883. This locomotive became No. 30 but was renumbered 43 in 1886. In 1894 it was put on the duplicate list and the added suffix 'A' was given whilst still in E&MR livery.

Heating surface and grate area are not known. They had been reboilered with Webb boilers and had his cab fitted, and the original four wheeled tenders were changed for McConnell six wheelers. The wheelbase was about 14 feet 3 inches being 6 feet leading to driving and about 8 feet 3 inches between coupled wheels. The 'about' dimensions were so shown on the diagram in Melton Drawing Office. Of the many diagrams of locomotives that the authors have seen, it is the only one with 'about' dimensions! They had Allan straight link motion reversed from the left side, but in 1891 No. 43 was rebuilt with Howe link motion reversed from the right, and the tender tank was renewed with a larger capacity. At some time a Melton chimney replaced the Webb chimney. No. 42 was similarly dealt with in 1893. They had no continuous brake – separate handbrakes for engine and tender being retained on both locomotives. The rebuilding was necessary because the engines were in a rundown condition when bought, though one wonders why it took the E&MR nearly ten years to undertake this work. No. 42 was at Norwich and worked the stopping goods train to Cromer and back each day, whilst No. 43 was at Melton and worked over the Yarmouth road. No. 42 was scrapped at Norwich about 1895 and No. 43 at Melton at much the same time.

PRINCIPAL DIMENSIONS FOR THE EX-L&NWR 2-4-0S				
Cylinders	Leading Wheel	Coupled Wheel	Boiler Pressure	Weight in Working Order
Outside 17in×20in	3ft 5in	5ft 2in	140 psi	22 tons 10 cwt

THE BEYER PEACOCK 4-4-0S

Of all the many and varied locomotives associated with the old M&GN, it is the authors' opinion that the Beyer Peacock 4-4-0s (known as Class 'A') can lay the most sound claim to have symbolised the difference of the system compared with its neighbours – including its two parent companies for that matter – if for no other reason than that they were neither MR nor GNR in lineaments. Even though the M&GN products of the latter companies were never quite like those of the owning company, they always had a strong family resemblance; but no matter how much subsequent modification was done to the 'Peacocks', they always remained quintessentially M&GN in character.

The story began in 1882, when the Lynn & Fakenham Railway received four outside cylinder 4-4-0s from Beyer Peacock & Co. (No's 21–24, works No's 2105–8 of 1881), which cost £3,000 each. They represented a tremendous step forward in terms of motive power and were quite sophisticated and contemporary locomotives. Though designed by the builders and carrying many of the characteristic Beyer Peacock 'trademarks' – including the distinctive concentric works plate on the outer edge of the leading coupled wheel splasher – they bore more than a slight resemblance to some of the contemporary William Adams designs for the London & South Western Railway.

Smaller than the contemporary Adams 4-4-0s, they shared the beautifully balanced and classical looks of the L&SWR product. Their front-end symmetry with a vertical line precisely bisecting chimney, cylinders and leading bogie was surely no accident, any more than was the descending height of the chimney, dome and cab roof from front to rear. Truly a classic-looking design, their performance in no way betrayed their lineaments until, in far more recent times, increasing train weights started to tax their absolute power and they began to be moved on to lighter services – but this is to anticipate. When built, they had 17 inches × 24 inches cylinders (massive by previous L&FR standards), bogie wheels of 3 feet 0 inches diameter and 6 feet 0 inches coupled wheels. The coupled wheelbase was only 8 feet 2 inches which prevented the later fitting of the Midland 'B' Class boiler. Bogie wheelbase was 6 feet 6 inches and between bogie and leading driving wheel, 6 feet 9 inches. The boiler, pressed to 140 psi, was 10 feet 3½ inches long and 4 feet 1 inch mean diameter and had 204 tubes of 1¾ inches outside diameter. This gave a heating surface of 988 square feet which, added to the 95 square feet of the firebox, was a quantum leap by previous standards. The grate area was 17.7 square feet. Six-wheeled tenders with a capacity of 2,000 gallons of water and three tons of coal ran on 3 feet 7½ inches wheels on a wheelbase of 11 feet equally divided. Weight in working order was, for the engine, 38 tons 7 hundredweight 1 quarter and, for the tender, 23 tons 9 hundredweight. Westinghouse brakes were fitted, but with no connection at the front. This first batch had copper capped chimneys and shorter domes than the subsequent batches. As built, the sophisticated compensating beams as seen on the Adams L&SWR 4-4-0s were not fitted between the coupled wheel springs but were added later, only to be removed still later.

Four more were delivered during 1883. They had been ordered by the Lynn & Fakenham Railway but the line had now become the Eastern & Midlands Railway. There were also slight technical differences from the earlier engines. The Westinghouse pump was placed forward into a more accessible position for attention and maintenance, but the most striking difference was in the height of the domes which were 9 inches higher in order to minimise the risk of priming, the water at Yarmouth being brackish. Provision was made at the front for the continuous brake and they were probably fitted with a built-up chimney similar to Stirling engines on the Great Northern. Again no compensating beams were fitted to the coupled wheels and they never were fitted to this batch. The running numbers of these engines were 25 to 28 (works No's 2338 to 2341 of 1883). They also cost £3,000 each.

No's 29–31 (works No's 2794, 2795 and 2798 of 1886) arrived in November 1886. Compensating beams were fitted from new on this and the final batch. For some reason that cannot be explained, it appears that they cost only £2,000 each. The final batch, No's 32–35 of 1888, arrived in May and June of that year. These engines were fitted with pipes and ejectors for the vacuum brake but had Westinghouse brakes like the others. These cost £2,300 each. They were useful engines and much more powerful than any of the previous engines as well as having a better turn of speed. They had regular crews and some drivers had a polished steel band fitted to the chimney, a practice that extended well into the later M&GN period. This feature can be seen at Plate 14, page 156.

Between 1895 and 1909 the whole class was reboilered with modified Midland Railway 'C' Class boilers. These were 10 feet 6 inches long with a mean diameter of 4 feet 2 inches and had 196 tubes of 1¾ inches outside diameter. These gave an almost identical boiler heating surface of 989 square feet and the firebox (which only had a grate area of 16 square feet) offered a further 104.4 square feet.

Plate 5
No. 29 was one of three, 29–31, that became E&MR stock in November 1886 and apart from the chimneys they were identical to the preceding batch. They were fitted with Westinghouse brakes, but following the formation of the M&GNJR, Midland practice prevailed and they were replaced with vacuum brakes. R.J. ESSERY COLLECTION.

Plate 6
No. 28 was the fourth engine of the second batch, No's 25–28, and entered traffic as an E&MR locomotive in 1883. The only difference between the first and second batch was the dome: they were higher on No's 25–28, as seen in this picture taken by the Midland Railway Photographer at Melton Constable in 1894. R.J. ESSERY COLLECTION.

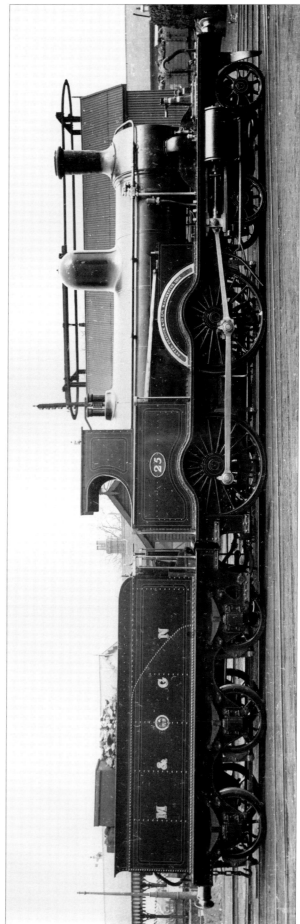

ABOVE: Plate 7
This picture was taken at Melton Constable at some time before No. 25 was reboilered in 1906 and shows the M&GN painting style after the company ceased to letter locomotives Jt M&GNR. R.J. ESSERY COLLECTION.

The working pressure was initially 140 psi, but after about 1906 it was increased to 160 psi. The standard steam/vacuum brake equipment replaced the Westinghouse brake after 1893 and the original boilers had the blower pipe on top of the boiler removed; they received plain cast Melton chimneys. From 1906, extended smokeboxes were fitted and a later Melton chimney, in some cases with a wind band, and extended cab roofs with an upright grab iron appeared on some. Three also received tender weatherboards for tender-first working, which could be moved from engine to engine when required.

No. 21 was rebuilt in 1914, with new straight-sided Midland pattern tender and new cab with round lookouts. The driving wheel splashers had sand boxes front and back, and the steam sanding applied for running either way. The two traversing jacks beside the smokebox, which had long been a feature of this class and the 4-4-0 tanks, were dispensed with. The original boiler centre height was retained at 6 feet 9 inches, but in subsequent rebuilds it was raised to 7 feet 3 inches above rail level. 'C' Class boilers were again used for this rebuilding. The new tender carried 3,000 gallons of water and 4 tons of coal, and the 3 feet 7½ inch wheels were on a wheelbase of 13 feet. It will be noted that these wheels differed in size from the true Midland tenders. No. 22 was similarly treated in 1915 (but as stated had the higher boiler centre) and No. 23 followed suit in 1919, No. 24 in 1914, No. 25 in 1920, No. 26 in 1923, No. 27 in 1927 and No. 28 in 1925.

Despite the considerable improvement on what had gone before, the riding qualities of these engines were far from good and, surprisingly, the engines that were not rebuilt and retained the compensating beams were far the worst. No. 24 remained at Melton and for a time worked through to Peterborough and back each day. The other rebuilds all found their way to South Lynn and the western section but were rarely seen on the Peterborough road. Only two were taken into L&NER stock, No's 25 and 27, and only No. 25 received the '0' prefix and had the initials of that company painted on the tender.

Withdrawal dates are given in the table. It should be stated here that the boiler of No. 24 was condemned and the frames No. 25 were broken, so the frames and wheels of No. 24 were united with the boiler and tender of No. 25 and the resultant hybrid became the new No. 25 – as a result, the official records gave the building date as November 1883 (old No. 25) rather than March 1882 (old No. 24). It should finally be added that the remains of some of these engines were laying about at Melton for some years before being cut up. All had worked for well over 40 years and the last survivor (L&NER No. 025) was 58 years old when withdrawn – no bad record for a relatively small class of engine.

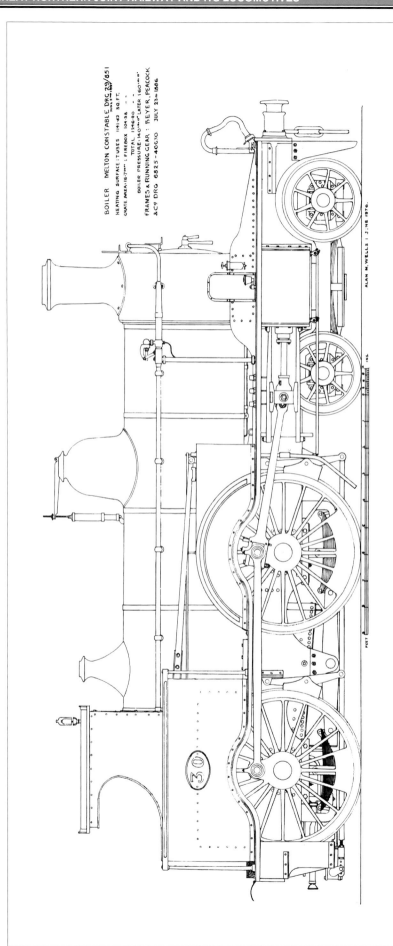

Plate 8
No. 30 as reboilered with 'C modified' boiler. The chimney is the first Melton pattern. Steam vacuum brake has superseded the Westinghouse, and it will be seen that the brake pull rods have been altered at the trailing end.

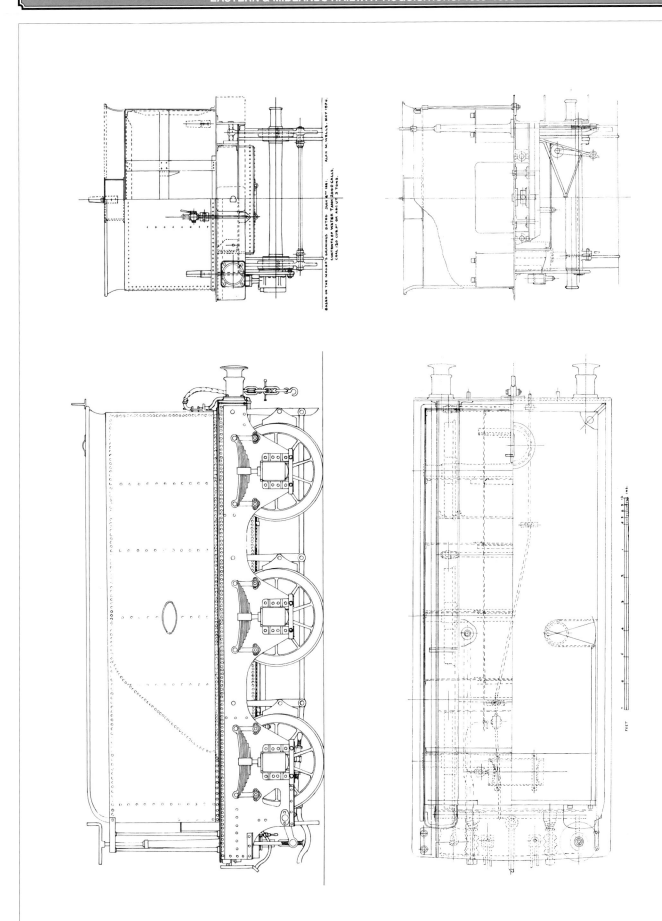

Plate 9
Drawing of the 2,000 gallon tender, as fitted to all of nos 21–35 when built. Built by Beyer Peacock & Co. Ltd, Gorton.

SUMMARY TABLE FOR THE BEYER PEACOCK CLASS 'A' 4-4-0

M&GN No's	DATE BUILT	REBUILT WITH MODIFIED MIDLAND 'C' CLASS BOILER, MIDLAND FITTINGS	SECOND REBUILDING	WITHDRAWN
21	1882	1896	1914	1936
22	1882	1898	1915	1936
23	3/1882	1895	1919	2/1937
24	1882	1898	1914	9/1936
25	11/1883	1906	1920	1941
26	11/1883	1904	1923	11/1936
27	11/1883	1905	1927	2/1937
28	11/1883	1905	1925	2/1938
29	1886	1906		1931
30	1886	1906		1933
31	1886	1906		1933
32	5/1888	1906		1933
33	1888	1908		1936
34	1888	1908		1936
35	1888	1909		1933

Engines No's 21–30 were rebuilt with modified Midland Railway 'C' Class boilers and later they received extended smokeboxes, but No's 31–35 received extended smokeboxes when they were rebuilt.

When first rebuilt No's 21, 26, 30, 31, 32, 33, 34 and 35 received extended cab roofs with grab irons, and No's 30, 33 and 34 were photographed with tender weatherboards for reverse running, later fittings being No's 32, 33 and 35.

Plate 10
This picture of No. 35 was taken at Melton Constable shortly before the engine was scrapped in 1933. When photographed it was fitted with a back weatherboard which, following withdrawal, was transferred to another locomotive. As can be seen, the Melton Constable coaling plant was rather primitive and entailed a lot of hard work on the part of the fireman. F.M. GATES.

Plate 11
No. 30 was one of the third batch, No's 29–31, and entered traffic in November 1886. Apart from the chimney they were identical with the previous batch. Following the formation of the M&GN, locomotives were lettered Jt M&GNR as shown, but later the initial Jt was discontinued. The locomotive is in immaculate condition. The reader's attention is drawn to the presence of two lifting jacks – one was more normal – and the arrangement of the front coupling where the three-link coupling has two long and one short link and there is also a screw coupling hanging over the coupling hook. R.J. ESSERY COLLECTION.

Plate 12
These two pictures, Plates 12 and 13, which have consecutive negative numbers, show the original and Midland Railway replacement boilers. There can be little doubt Plate 12 shows the original boiler, which was fed by two injectors – note the steam valves, two large wheels above the regulator. Unlike the replacement boiler there were two boiler water gauges, but in keeping with the current practice they were not fitted with a protector. The firedoors are similar to the type used by the LM&S in the Stanier era, but cushions on the top of the toolboxes were something that would not be found on a Midland locomotive. The first locomotive to be rebuilt was No. 23 in 1895 and it is possible this is the locomotive that was the subject of both photographs. Although the Midland Railway Photographer took many pictures following the formation of the M&GNR, he undoubtedly made other visits to the Joint line. Research indicates that the negative numbers given may not be indicative of the date the picture was taken, the result of a renumbering that took place to put all the M&GN numbers into a single series. R.J. ESSERY COLLECTION.

Plate 13
This shows the cab interior of a locomotive that has been fitted with a Midland Railway modified 'C' boiler but, unlike the boilers used on the Midland system, the M&GN boiler had a shorter firebox with 1¾ inch tubes instead of 1⅝ inch. Until about 1906 the earlier boilers were pressed at 140 lb per square inch, but the replacement boilers were pressed at 160 lb per square inch. Johnson pattern mountings were used and combination injectors on the firebox backplate replaced the original type with independent clackboxes. With the exception of the reverser and the absence of a boiler water gauge glass protector the layout is similar to the 'B' Class boiler 0-6-0s that were still in service during the early days of British Railways, although padded seats were unknown. R.J. Essery collection.

Plate 14
Only two of the Beyer Peacock 4-4-0s survived long enough to receive the '0' prefix by the L&NER: No's 25 and 27. No. 27 is seen here at Yarmouth Beach on the 24th October 1936 with Fireman A. Walker in the cab. This picture shows the second rebuilding of the engine carried out in 1927, with the replacement straight-sided tender which could carry 4 tons of coal and 3000 gallons of water. The new cabs, while not as aesthetically pleasing as the originals, offered better protection to the driver and fireman. W.A. CAMWELL.

CHAPTER 6

THE 'MIDLAND' 4-4-0S

The Midland Railway had not long been in charge of locomotive affairs on the M&GN before it began to inject its own characteristic ideas on to the scene. Indeed, as the previous chapters have half-hinted, the engines on hand in 1893, even including the Beyer Peacock 4-4-0s, could barely cope with the traffic on offer in the eastern section, let alone elsewhere, so the lines west of Lynn continued to be worked for a year or so by Great Northern and Midland engines as before. In fact, such was the situation that several Midland engines were transferred into the eastern section. Amongst them, according to reliable sources, were 4-4-0 engines of the '1738' Class (see *Midland Locomotives, Volume 2*), of which No's 11 and 14 were for some time at Norwich. At least one 2-4-0, No. 233A (a rebuild of a Kirtley double framed tank engine), was also at Norwich and another 2-4-0, No. 198, was photographed at Cromer Beach. Some GNR engines were also on loan at the time.

Not surprisingly, the MR took action and as early as 1894 Messrs Sharp Stewart and Co. supplied the first twenty-six of an eventual forty-strong class of typical Johnson Midland type 'slim boiler' 4-4-0s for service on the Joint line. Known as M&GN Class 'C', these engines were, to all intents and purposes, identical to the MR '1808' Class 4-4-0s of 1888 and 1891 (see *Midland Locomotives, Volume 2*, page 100) and every bit as handsome in their 'as built' form. The class was completed by seven further examples each in 1896 and 1899 from Sharp Stewart and Beyer Peacock respectively.

We review below the gradual progression of the engines' detailed evolution; but at this stage it will be helpful, by way of comparison, briefly to recall the normal Midland development of most engines of the Johnson slim boiler type. On the Midland the first normal change was to replace the original slim boiler by the larger Deeley saturated steam round-topped 'H' boiler. This was often but not always followed by a further reboilering using the saturated 'G7' Belpaire boiler, but always retaining the original wheel size and wheelbase. The final change, applied to most but by no means all of the original Johnson engines, was a more extensive rebuild – in most cases it amounted to a full renewal often including a change in driving wheel diameter and coupled wheelbase – to the '483' Class form, using the superheated 'G7S' boiler. These superheated and so-called 'rebuilds' were the progenitors of the familiar LM&SR standard Class '2P' 4-4-0s.

The progression on the M&GN was rather different. The first change, beginning in 1907 and continuing to 1919, was to fit an extended smokebox to the original Johnson slim boiler – an alteration which did little for their looks and which was only applied to one MR slim boiler 4-4-0 – No. 323, formerly No. 1341 (see *Midland Locomotives, Volume 2*, page 84). No. 323 ran in the M&GN area and this may have been significant. After the extended smokeboxes on the slim boiler engines, the 'H' and 'G7' variants duly made their appearance on the Class 'C' 4-4-0s, just as on the parent MR system. Once again, extended smokeboxes appeared with the round top 'H' boilers on the M&GN, unlike the MR itself, but engines with 'G7' boilers had extended smokeboxes on both systems. However, the superheated 'G7S' boiler and the '483' Class form was never adopted for the M&GN series; instead, a number were rebuilt in later years with the smaller 'G6' Belpaire saturated boiler, something that was never done with the original MR 4-4-0s though it was common enough on the broadly contemporary 0-6-0 goods engines. As always, and again in contradistinction to the MR (by now LM&SR) system, the M&GN adopted an extended smokebox with the 'G6' boiler.

As with the Midland engines, the various post-Johnson era rebuilds also went hand in hand with various changes in cab style – usually

Plate 1
This picture of No. 44 was taken by the builders, Sharp Stewart & Co., and shows one of the first batch, built in 1894 and lettered 'J⸏M&GNR'. Some sources refer to them as being like the Midland Railway '2203' Class, but this is not correct; they were in fact like the '1808' Class, which had entered service on the Midland in 1888, with a further batch built in 1891. ALAN WELLS COLLECTION.

Plate 2
This picture of No. 54, built by Sharp Stewart & Co. in 1896, shows the locomotive in its original condition. In 1914 it was rebuilt with a 'G7' boiler and as L&NER No. 054 it was withdrawn in October 1939. P.C. DEWHURST.

occasioned by the changed boiler shape and/or the need to give greater crew comfort, although the Deeley-style cabs on the 'G7' rebuilds, unlike the Midland, had no roof vents. In one further respect, there was also much common ground: just as with the proper MR 4-4-0s, so too with the M&GN Class 'C's – there was never total consistency of appearance or boiler type once the rebuilding had commenced. Thus, just as on the MR itself, the once tidy pattern of broadly homogeneous engines quite soon became a fascinating mixture of all manner of variants. With this in mind, we will now attempt to unravel the story of the Class 'C' 4-4-0 locomotives, starting with a summary of building dates and principal dimensions as built.

SUMMARY OF ENGINES BUILT

No's 36–39, 42–50, 1–7, 11–14, 17 and 18. Sharp Stewart & Co. in 1894. Makers No's 3988–4013.
No's 51–57. Sharp Stewart & Co. in 1896. Makers No's 4190–4196.
No's 74–80. Beyer Peacock & Co. in 1899. Makers No's 4066–4072.

The principal dimensions were as follows. Inside cylinders 18 inches × 26 inch stroke with valves between. Bogie wheels 3 feet 3 inches diameter, coupled wheels 6 feet 6 inches diameter, tender wheels 4 feet 2½ inches diameter. Boiler pressure 160 psi. Total heating surface 1240 square feet (later reduced to 1150 square feet). Grate area 17.50 square feet. Engine weight in working order 42 tons 12 hundredweight. Tender with 2950 gallons of water three tons of coal: 33 tons 10 hundredweight 3 quarters. Centre line of boiler above rail level 7 feet 4 inches. Height to chimney top 13 feet 1³/₁₆ inches. Height to top of cab 11 feet 3 inches above rail level. Length over

engine and tender 52 feet 9½ inches. Wheelbase; engine bogie 6 feet, trailing bogie to driving 7 feet 0½ inches, coupled 8 feet 6 inches. Leading overhang 2 feet 2 inches, trailing overhang 4 feet 1 inch. Tender wheelbase 13 feet equally divided with leading overhang 4 feet and trailing 3 feet 8 inches.

There was little difference between the engines built by Sharp Stewart and Beyer Peacock except in the painting details. The Beyer Peacock batch had the Furness cylinder lubricators on the smokebox in line with the chimney; those by Sharp Stewart had them behind the smokebox. Midland brass cut-out numerals were used – these, as usual, being supplied by the Midland itself. The two plates on the back of the tender were identical to those used by S.W. Johnson on all Midland Railway locomotives. The lamp brackets were the same as for the Midland; that is, two up top – one at the base of the chimney the other on the top half of the smokebox door – one over the right buffer and two over the left buffer (looking from the cab). These were changed to four, one up top and three above the buffer beam in 1903. The first batch were lettered JᵀM&GNR as built, but this was altered to M&GN later and other batches were so lettered as built.

Unlike the Somerset & Dorset and the Midland, the buffer planks did not carry the company's initials, but had 'No' on one side of the coupling hook and the digits on the other. There were slight differences between the tenders of the Sharp Stewart and Beyer Peacock engines; the latter did not have the handrail across the back of the tender, as did the Sharp Stewart engines. Some round-headed rivets were used on the Beyer Peacocks, but all others were countersunk.

When reboilering became necessary, boilers were made at Melton Constable, except for 'H' and 'G7' types, these being supplied from

Derby (the 'GN' type boiler replacements for the 'DA' Class came from Doncaster). The original boilers were the Johnson Midland Railway 'B' Class. As built they required careful firing but with the alteration to the tubeplates a better circulation was given and from then on there was not much trouble with steaming. The Midland ran all the engines for a trial of 1,000 miles as laid down in the specifications before they were delivered to the M&GN.

The boilers were lagged with silicate cotton when built, but this was later changed to wood lagging. For many years the front coupling was of the three link type and most engines had a screw coupling over the lamp bracket on the footplate. Needless to say, a change to screw coupling was made, but the exactly when this took place is not known. From 1906, extended smokeboxes began to be fitted to the 'B' boilers; some had Johnson 3 feet 4 inches chimneys but generally a pattern designed at Melton Constable was used with a 2 inch windband. The smokeboxes were 4 feet 3 inches in length. No. 79 was the only locomotive on the Midland or M&GN with a windband fitted to the Johnson chimney.

Between 1906 and 1908, Whittaker Tablet Exchanging Apparatus was fitted (see Appendix B), in some cases for either way running. These were carried on the tender, as the oscillating of the engine was liable to result in the dropping of the tablet, and were operated by a slide – except on the 'H' and 'G7' rebuilds which had a jointed arrangement because of the raised cab floor.

No. 39 was rebuilt in 1908 with a Midland 'H' boiler of 4 feet 8 inches diameter and Deeley cab. The boiler centre line was set at 8 feet 3 inches above rail level and circular cab spectacle windows were retained. No. 55 was similarly rebuilt the same year but had a Johnson tapered chimney. The heating surface for No. 39 was 1428

square feet and that for No. 55 was 1347 square feet. Both received extended smokeboxes of Melton pattern, 4 feet 3 inches in length. The top lamp bracket was fitted above the smokebox and to reach it the fireman had to stand on the vacuum standpipe. This lamp bracket was later put on to the smokebox door.

The painting of the 'H' boiler rebuilds was as for the Sharp Stewart engines except that the device was enclosed in a shield-shaped motif. These two engines were the only ones to be so treated (see Chapter 11). They were stationed at Norwich to work the express to Leicester on alternate days. They both later received 'G7' boilers, No. 39 in 1924 and No. 55 in 1925. For a short time No. 55 ran with its cylinders lined up to 17 inches diameter as an experiment, but this not proving useful it had the cylinders opened out to 18½ inches.

No's 45 and 53 were rebuilt in 1909/10 with 'G7' boilers with Deeley parallel chimneys and cabs, and extended smokeboxes in which the two handle fastening gave way to a wheel and the Johnson plate hinge was replaced by two straps. Unfortunately, the chance was not taken to enlarge the tanks and the two coal rails remained until about 1921 when a third was added. Whereas the old type ejectors were fitted to No's 39 and 55, all the later 'G7' rebuilds had the combined type. No's 38 and 55 retained the old type to scrapping. Larger cut-out figures were used at the rebuilding. They were of the same shape as the originals. The boiler pressure was 175 psi for both 'H' and 'G7' rebuilds and the locomotives then became Power Class 2 for loading purposes. No's 56 and 57 were rebuilt to 'G7' in 1912, No. 52 in 1913, No. 54 in 1914, and No's 46 and 51 in 1915. In these first 'G7' boiler rebuilds, the mudholes on the upper edges of the Belpaire were covered with doors and the firedoors were of the sliding pattern, whilst later 'G7' boilers had plugs on the side

Plate 3
This view of No. 46 shows the locomotive at Holt after it had been fitted with an extended smokebox. It was rebuilt in 1915 with a 'G7' boiler and withdrawn in March 1943 as L&NER No. 046. E. BOLTZ.

of the firebox and Johnson firedoors. Likewise, the early boilers had open Ramsbottom safety valves with a lock up behind and later ones had Ross Pop valves which were changed to Ramsbottom valves later.

Unlike the Midland engines rebuilt with 'G7' boilers, which generally received new frames, the M&GN engines retained their original frames. Also unlike the Midland, all of these rebuilds were fitted with smokebox doors secured with a centre locking handle and handwheel rather than by dogs held by ⅞ inch nuts. These doors must have shown problems with air tightness, because in the 1920s many of them were fitted with dogs around the lower edge. Their ultimate fate was of course to receive Deeley doors.

All the engines were fitted with Midland type steam heating gear that was carried on the front of the tender. At first the pipe was only on the tender, but in Mr Nash's time some were fitted for either way running or when the train was doubleheaded. Between 1929 and 1930, seven of the unrebuilt engines were fitted with LM&SR 'G6' Belpaire boilers; No's 36 and 50 in 1929, No's 6, 44 and 77 in 1930, and No's 2 and 49 in 1931. They had Ross Pop valves and new cabs, which were extended and had upright handrails. The front lookouts were circular and above the Belpaire and it was virtually impossible to look through them. As a consequence the driver had to wedge himself between the reversing handle and the cab side when braking into a station. Needless to say they were not popular. Again the Pop valves were changed to open Ramsbottom, said to be done to avoid startling the large number of horses and other animals in the agricultural area that the railway passed through. Although some sources suggest that No. 2 kept the Pop valves until withdrawal, a photograph taken at Stratford when it was awaiting scrap shows Ramsbottom valves.

After these seven had been fitted with 'G6' boilers it was decided from 1931 to use 'B' boilers from the Derby Boiler Bank for all future boiler replacements, and these of course had Salter Spring Balance safety valves. They had slightly larger fireholes and did not steam as well as the M&GN-made 'B's. The boilers themselves were mostly recovered serviceable from withdrawn Kirtley double-famed 0-6-0s. From 1927 to about 1934 all the engines received Deeley-type smokeboxes with snap-head rivets and doors fitted with bolts and clips. The handrails finished near the front of smokebox and a straight handrail went across the door. Two straps replaced the Johnson plate hinges.

Mr A.H. Nash became Resident Mechanical Engineer in 1932 and he made alterations to several of the engines. He further extended the smokeboxes with jumper top blastpipes and plates over the tubes, but these features did not help. Neither did his short chimneys as fitted to the small boilered engines. A few engines were fitted with stovepipe chimneys which, whilst leaving the steaming unaffected, spoiled their appearance. With the small boilered engines the steam beat down in front of the cab and the engines did not steam as well as previously. The driver's seat on the 'G7' rebuilds was on top of the reversing gear and Mr Nash fitted a small tip-up seat near the cab opening on the right side, thus saving the driver the job of carrying his own portable seat around. One good thing he did was to cut slots in the splashers above the coupled axleboxes which made it possible to see into them without the driver having to wedge himself up inside the splasher when oiling up.

Plate 4
When this picture was taken at Bourne in 1906, No. 79, working a Yarmouth–Birmingham train, had been fitted with a chimney with a 'windband'; it was the only one of the class to be so equipped. Other points of interest include the use of a sack placed between the engine and tender handrails to reduce the draught on the fireman's side of the engine; the front coupling is still three links – later, screw link coupling were fitted. On the other side of the platform can be seen part of a Midland Railway 0-4-4T engine, which may have been one sent to the M&GN in exchange for the 4-4-0Ts, see Appendix A. No. 79 was withdrawn in February 1937 as L&NER No. 079. P.C. DEWHURST.

ABOVE: Plate 5
No. 55 was built by Sharp Stewart & Co. in 1896, but this picture was taken at Holt after it had been rebuilt in 1908 with a Midland 'H' Class boiler, the centre line set 8 feet 3 inches above rail level. Two engines were rebuilt, but while No. 39 had a parallel type chimney as used on the 'G7' rebuilds, No. 55 was fitted with a Johnson tapered chimney. The driver, seen in the cab, was Jack Loynes, and the fireman, standing on the platform, often referred to as the framing, was 'Punch' Walpole. In 1925 a 'G7' boiler was fitted, the locomotive was withdrawn as L&NER No. 055 in November 1943. ALAN WELLS COLLECTION.

BELOW: Plate 6
This picture illustrates the other Class 'C' locomotive to be rebuilt with an 'H' Class boiler. No. 39 was one of the first batch built by Sharp Stewart & Co. in 1894. It was rebuilt as seen here at Melton Constable in 1908, and reboilered again 1924 when it received a 'G7' boiler. Note the shield surround to the device, which is also visible on the picture of No. 55, Plate 5. Withdrawal came in February 1937 as No. 39, before the L&NER '0' prefix was applied. P.C. DEWHURST.

ABOVE: **Plate 7**
The 'C' Class locomotives that were rebuilt with 'G7' boilers and extended smokeboxes and stovepipe chimneys were not aesthetically pleasing. No. 56 received its first 'G7' boiler with an extended smokebox in 1912. There additional tender coal rail would have been helpful when the tender was coaled to its maximum capacity. When working onto a foreign system any water or coal taken would be charged, and while there was a limit to the amount of water that could be carried in the tank it was the usual practice to coal to the maximum so that the locomotive could work 'out and back' without the need to take further coal during the course of the journey. No. 56 was built by Sharp Stewart & Co. in 1896 and became No. 056 in February 1939, before being withdrawn in November 1943. ALAN WELLS COLLECTION.

Plate 8
This photograph of No. 053 was taken at South Lynn after the locomotive was renumbered by the L&NER in July 1937, but before it was withdrawn in January 1940. It should be pointed out that the windguard is missing from the chimney. P.C. DEWHURST.

The London & North Eastern Railway assumed management of the line on the 14th September 1936 and the footplate staff were transferred to that company along with the locomotives. At first all engines carried the '0' prefix to the M&GN numbers and the old brass numerals were taken off. The engines were still classed 'C' or 'C Rebuilds', but in 1942 became 'D52' for unrebuilt engines, 'D53' for those with 'G6' boilers and 'D54' for 'G7' rebuilds. Although seven of the class were allocated L&NER numbers, none did in fact carry them.

The L&NER diagrams show all the Class 'C's with Nash short wide chimneys, but none of the 'G6' engines had them, nor did many of those fitted with 'B' boilers. These later were shown with a single Salter Balance Valve, but at least a front elevation was given which the M&GN diagrams did not include. When rebuilt with 'H' and 'G7' boilers, independent blowers were fitted, but those with 'B' and 'G6' boilers retained the combined small ejector and blower. The small ejector wheel was moved 180 degrees and vacuum at 21 inches should have been maintained when the blower was opened, but in practice the vacuum dropped, so to keep down smoke when coasting, the ashpan damper and firedoor were opened rather than to just rely upon the blower. The first alteration made by the L&NER was to fit independent blowers operated by a rod above the right handrail. The blower operated in the ring in the base of the chimney and the ejectors exhausted up the side of the chimney, making a lot of noise.

In view of the reduced level of passenger traffic in the closed season the Class 'C' engines were used for both passenger and goods work, often being diagrammed for a goods out and a passenger back or vice versa. It says much for their construction and maintenance that they lasted as long as they did. The eastern section was heavily graded and with 6 feet 6 inch wheels it meant hard work. Excursion traffic was heavy in the summer and frequently trains would come into South Lynn behind two Class '4F's, then to be taken over a heavy road by a single Class 'C' engine. The heaviest load that one former M&GN employee ever saw single headed was of seventeen LM&SR bogies and this occurred on several occasions. Time was not always kept, especially in view of the large amount of single line involved, and in the circumstances this was not surprising. Perhaps more than anything that contributed to this sort of working was the quality of the coal and the use of the tablet exchange gear, which allowed the exchange to be taken at higher speed than if it was a hand exchange

between the signalman and fireman. This was supplemented by the skill of the enginemen whose exploits were highly spoken of.

On average, they did not last quite as long as the earlier Beyer Peacock 4-4-0s (Chapter 5), but they gave good service, especially for such relatively low-powered engines, most of them putting in at least forty years before they were withdrawn.

From about 1907, extended smokeboxes were fitted to the unrebuilt locomotives with 'B' Class boilers, but the chimneys varied. Some locomotives retained the original Midland chimney but others received various styles of Melton chimneys and some details are given below.

EXTENDED SMOKEBOXES WITH MELTON CHIMNEY EXCEPT (J)=JOHNSON CHIMNEY	
1907	14 (J), 17, 46
1908	13, 37, 47
1910	3, 38, 42
circa 1910	1, 2, 8, 18 (J)
1911	4, 5, 12, 36, 43, 44, 49, 50
1912	6, 48
1914	7, 77 (J)
1916	75, 76, 78
1917	79 (J)
1918	74
1919	80
NASH CHIMNEYS, (S)=STOVEPIPE	
1934	45 (S), 55 (S), 56 (S)
1935	1, 4, 12,
1936	38 (reverted to Melton chimney 1938), 42, 48, 56 (Nash flowerpot), 78

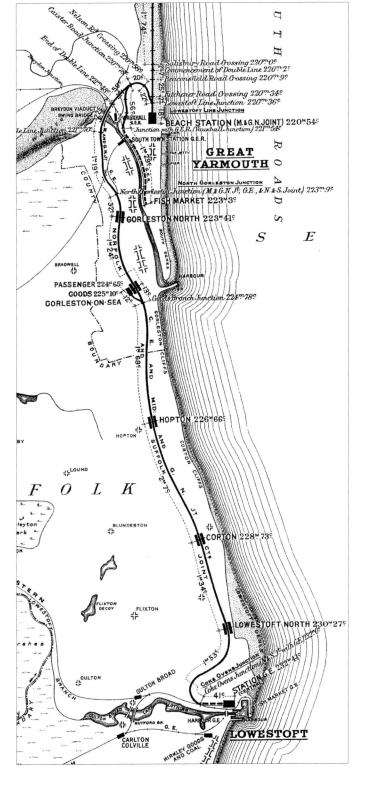

Plate 9
A number of 'C' Class locomotives were rebuilt with 'G6' Belpaire boilers, as seen in this picture of No. 36 photographed at Spalding on the 22nd October 1936. A note on the reverse of the print states that it is Driver H. Dawson in the cab. No's 36 and 50 were the first to be rebuilt in 1929, and the new cab was fitted at the same time. This locomotive was the first of the class to enter service in 1894 and it was withdrawn January 1937. W.A. CAMWELL.

Summary of Class 'C' 4-4-0

M&GN No.	Built by	Date Built	Rebuilt H Boiler	Rebuilt G7 Boiler	Rebuilt G6 Boiler	L&NER Number	Month Applied	Month Withdrawn
36	Sharp Stewart & Co.	14/5/1894			1929			1/37
37	Sharp Stewart & Co.	17/5/1894						2/37
38	Sharp Stewart & Co.	21/5/1894				038	12/37	9/43
39	Sharp Stewart & Co.	24/5/1894	1908	1923				2/37
42	Sharp Stewart & Co.	29/5/1894				042	11/36	6/40
43	Sharp Stewart & Co.	30/5/1894				043	9/37	6/45
44	Sharp Stewart & Co.	7/6/1894			1930	044	7/37	8/41
45	Sharp Stewart & Co.	8/6//1894			1909			11/36
46	Sharp Stewart & Co.	12/6/1894		1915		046	3/37	3/43
47	Sharp Stewart & Co.	20/6/1894				047	7/37	4/42 Destroyed by enemy action
48	Sharp Stewart & Co.	7/7/1894						11/37
49	Sharp Stewart & Co.	11/7/1894			1931	049	10/37	9/41
50	Sharp Stewart & Co.	27/7/1894			1929	050	9/37	1/45
1	Sharp Stewart & Co.	1/8/1894				01	10/36	1/37
2	Sharp Stewart & Co.	3/8/1894			1931	02	7/37	5/43
3	Sharp Stewart & Co.	22/8/1894						10/37
4	Sharp Stewart & Co.	24/8/1894						2/38
5	Sharp Stewart & Co.	24/8/1894	1908	1925		05	11/36	7/37
6	Sharp Stewart & Co.	30/8/1894			1930	06	10/37	3/44
7	Sharp Stewart & Co.	31/8/1894				07	10/36	6/37
11	Sharp Stewart & Co.	13/9/1894				011	9/37	8/42
12	Sharp Stewart & Co.	16/11/1894				012	11/37	8/42
13	Sharp Stewart & Co.	20/11/1894				013	5/37	9/41
14	Sharp Stewart & Co.	23/11/1894						2/37
17	Sharp Stewart & Co.	27/11/1894						10/37
18	Sharp Stewart & Co.	29/11/1894						2/37
51	Sharp Stewart & Co.	29/8/1896		1915		051	9/37	5/43
52	Sharp Stewart & Co.	29/8/1896		1913		052	10/36	2/43
53	Sharp Stewart & Co.	31/8/1896		1910		053	7/37	1/40
54	Sharp Stewart & Co.	5/9/1896		1914		054	1/37	10/39
55	Sharp Stewart & Co.	7/9/1896	1908	1925		055	4/37	11/43
56	Sharp Stewart & Co.	11/9/1896		1912		056	2/37	11/43
57	Sharp Stewart & Co.	17/9/1896		1912				2/37
74	Beyer Peacock	12/10/1899						5/37
75	Beyer Peacock	19/10/1899						2/37
76	Beyer Peacock	26/10/1899				076	11/37	7/43
77	Beyer Peacock	3/11/1899				077	10/37	1/45
78	Beyer Peacock	15/11/1899				078	11/36	2/37
79	Beyer Peacock	24/11/1899				079	11/36	2/37
80	Beyer Peacock	30/11/1899						2/37

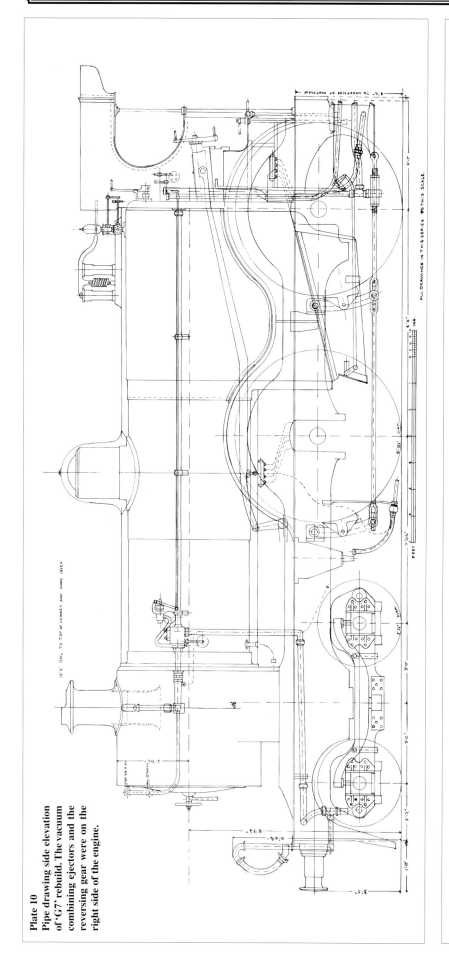

Plate 10
Pipe drawing side elevation of 'G7' rebuild. The vacuum combining ejectors and the reversing gear were on the right side of the engine.

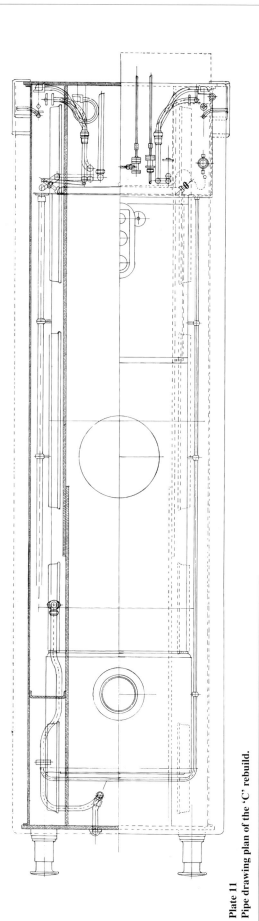

Plate 11
Pipe drawing plan of the 'C' rebuild.

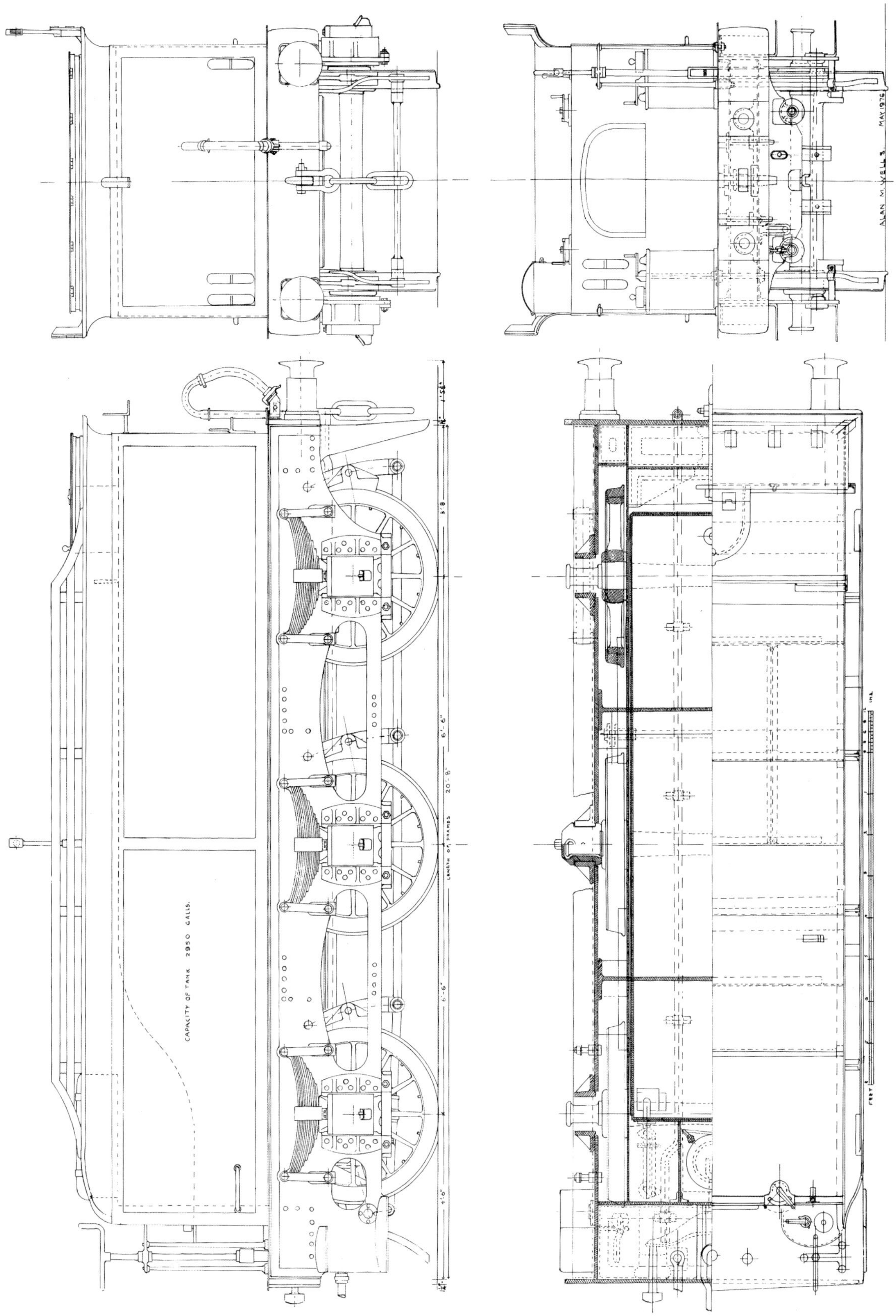

Plate 12
M&GNJ'R tenders for engines of Classes 'C' and 'D', based on
drawings supplied by Beyer Peacock & Co. dated 19th October 1893.

CAPACITY OF TANK 2950 GALLS.

ALAN M. WELLS. MAY 1976

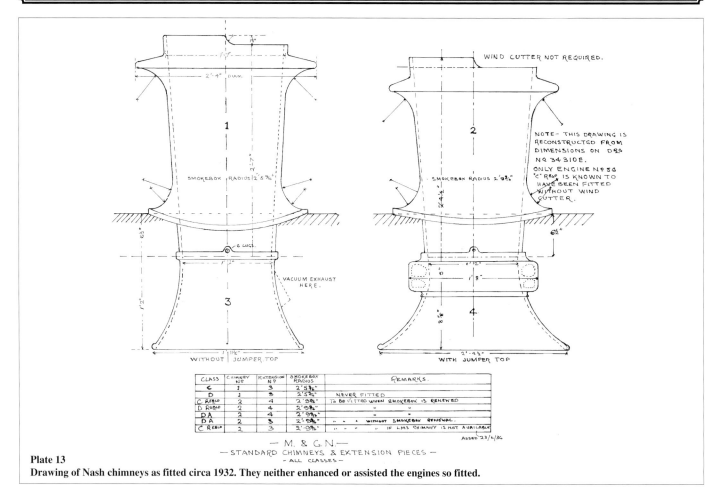

CLASS	CHIMNEY Nº	EXTENSION Nº	SMOKEBOX RADIUS	REMARKS.
C	1	3	2'5⅞"	
D	1	3	2'5⅞"	NEVER FITTED
C REBLD	2	4	2'9½"	To BE FITTED WHEN SMOKEBOX IS RENEWED
D REBLD	2	4	2'9½"	" " " "
DA	2	4	2'9½"	" " " "
DA	2	3	2'9½"	" " WITHOUT SMOKEBOX RENEWAL.
C REBLD	2	3	2'9½"	" " IF LMS CHIMNEY IS NOT AVAILABLE

— M. & G.N.—
— STANDARD CHIMNEYS & EXTENSION PIECES —
— ALL CLASSES —

Added 23/6/36

Plate 13
Drawing of Nash chimneys as fitted circa 1932. They neither enhanced or assisted the engines so fitted.

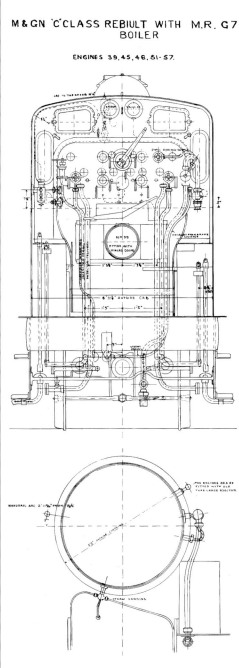

M & GN 'C' CLASS REBUILT WITH M.R. G7 BOILER

ENGINES 39, 45, 46, 51-57.

Plate 15
Pipe drawings taken from M&GN Drawing No. 39/2137 of 13th January 1910. The lower drawing includes the positions of the hand rails. No's 39 and 55 had the old-type large ejector and the handrails were higher up.

FACING PAGE: Plate 14
This undated picture of No. 047 was taken after it was renumbered by the L&NER in July 1937, but before it was destroyed in an air raid and withdrawn in June 1942. The locomotive is generally in the original condition other than being fitted with an extended smokebox. Built by Sharp Stewart & Co. in 1894. R.J. ESSERY COLLECTION.

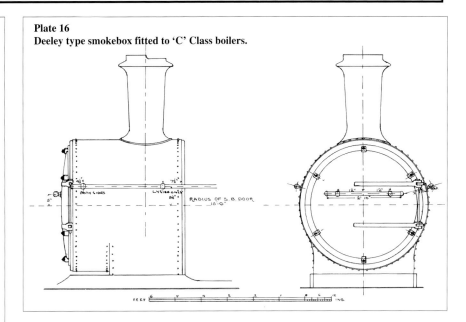

Plate 16
Deeley type smokebox fitted to 'C' Class boilers.

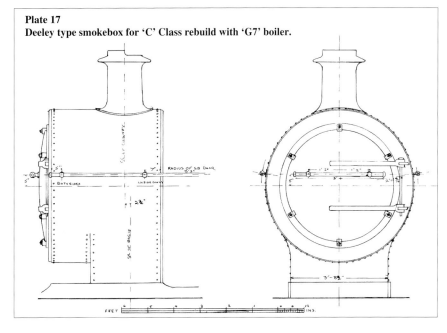

Plate 17
Deeley type smokebox for 'C' Class rebuild with 'G7' boiler.

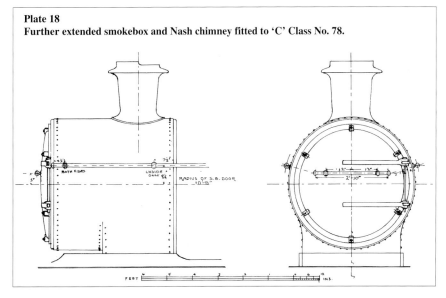

Plate 18
Further extended smokebox and Nash chimney fitted to 'C' Class No. 78.

Plate 19
Photographed at Melton Constable on the 23rd October 1936, No. 2 was built by Sharp Stewart & Co. in 1894 and rebuilt with a new cab and 'G6' boiler in 1931. In 1937 it became L&NER No. 02, and remained in service until it was withdrawn in May 1943. W.A. CAMWELL.

CHAPTER 7

THE 'MELTON' 0-6-0TS

Melton Constable works must have been a very versatile place given its size, and we have already seen the extent to which its rebuilding and other activities contributed to the nature of the line. One of the most enterprising results of this situation was that the M&GN actually constructed its own locomotives from time to time. This was rare indeed for a small concern, but Melton Constable was to do so twice during the period of MR supervision. Although the boiler drawings were made at Derby and other features were similar to Derby practice, they were M&GN designs. The rate of output was not exactly at the Derby or Doncaster level, but the engines concerned gave very good service over a long period of time. Two designs were produced at Melton Constable, of which the neat 0-6-0Ts, the subject of this chapter, were the more numerous. Nine were built from 1897 to 1905, approximately one per year.

It could be said they were 'M&GN style' in the form inherited from the E&MR and its various predecessors. Thus outside cylinders typified the E&MR but the boiler mountings were Midland. Tank and cab detail had a distinctly 'Johnson' feel to it but the chimneys were Melton Constable. In fact, they rather gave the appearance of an outside cylindered version of the familiar Class '1' Johnson shunting tanks of the parent system but with distinct local overtones. Amongst their detail fittings may be noted their above-axle springs and below-tank injectors, while a vertical hand wheel in the cab applied the steam brake, rather like that of the 4-4-0Ts. The sandboxes were operated by a rod (located at the front and rear below the running plate) and were placed so as to allow sanding when running in either direction. In order to clear the smokebox door the front vacuum pipe was mounted on a swivel connection (as was the centre lamp iron), but from about 1930 this arrangement was replaced on No's 15, 16, 94, 97, 98 by a fixed pipe mounted lower on the bufferbeam.

They were quite handsome engines and, for their size, very strong. Officially they were rebuilds and carried plates 'Rebuilt Melton Constable' but, except for some wheels recovered from the withdrawn ex-Cornwall Minerals Railway engines, they were in fact

Plate 1
No. 1A was built at Melton Constable in August 1898 and renumbered in 1907, when it became No. 93; the locomotive was withdrawn in June 1944. Although described as 'rebuilds of the Cornwall Mineral Railway engines', they were in effect new engines but some parts of the CMR locomotives were used. The most obvious were the locomotive wheels, and this undated picture shows them to good effect. The locomotive is in pristine condition and, although designated as a 'shunting' locomotive, the class was equipped with vacuum brakes and also used on passenger trains. Note the polished steel band on the chimney – a driver's decoration. R.J. ESSERY COLLECTION.

Plate 2
This picture of No. 97 has been included to show the difference between the wheels recovered from withdrawn CMR locomotives as seen in Plate 1 and the Melton Constable wheels seen here. The picture was taken at South Lynn circa 1925, when the locomotive was in the light yellow-brown livery. Built in 1902 as No. 12A, it became No. 97 in 1907 and L&NER No. 097 in February 1938, before it was withdrawn from service in March 1943. R.J. ESSERY COLLECTION.

new. Some of the dimensions supplied by the late Alan Wells differ from the standard L&NER dimensions as published by the RCTS in Part 8B of *Locomotives of the LNER*. Where there is a difference the dimensions published by the RCTS are shown in brackets.

One engine was rostered to work a shuttle passenger service between South Lynn and King's Lynn. Those fitted with wheels from the Cornwall Minerals Railway had the left crank leading in fore gear,

whilst the others had 12 spoke wheels of oval section and led off with the right crank. The wheelbase was 6 feet 3 inches leading to driving and 7 feet 6 inches driving to trailing. The valve gear was Howe Link motion and driven from the right side. The leading sand boxes were fed through the side tanks and brake blocks were only fitted to driving and trailing wheels. Most were numbered in the duplicate list from the outset and building was as shown in the table.

PRINCIPAL DIMENSIONS OF THE 'MELTON' 0-6-0Ts							
Cylinders	Wheels	Boiler Pressure	Heating Surface	Grate Area	Water Capacity	Coal Capacity	Weight in Working Order
Outside, 16in×20in	3ft 6½in (3ft 7in)	140 psi (150 psi)	882.43 sq ft (729.8 sq ft)	11.3 sq ft	800 gallons	30 cwt, or 2 tons with bunker hopper	37 tons 13 cwt 3 qtr

M&GN No.	**DATE BUILT**	**RENUMBERED IN 1907**	**1937 L&NER NUMBER**	**MONTH APPLIED**	**1946 L&NER NUMBER**	**MONTH APPLIED**	**MONTH WITHDRAWN**
14A	10/1897	98	098	8/37	8482	8/46	1/47
1A	8/1898	93	093	12/37			6/44
11A	8/1899	96	096	3/37	8484	8/46	5/48
3A	12/1899	95	095	5/37	8485	8/46	12/47
15	1/1901		015	11/37			12/45
17A	3/1902	99	099	3/37			7/45
12A	12/1902	97	097	2/38			3/43
2A	1/1904	94	094	12/37	8488	8/46	1/48
16	30/5/1905		016	5/38	8489	12/46	8/49

Plate 3
This photograph shows No. 95 at South Lynn on the 22nd October 1936. Built as No. 3A in 1899, the engine was renumbered as seen here in 1907. In L&NER ownership it was renumbered as 097 in 1937, became 8485 in 1946 when the L&NER renumbered their locomotive stock, and was withdrawn in December 1947. Note the locomotive retains the Cornwall Mineral Railway wheels which meant the left hand crank led in forward gear. W.A. CAMWELL.

Plate 4
This delightful view of a rather grubby No. 15 was taken at Yarmouth Beach on the 24th October 1936. Built in December 1900, it became L&NER No. 015 in 1937 and was withdrawn in December 1945. Note the bunker hopper that was fitted to assist coaling at the new Yarmouth and South Lynn coaling plants. W.A. CAMWELL.

From about 1929 most were fitted with Deeley type smokeboxes, but No. 96 was still fitted with a Melton pattern smokebox in 1937. Those placed on the duplicate list were renumbered from 93 to 99 as shown above, but the stock numbers of No's 15 and 16 were not changed. The reason for the apparent random numbering was because the engines were built as replacements of nine engines whose numbers they then took. These were six of the Cornwall Mineral Engines (No's 1A, 2A, 3A, 11A, 13A and 14A), one Black Hawthorn tank (No. 17A) and the two remaining Fox Walker tanks (No's 15 and 16). Not all the replaced engines were withdrawn, of course, being either sold out of service or retained for internal works use.

When mechanical coaling plants were installed in 1930/31 at South Lynn and Yarmouth, a hopper was fitted above the bunker and whilst useful for coaling it did not improve the appearance of the engines. Most retained the hopper until withdrawal, but it was removed from No. 16 after 1938. From the 1st October 1936 the L&NER began to renumber them by applying an '0' prefix to their M&GN numbers and later, in July 1942, they were designated Class 'J93'. Prior to that date they were shown on M&GN and L&NER Engine Diagrams as Class 'Shunting Engines'. They were also sometimes referred to as Class 'MR', standing for Melton Rebuild!

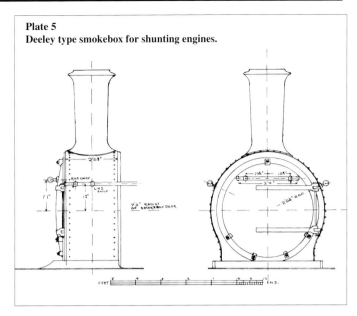

Plate 5
Deeley type smokebox for shunting engines.

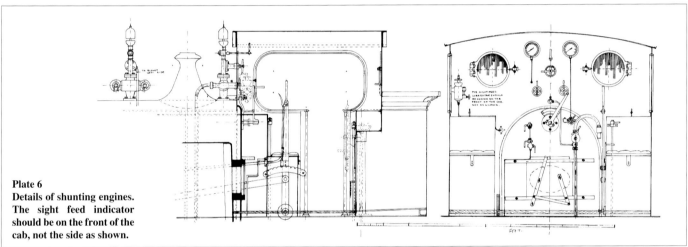

Plate 6
Details of shunting engines. The sight feed indicator should be on the front of the cab, not the side as shown.

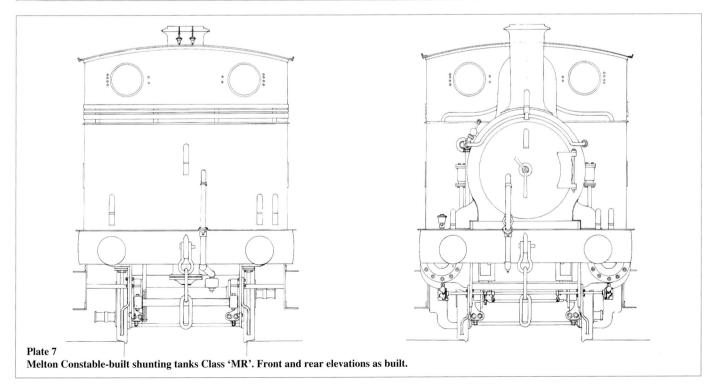

Plate 7
Melton Constable-built shunting tanks Class 'MR'. Front and rear elevations as built.

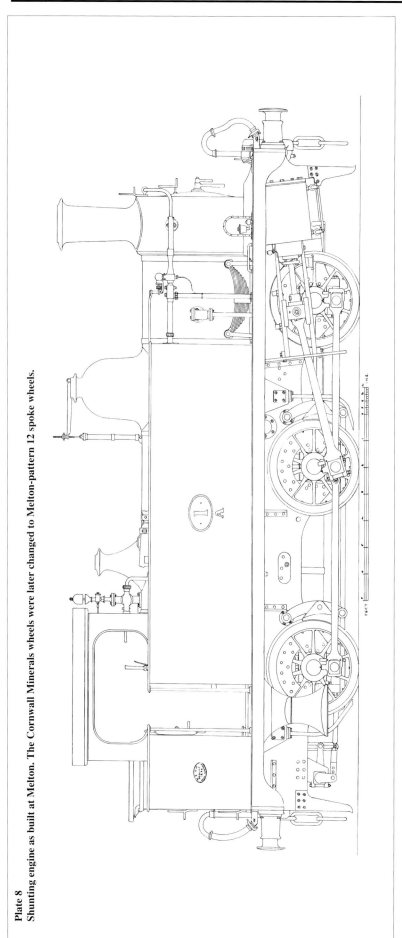

Plate 8
Shunting engine as built at Melton. The Cornwall Minerals wheels were later changed to Melton-pattern 12 spoke wheels.

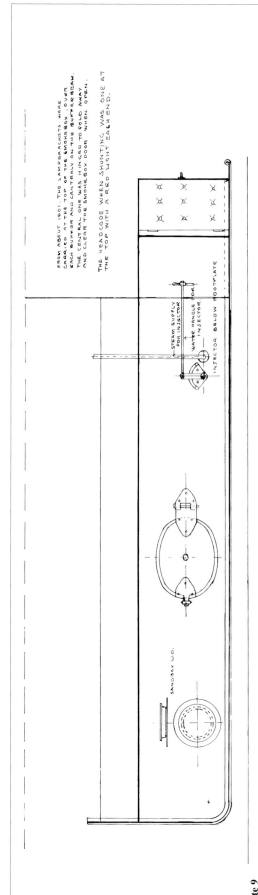

FROM ABOUT 1901. THE LAMPBRACKETS WERE
CARRIED AT THE TOP OF THE SMOKEBOX, OVER
EACH BUFFER AND CENTRALLY ON THE BUFFERBEAM.
THE CENTRAL ONE WAS HINGED TO FOLD AWAY
AND CLEAR THE SMOKEBOX DOOR WHEN OPEN.

THE HEAD CODE WHEN SHUNTING WAS ONE AT
THE TOP WITH A RED LIGHT EACH END.

Plate 9
Position of sand and water fillers; also showing the steam and water controls, the ejectors being
below the tanks. Note the alternative lamp brackets and the shunting codes for lamps.

Plate 10
This picture of No. 15 has been included to give a clear view of the bunker hopper that was fitted to all the class, but the precise date of fitting is not known. The RCTS Part 8B of *Locomotives of the LNER* suggests this was done between 1930 and 1934. They were intended to ease coaling at the new coaling plants at South Lynn and Yarmouth Beach and held an additional ten hundredweight of coal, making the coal capacity two tons. R.J. ESSERY COLLECTION.

Above: **Plate 11**
L&NER No. 096 was built in 1899 as M&GNJR No. 11A and became No. 96 in 1907. When this picture was taken it had received a bunker hopper and been renumbered by the L&NER, but still retained the old Cornwall Mineral Railways wheels. This locomotive was one of three to be allotted British Railways numbers, in this case 68484, but it was not applied and the locomotive was withdrawn in May 1948 carrying its final L&NER number 8484. R.J. Essery collection.

Below: **Plate 12**
The final picture of a 'Shunting' Class locomotive is No. 8485. It is seen here with a tall stovepipe chimney, but when it arrived at Stratford for scrapping it was carrying a shorter one. Built in 1899 as No. 3A, it became No. 95 in 1907, L&NER No. 095 in 1937 and, when renumbered by the L&NER in August 1946, it was No. 8485, which helps to date the photograph since it was withdrawn in December 1947. The enginemen have rigged up a screen to protect them from the weather, probably side winds judging by the direction the smoke is blowing. R.J. Essery collection.

CHAPTER 8

THE 'MIDLAND' 0-6-0s

An interesting aspect of the M&GN at the time of its formation was that it possessed no goods engines as such – save perhaps the rather feeble former Cornwall Minerals Railway 'tender tanks'. To these one might also perhaps add the two former L&NWR 2-4-0s which when originally built were usually regarded as being goods rather than passenger types – the L&NWR often tending to prefer the 2-2-2 'Crewe' type for its passenger trains, especially south of Crewe. But even so, these engines were already very old by 1893 and worn out. Furthermore the general way of operating on the E&MR and fledgling M&GN was for so-called passenger engines to work goods trains one way and a passenger train on the return – or vice versa. Some of the passenger engines were employed wholly on goods work, which meant the load they could haul was less than would be the case for a similar power capacity goods engine. On the other hand, the Midland Railway goods engines working passenger trains on branch lines could take a heavier load, generally about 10 per cent more than an equivalent power class passenger engine. It is possible that the same rules applied on the Joint line.

Not surprisingly, therefore, Derby addressed the problem quite soon after 1893, if not with quite such urgency as with the Class 'C' 4-4-0s (Chapter 6). The result was just as predictable, and the M&GN soon found itself in possession of a class of typical 'state of the art' Johnson 0-6-0 goods engines. Known on the M&GN as Class 'D', eight each were built in 1896 and 1899 and at the time they represented the latest Derby thinking. They were in fact identical to the Class 'M' 0-6-0s which have been described elsewhere (*Midland Locomotives, Volume 4*, page 65) and were built alongside identical batches from the same makers for the Midland itself. As it turned out, the M&GN never did abandon the use of passenger engines hauling goods trains and vice versa.

When it came to rebuilding, relatively few were involved compared with the Midland's own stock of these locomotives. Details are given below, and this time it is worth noting that the modest amount of reconstruction mostly mirrored traditional MR practice. There was, for example, no use of the extended smokebox on any of the original small boiler examples – or the two 'H' boiler rebuilds either. But the four which eventually received 'G7' Belpaire boilers, thus making

Plate 1
This picture of No. 58 was taken circa 1906 and shows the locomotive in pristine condition. Note the jaws for the tablet exchanger have been removed.
P.C. DEWHURST.

them akin to the familiar MR/LM&SR Class '3F', did receive extended smokeboxes thus making them immediately recognisable compared with the Derby-built engines. For the most part other detail changes also mirrored traditional Derby practice. For example, even on the unrebuilt engines, the original Johnson chimneys and smokeboxes eventually gave way to the Deeley pattern smokebox, though the chimneys were 'Melton' (below). But there were inevitable individual variations and these are shown though the pictures.

Building dates and original dimensional details, as shown on engine diagram No. 29/3150, were as follows:

- No's 58–65 by Neilson & Co. in 1896. Makers No's 5032–5039.
- No's 66–73 by Kitson & Co. in 1899. Makers No's 3873–3889.

Of standard Midland design, they were fitted with the combined steam/vacuum brake and often worked passenger trains, particularly excursions. The only difference in the two batches was in the cylinder drain cock control – the Neilson engines had a rod visible above the reversing reach rod whereas the Kitson batch had a rod running under the platform and operated by a handle that was moved up and down. Passenger communication was by a bell in the cab on the right side. They had steam sanding for forward and reverse running.

No. 62 was rebuilt with a Midland 'H' Class boiler in 1906 but had a 'G7' boiler as replacement in 1924. With the 'H' boiler the cab sides were enlarged and a taper chimney fitted. No. 69 also received an 'H' Class boiler in 1909 (this time, uniquely for other MR or M&GN,

PRINCIPAL DIMENSIONS FOR THE 'MIDLAND' 0-6-0s, ENGINE				
Cylinders	Driving Wheel	Boiler Pressure	Weight in Working Order	Wheelbase
18in×26in	5ft 2½in Later 5ft 3in with thicker tyres	150 psi Later 160 psi	38 tons 16 cwt 1 qtr	8ft + 8ft 6in 7ft 0⁵/₁₆in overhang at front

PRINCIPAL DIMENSIONS FOR THE 'MIDLAND' 0-6-0s, TENDER				
Wheel	Weight in Working Order	Water Capacity	Coal Capacity	Wheelbase
4ft 2½in	33 tons 10 cwt 3 qtr	2950 gallons	3 tons	6ft 6in + 6ft 6in 5ft 5in trailing overhang

The engines later became Power Class 2. With the leading engine buffer beam 6 inches wide, the length overall was 50 feet 2¹/₁₆ inches.

Plate 2
Here we can see Class 'D' locomotive No. 72, which was photographed circa 1930. Note the spare coupling hooked over the left hand lamp holder and the Melton chimney that replaced the original chimney. P.C. DEWHURST.

ABOVE: Plate 3
This shows No. 63 in the 'as built' condition at an unidentified location. ALAN WELLS COLLECTION.

BELOW: Plate 4
Here we can see the opposite side of Class 'D' locomotive No. 67, photographed at Melton Constable. G.F. BURT.

with a taper chimney with wind guard) and a 'G7' replacement in 1921. This locomotive also had the enlarged cab, and the smokebox door had strap hinges and a wheel for fastening. When fitted with the 'G7' boiler the above engines had the chimney altered to the Deeley parallel type and received a Class '3' type Deeley cab. No's 68 and 71 were similarly rebuilt in 1921 with 'G7' boilers. All four 'G7' rebuilds were similar to what became the MR/LM&SR Class '3F' but had extended smokeboxes. As built, the boiler centre line was 7 feet 1 inch above rail level and this was increased to 7 feet 7 inches when fitted with larger boilers. With the larger boilers, the trailing end was extended a further 1 foot 1½ inches, giving an overall length of engine and tender of 51 feet 8½ inches. Heating surface increased as a result of rebuilding and the increase of boiler pressure to 175psi caused their upgrading to Power Class 3.

From about 1908, new chimneys of Melton pattern began to replace the Johnson chimneys. These chimneys originally had a 2 inch wind-guard but this was later removed. Extra coal rails were added to the tenders after 1921 for all engines and the older type of tablet exchanger was fitted to the rebuilds. All but two engines had the original wooden buffer planks replaced, the two exceptions having the original fitting retained for use with the South Lynn snowplough.

During Mr Nash's term of office No. 58 received an extended cab roof with upright handrails. No's 69 and 71 had the smokebox

further extended and were fitted with stovepipe chimneys. A jumper top blastpipe was fitted to No. 71 and later was retained but bolted down. Steam heating was applied to some, and all received Deeley smokeboxes with bolt and clip door fastenings. It is interesting to note that whereas the larger smokeboxes only had six dogs, the smaller ones had seven – four below the centre. Their duties were similar to the Class 'C' 4-4-0s and they did a lot of passenger work, especially on the western section. When coupled as a pilot engine to a 'C' Class on heavy excursions they proved most useful. Their speed was high and riding qualities very good. The rebuilds would have been better had the water capacity been increased.

They were little altered by the L&NER. The principal change being the fitting of independent blowers to the 'B' boilers and these were operated like those on the 'C' Class. On coming under the L&NER the prefix '0' was given to all except No's 66, 67 and 72, while No's 59, 64, 65 and 70 were allocated L&NER numbers but did not carry them. In July 1942 the surviving small boilered engines were reclassified 'J40' and the remaining 'G7' boilered engines No's 069 and 071 became Class 'J41'. The rebuilds with 'G7' boilers retained their original frames. A number were fitted with carriage warming apparatus; in some cases it was only fitted to the tender but others carried it at both ends – records show that at one time No's 59, 60, 61, 64, 65, 70 and 73 only had a fitting on the tender, but No's 61, 62, 65, 69 and 73 ran with fittings at both ends. Whilst the author has

Plate 5
By the time this picture was taken, No. 58 had received a Deeley smokebox, Melton chimney and the cab roof had been extended. From the enginemen's point of view the cab was the most beneficial improvement, the protection offered by the original Johnson cab was limited. The Midland version was referred to as the 'fair weather engines' at Saltley circa 1950. The engine has been renumbered by the L&NER, but the new number 058 has been applied at Melton paint shop on the dark brown livery. The note on the reverse of the print states Yarmouth Beach, 24th October 1936, No. 4 at rear. W.A. CAMWELL.

not found any Melton works orders regarding the fitting or removal of carriage warming apparatus, it was not uncommon for Derby Works orders to be issued for changes to be made to Midland and, in particular, LM&SR locomotives, and for the apparatus to be added to the front of the locomotive. The L&NER engine diagram shows the small-boilered engines with Nash chimneys but fortunately, from the aesthetic standpoint, none had them. The front elevation also shows a single spring balance safety valve but this was also wrong.

On average, the M&GN engines lasted rather less well than their Midland contemporaries; their latter-day L&NER ownership may well have been the explanation, along with the fact there was no suitable 'Doncaster' or 'Stratford' boiler that could be used when replacements were required.

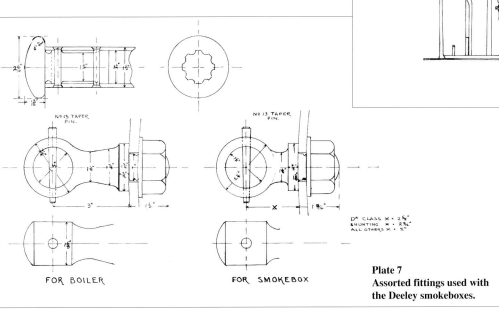

Plate 6
Cab of Class 'D' locomotives as built.

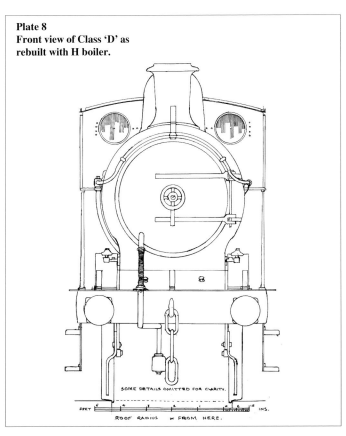

Plate 7
Assorted fittings used with the Deeley smokeboxes.

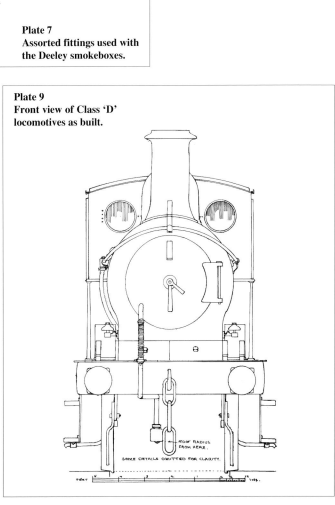

Plate 8
Front view of Class 'D' as rebuilt with H boiler.

Plate 9
Front view of Class 'D' locomotives as built.

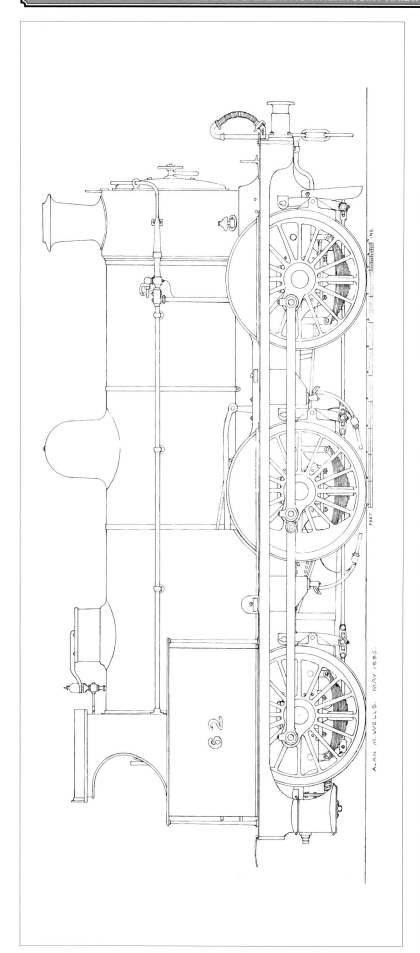

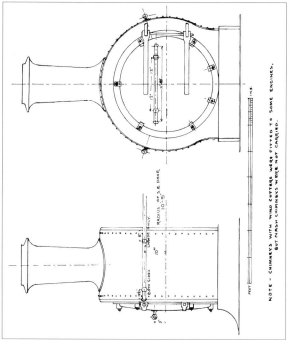

NOTE – CHIMNEYS WITH WIND CUTTERS WERE FITTED TO SOME ENGINES, BUT NASH CHIMNEYS WERE NOT CARRIED.

ABOVE: Plate 10
Class 'D' locomotive as rebuilt with 'H' Class boiler.

LEFT: Plate 11
All of the Class 'D' locomotives with 'G7' boilers had extended smokeboxes.

RIGHT: Plate 12
Drawing of the Deeley smokebox fitted to 'D' Class engines with Melton chimney.

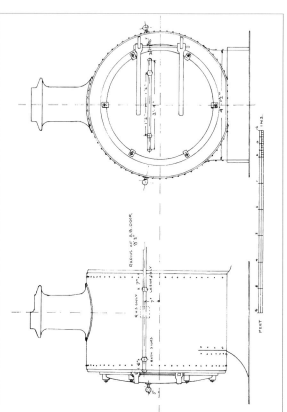

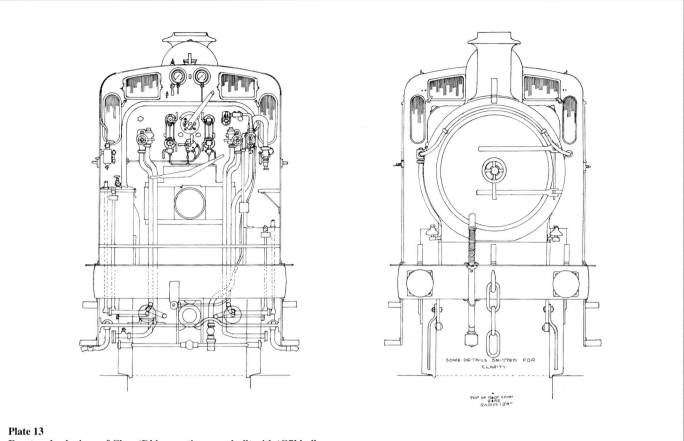

Plate 13
Front and cab views of Class 'D' locomotives as rebuilt with 'G7' boiler.

SUMMARY TABLE

M&GN No.	BUILT BY	DATE BUILT	REBUILT H BOILER	REBUILT G7 BOILER	L&NER No.	MONTH APPLIED	MONTH WITHDRAWN
58	Neilson & Co	27/8/1896			058	10/36	9/38
59	Neilson & Co	29/8/1896			059	8/37	6/44
60	Neilson & Co	28/8/1896			060	11/37	5/41
61	Neilson & Co	31/8/1896			061	1/37	12/42
62	Neilson & Co	31/8/1896	1906	1923	062	5/37	10/39
63	Neilson & Co	5/9/1896			063	10/36	2/37
64	Neilson & Co	8/9/1896			064	by 5/37	3/44
65	Neilson & Co	8/9/1896			065	9/37	3/44
66	Kitson & Co	30/3/1899			Not to L&NER stock		10/37
67	Kitson & Co	31/3/1899			Not to L&NER stock		1/37
68	Kitson & Co	4/4/1899		1921	Not to L&NER stock		11/36
69	Kitson & Co	14/4/1899	1909	1924	069	3/37	7/42
70	Kitson & Co	16/4/1899			070	1/38	3/44
71	Kitson & Co	20/4/1899		1921	071	5/37	7/43
72	Kitson & Co	16/4/1899			Not to L&NER stock		10/37
73	Kitson & Co	30/4/1899			073	9/37	5/41

Plate 14
This view of No. 71, taken after 1926, shows the locomotive as it was rebuilt in 1921. The extended smokebox and chimney variations resulted in a 'different look' to the Midland engines that were at Saltley. P.C. DEWHURST.

Plate 15
The L&NER classified the 'G7' boiler rebuilds of the 'D' Class as 'J40'. This picture of No. 062 was taken at South Lynn after its repainting at Stratford in 1938; the locomotive was rebuilt with a 'H' Class boiler in 1906, and then with a 'G7' boiler in 1924. P.C. DEWHURST.

CHAPTER 9

THE 'GREAT NORTHERN' 0-6-0s

The year 1900 marked a point when British locomotive building was at one of its periodic peaks and as far as the Midland was concerned, the company could not manage to find enough outside builders in the country (in addition to the output of Derby) to satisfy its own needs, leave alone those of the Joint lines. As is quite well known, the solution to its own problems (and those of some other railways as well) was partly solved by the importation of American-built 2-6-0s. It seems likely, therefore, that this inability of either Derby or any of the outside contractors to take on new work may have been the reason why the continuing need for further goods engines on the M&GN was met by its other joint partner, the GNR. The GNR was not responsible for locomotive matters on the M&GN as such, but the company agreed to release a dozen engines from its own order from Dübs and Co. to meet the need – clearly Doncaster had no spare building capacity either.

No other reason has been discovered as to why the M&GN increased its already considerable variety of locomotives by adding yet a different type to its list. The logical solution would clearly have been to add more Johnson goods engines to the existing 'D' Class (as had been the case with the 4-4-0s when 'more of the same' were needed) and the fact that the GNR design was classified Class 'DA' on the M&GN rather than given a new type letter, somewhat suggests that the engines were regarded as being 'in lieu' of further Midland 0-6-0s. We shall probably never know, but the end result was to add Great Northern lineaments to those of Melton Constable and Derby. The existence of these 0-6-0s also meant that in spite of its overall responsibility for M&GN locomotive matters, Derby had in fact designed only two out of the five classes of engine built for the Joint line after its formation. In pure numbers of course (fifty-six out of the eighty new engines added), Derby clearly held the ascendancy, but this Great Northern injection added to the already distinctive nature of the M&GN.

As with their Class 'D' predecessors, the new 0-6-0s were identical to those provided for the particular parent company, this time the GNR Class 'J4' (later to become L&NER Class 'J3'). They were

Plate 1
Photographed at Yarmouth, this picture illustrates No. 88 in its original condition. It was rebuilt with a larger boiler in 1920 and remained in service until 1949. ALAN WELLS COLLECTION.

Plate 2

This broadside picture of No. 81 was taken at the Dübs & Company works where it was built in 1900. Note the lamp holder on the chimney; also that, unlike the Midland 0-6-0s which were fitted with steam sanding, this class was fitted with hand sanding – when running forward the sand was dropped in front of the leading wheels, and in front of the trailing wheels when in reverse. The photographic grey livery shows how the engines arrived on the M&GN. Their livery was adjusted very quickly to the form seen in Plate 1. R.J. ESSERY COLLECTION.

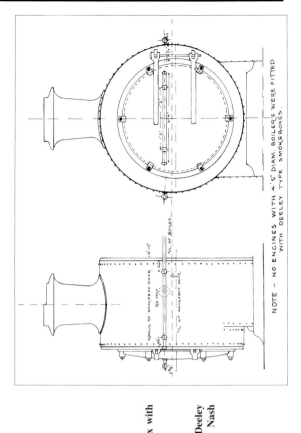

NOTE – NO ENGINES WITH 4.5' DIAM. BOILERS WERE FITTED WITH DEELEY TYPE SMOKEBOXES.

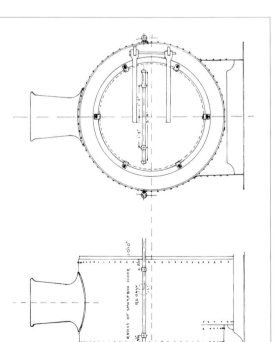

LEFT: Plate 3
DA type Deeley smokebox with Nash stovepipe chimney.

RIGHT: Plate 4
Type DA with off centre Deeley smokebox door and Nash chimney.

Plate 5
Here we see No. 82 at Peterborough Spital shed after it had been rebuilt with a larger boiler in 1921. In 1937 the engine was rebuilt as a 'J4' and ran as L&NER No. 4157 before being withdrawn in 1947. R.J. ESSERY COLLECTION.

just as recognisably Doncaster in style as the Class 'D's were self evidently Derby in appearance. Nominally designed by Henry Ivatt of the GNR, their origins in fact went back to Patrick Stirling's time on the GNR and in concept they were the GNR design equivalent of the Johnson 0-6-0s as near as made no difference. They would clearly be expected to do the same sort of work on the Joint line as did the Johnson engines.

Although delivered in 1901, they were built in 1900 (Dübs works No's 3933–44) as part of the aforementioned GNR order for twenty-five engines. They carried M&GN numbers 81–92 and were the only M&GN engines to have the Automatic Vacuum Brake on engine and tender. They had 17½ inch × 26 inch cylinders (inside) and coupled wheels were 5 feet 2 inches diameter. The leading to driving wheelbase was 7 feet 3 inches and driving to trailing 8 feet 3 inches. The boiler pressure was 160 psi and the total heating surface 1123 square feet, the grate area being 17.8 square feet. The tenders had wheels of 4 feet 2 inches diameter on a wheelbase of 13 feet equally divided. It carried 3170 gallons of water and 5 tons of coal and weighed 37 tons 15 hundredweight 2 quarters full, and the engines weighed 40 tons 12 hundredweight in running order. Extended smokeboxes were fitted in 1907 to accommodate a spark-arresting device. Between 1920 and 1927, larger boilers of 4 feet 8 inches diameter were fitted and they were classified as 'DA Rebuild'.

From about 1933, Deeley pattern smokeboxes and doors began to be fitted and this resulted in some strange and not altogether beneficial changes to their appearance. For one thing, the smokebox door centres were often set below the boiler centre line with curious aesthetic results. It was not too bad where the original and rather handsome GNR built-up chimney was retained – especially if combined with properly central smokebox door. But the marriage

of an off-centre door with the later chimney (which sometimes happened) was not pleasing to the eye, especially if the Nash chimney was of the stovepipe kind. Locomotive appearance is, of course, a rather personal thing, but in one respect the new larger boilers with their consequentially taller cabs gave them a more balanced look in relation to the tender. Some chimney and smokebox variations are noted below. As built, the tenders rather swamped the ensemble and in this respect parallels may also be drawn with the Midland where large tenders were sometimes coupled to very small engines. Most people considered that they looked their best with large boilers and GNR-type front ends. With the fitting of the larger boilers the pressure was raised to 175 psi. They were quite powerful engines and capable of fast running, so were used for passenger as well as goods work and were ideal for working the heavy fish-workers' trains. Like most GNR engines they were very free steaming. With the higher boiler pressure they should have been upgraded to Power Class 3 but for some unknown reason they never were.

An attempt to fit the Derby G5½ boilers was resisted and never done. It was not in fact possible without major modification and expense to put any bigger Midland boiler between the frames than this small type. Had it been carried out it would have rendered the engines next to useless. This idea was first proposed in 1919 and the matter was again raised in 1925, but by then eight of the engines had received the larger Doncaster boilers. Facsimile copies of the correspondence from the Melton end are included here. It makes interesting reading and rather supports the conjecture (above) that the engines were only obtained because it was impossible to procure more Johnson 0-6-0s in the first place.

Between 1936 and 1938 all received the prefix '0' from the L&NER, which designated them Class 'J3'. The details are given below.

SUMMARY TABLE

M&GN No.	BUILT BY	DATE BUILT	REBUILT TO DA BY M&GN	L&NER 1937 NUMBER	MONTH APPLIED	REBUILT TO J4 BY L&NER	L&NER 1946 NUMBER	MONTH APPLIED	BR NUMBER	MONTH APPLIED	MONTH WITHDRAWN
81	Dübs & Co	10/1900	6/27	081	4/38		4156	6/46			9/47
82	Dübs & Co	10/1900	8/21	082	3/37	3/37	4157	8/46			8/47
83	Dübs & Co	10/1900	1/21	083	1936		4158	6/46			7/51
84	Dübs & Co	10/1900	12/24	084	1/37	1/37	4159	8/46			8/47
85	Dübs & Co	10/1900	4/26	085	2/37	2/37	4160	8/46	64160	11/48	12/51
86	Dübs & Co	10/1900	10/27	086	1/37		4161	1/37			9/47
87	Dübs & Co	10/1900	5/25	087	6/37	6/37	4162	12/46			12/50
88	Dübs & Co	10/1900	11/20	088	1936		4163	6/46			1/49
89	Dübs & Co	10/1900	2/26	089	4/37	4/37	4164	4/37			8/47
90	Dübs & Co	11/1900	12/26	090	2/37	2/37					7/46
91	Dübs & Co	10/1900	1/27	091	5/37	5/37					1/46
92	Dübs & Co	11/1900	10/21	092	2/37	2/37	4167	6/46			7/48

DA rebuild: locomotives rebuilt by M&GN with larger boilers similar to L&NER 'J3', classified as 'DA'.
Circa 1930, Deeley smokebox doors not central: No's 82, 85, 87, 89, 92.
Circa 1935, Nash Chimneys, (S)=stovepipe: No's 81, 83, 84(S), 86(S), 88, 92.

ABOVE: **Plate 6**
Photographed in 1934 at Melton Constable shed, this picture shows the rear of the tender that was coupled to No. 87. The locomotive was rebuilt as a 'J4' in 1937 and became L&NER No. 4162 in 1946, before being withdrawn at the end of 1950. R.J. ESSERY COLLECTION.

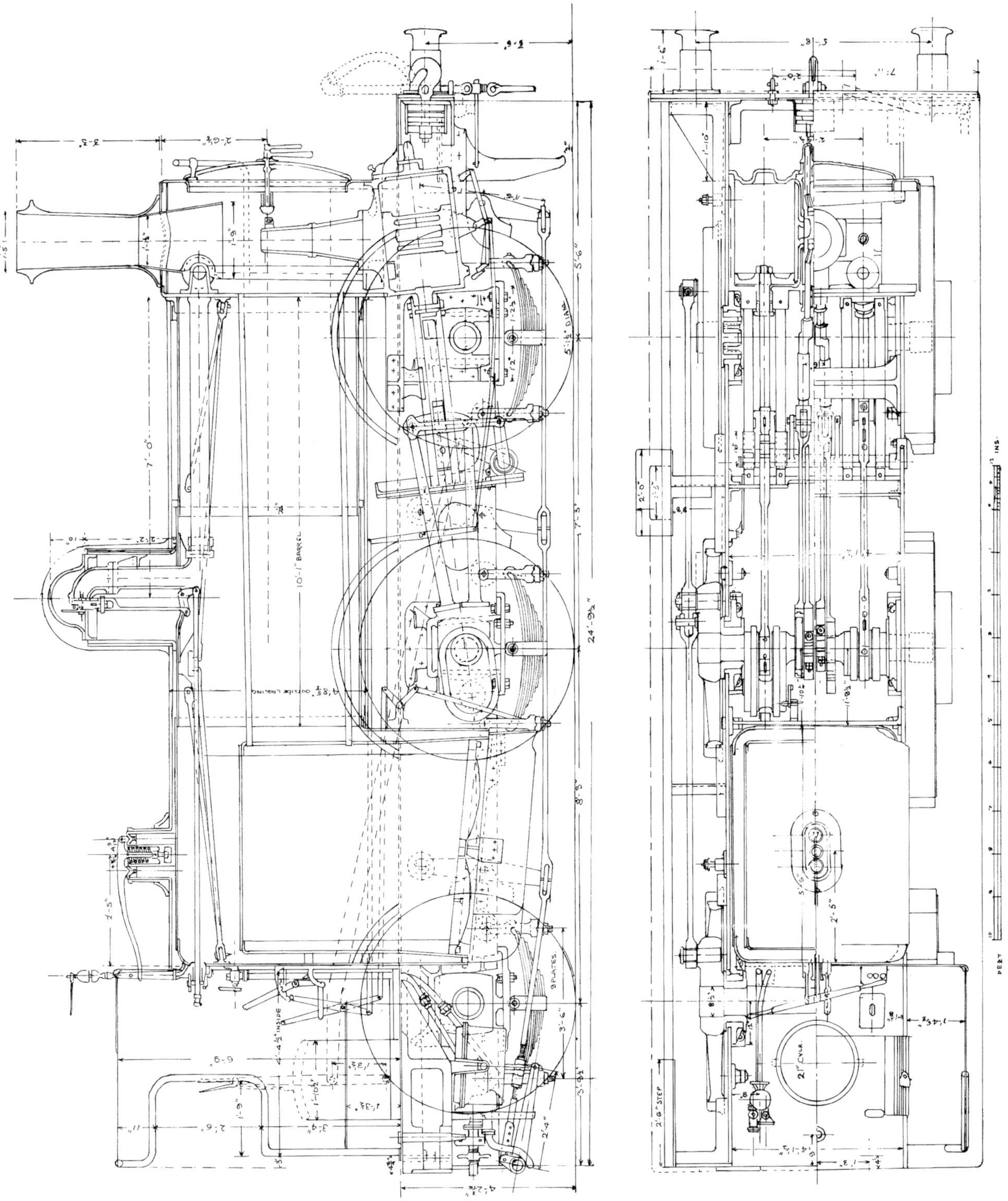

Plate 7
General arrangement of Class 'DA' locomotive as built.

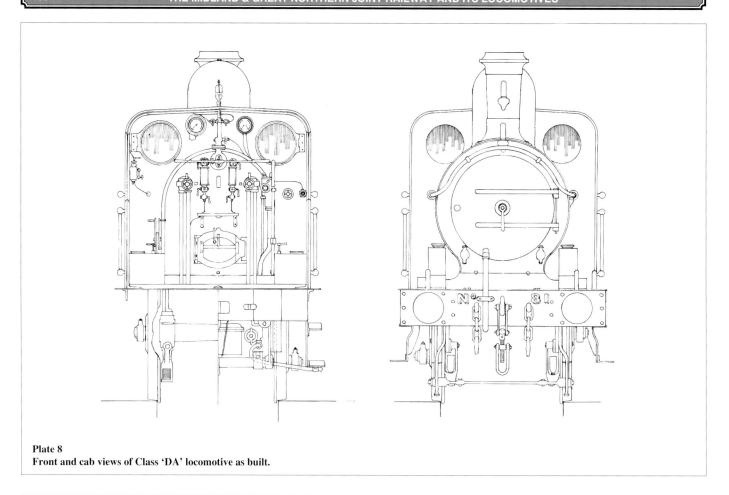

Plate 8
Front and cab views of Class 'DA' locomotive as built.

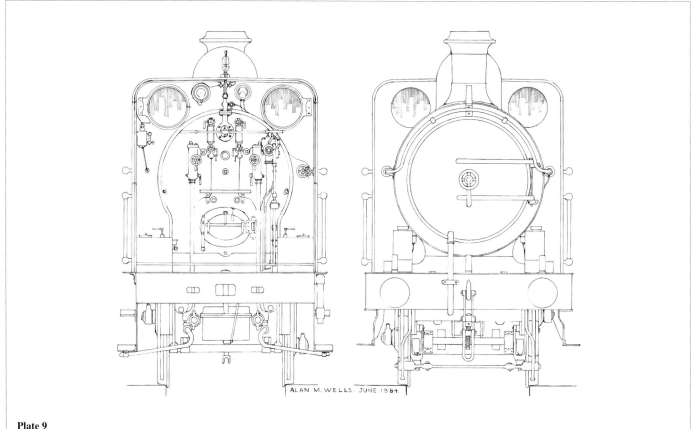

Plate 9
Front and cab views of Class 'DA' locomotive when reboilered.

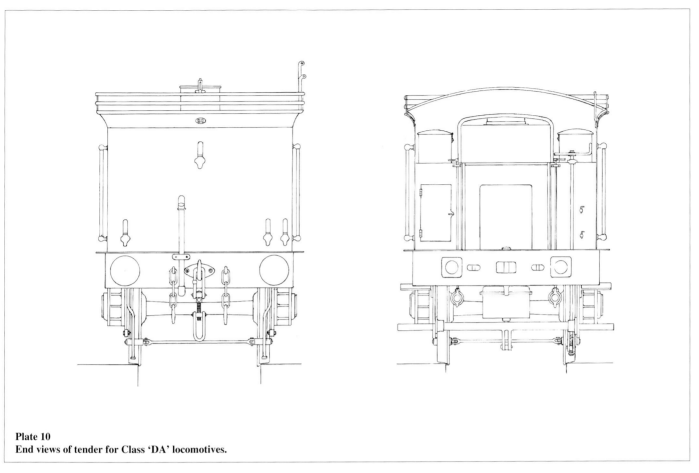

Plate 10
End views of tender for Class 'DA' locomotives.

BELOW: **Plate 11**
No. 088 was rebuilt with a larger boiler in 1920 and renumbered as seen here in 1936. Ten years later it was renumbered again and became L&NER No. 4163, before being withdrawn by British Railways in 1949. D. IBBOTTSON COLLECTION.

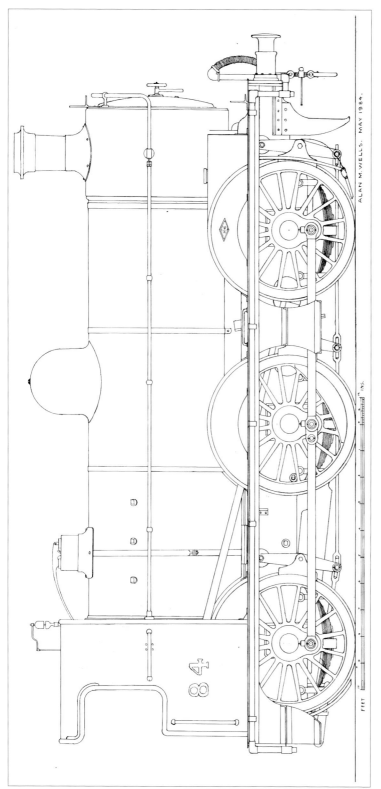

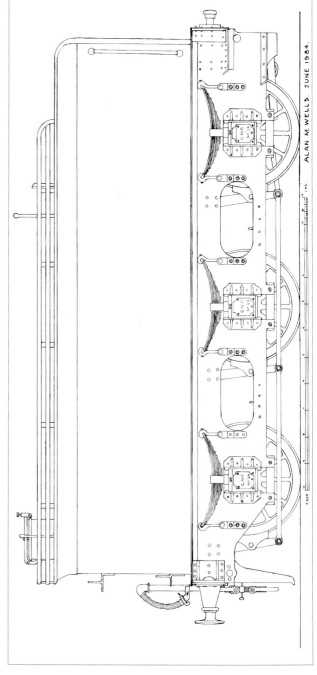

ALAN M. WELLS. MAY 1984.

ALAN M. WELLS. JUNE 1984.

ABOVE LEFT: Plate 12
Part section of frame at motion plate.

ABOVE RIGHT: Plate 13
Side elevation of M&GN Class 'DA' as rebuilt with longer boiler.

RIGHT: Plate 14
Side elevation of 3170 gallon tender as fitted to 'DA' Class engines.

ABOVE: **Plate 15**
This picture of No. 090 was taken after the locomotive was renumbered by the L&NER but before it was rebuilt as a 'J4' in 1937; but it did not remain in service long enough to carry its L&NER 1946 stock number, being withdrawn before it could be applied. H.C. CASSERLEY.

Plate 16
We conclude with this view of No. 4161, taken at Doncaster works yard on the 21st September 1947 when this locomotive was taken out of service. As M&GN No. 86 it had been rebuilt with a larger boiler in 1927. D.F. TEE.

MIDLAND & GREAT NORTHERN RAILWAY JOINT COMMITTEE.

Locomotive & Way & Works,

Reference   COPY   Engineer's Office,
N. 16-6.

MELTON CONSTABLE.   June 16th 1919.

Dear Sir,

Boilers for O-6-O Engines Class "Da"
G.N.R. Built supplied in 1900.

With reference to your letter DA 8980/2 - 87 of the
12th inst. The two prints Nos 18-9993 & 18-9992 of the proposed
M.R. boilers have come to hand and I herewith offer my observations
on same.

As you are aware we have fitted the H. boilers and
propose putting at the first opportunity some G.7. boilers into
the M.R. type 6 wheel Goods Engines these boiler barrels are 4'-8"
dia'r inside the large ring and carry 242 and 254 tubes, The boilers
you now propose to fit into the G.N. class goods engines have a
boiler barrel 4'-1" dia. inside the large ring and fitted with a less
number of tubes (the number not being shown on the prints sent). The
frames of the G.N. built engines are deeper and heavier and are
certainly quite suitable to carry the larger M.R. type boiler especiall
when compared with the frames of the M.R. type goods engine in which
we have already put these large dia'r boilers and I would propose that
instead of the small boilers being used that we adopt the ordinary
G.7. arrangement modified to suit the dimensions at our disposal, but
to this suggestion there is a serious obstacle, the G.N. pattern
rounded cab is unsuitable to meet the shape of the square top belpaire

ABOVE AND FOLLOWING PAGES: Plate 17
The letters between W. Marriott (16th June and 27th June 1919) and the Midland Railway Chief Mechanical Engineer, Sir Henry Fowler, reproduced
here, together with the later letter from W.E. Newman to Sir Henry, clearly show the Joint line local management 'stood their ground'. The letters
are reproduced as written, typing errors and annotations included.

June 16/1919

2.

type firebox and would if adopted necessitate renewing the cab
entirely. I estimate the cost of fitting the G.7. boiler to be
anything from £100 upwards in excess of the cost for putting in the G.
G.N. standard 4'-8" dia'r boiler, but admit against this there is the
the desirability for the standardization of the fittings etc.
I feel sure it is not your wish that we should make the G.N. built
engines less efficient than the M.R. built engines which necessarily
would be so with presumably 196 tubes in the boiler against 238 in the
G.N.Boiler or 254 in the M.R. G.7. besides having 160 lbs per sq inch
working press compared with 175 lbs per sq inch and further the boiler
you now suggest is 3" less in diameter than the present or original
boiler.

I must leave the question open to be decided by your-self & hope that
you will give me your decision quickly for I want to feel that the
best will be done to provide the boilers by the time we shall want
them.

> Yours faithfully,
>
> (signed) W. Marriott.,

Chief Mechanical Engineer,
    Midland Railway,
        DERBY.

P.S. If you decide in favour of midland boiler we shall standardise the brake & fittings and this of course mounts up the cost but should be done.

MIDLAND & GREAT NORTHERN RAILWAYS JOINT COMMITTEE.

COPY

Locomotive & Way & Works,

Reference
E. 4514
GO/27/6

Engineer's Office,

MELTON CONSTABLE. June 27th, 1919.

Dear Sir,

        Boiler for 0-6-0 Engines, Class "Da",
        G.N.R. built, supplied in 1900.
        -------------- ----

CA/8980/2
88/16. Referring to your letter of the 25th inst. and our

conversation.) You know our position as regards arrears of work

and necessity for stringent economy, and therefore I venture to put

the case of these boilers plainly before you, telling you frankly what

my opinion is, but knowing that you understand I will at once loyally

accept your decision in the matter.

        To change the "H" Boiler into the G.N. type of Goods

Engine from our Midland type 6-wheel Goods Engines, while it would

be very useful in giving is more of our standard G.7 boilers, would

cause us double work. We should have to pull the "H" boilers out

of the two engines that are at present running and useful, and have

only just been turned out of the shops after heavy repairs, and we

should have to alter the Cabs etc. again to suit the G.7 boiler,

meaning double work at this time, which I am very anxious to avoid.

        Personally my view is this. I always thought it was a

very great mistake having the G.N. type of Engine. We have always been

attached for Loco purposes to the Midland at Derby, and I have acted

loyally throughout with them, as we have in Permanent Way matters with

June 27/1919

2.

The Gt. Northern. As, however, we have the Engines, my view is for
the sake of economy we should stick to the G.N.type just for that class
numbering 12.   If we put the Midland boiler in we must alter the Cabs,
giving is extra work. We should also have to alter the brake and
fittings, and we should get as a result an Engine which is neither
Midland nor Gt. Northern but a kind of bastard. These are very good
Engines although there are some things which I do not like, for instance,
I much prefer the Midland type of regulator, And I think the brake is
not anything like as good an arrangement as the Midland type, but I
strongly recommend you, for the sake of economy, to let us keep these few
Engines distinctly as G.N.type Engines, so that in case of an allocation
of our Engines later on by the Government, they could go back to the
Gt. Northern and you could take your own type.

Perhaps you will kindly consider the reasons I have given
you, remembering that the boiler you suggested previously, No.G.5½, was
only demurred to as having less heating than the existing boilers, and
I do not wish to have the Engines any less powerful.

I notice you may have thought from my letter of the 16th
inst. that I was going to take out the "H" boilers, but we only mean
to replace some more of the ordinary Midland Goods Engine Boilers with
G.7 boilers when they come in for renewal.

Yours faithfully,
(signed) W. Marriott.,

Sir Henry Fowler,
     Derby.

MIDLAND & GREAT NORTHERN RAILWAYS JOINT COMMITTEE.

RESIDENT MECHANICAL ENGINEER,

MELTON CONSTABLE.   April 9th, 1925.

` Ref. J./5796.

3 Enclosures.

Dear Sir,

Proposed Rebuilding O-6-O G. N. DA Type
Engines.

Your letter DA.8980/2 of the 3rd instant.- I am sorry
to have to state the general arrangement drawing we have of this
class engine is by no means complete and I am sure would be of
little use for your purpose, and I have traced on the trailing
horn blocks and sent you another print also detail drawings of
Horn blocks and axleboxes.

May I call your attention to previous letters on the
proposal to fit a M.R. G.5½ boiler, your reference A88/8980/2/781
of July 8th 1919 and my letters of June 16th 1919 and June 27th 1919.
The position at present is, we have twelve engines of this class
six of these engines have already been fitted with the L. & N. E.
standard boilers and we have two new boilers on hand so that 8 of the
engines are provided for and will not require to be considered for
some years.   The remaining four engines I do not propose to reboiler
until next year and I recommend you for several reasons to not
countenance these four engines being made less effective than the
eight already dealt with.   I know your difficulty is the creation of
an odd size boiler, but may I point out that if you will allow a
requisition to be passed say in September next for four boilers
without Tubes to be made by the L. & N.E. early next year it will
be a great saving in expense to us here and the Boilers being a
L. & N.E. standard will in my opinion be quite reasonable as regards
cost.

Yours faithfully,

(signed) W. E. Newman.

M&GN drawings, to:-
No 3/887 Arrangt class DA engines
No 3/894 Axle boxes for same
No 3/895   "   guides for same.
Returned to LDO

Sir Henry Fowler, K.B.E.
L. M. & S. Railway,
DERBY.

CHAPTER 10

THE CLASS 'A TANK' MELTON 4-4-2Ts

In 1904 there emerged from Melton Constable works the first of an eventual series of three 4-4-2Ts that were undeniably amongst the most handsome of the genre – but arguably amongst the least successful. Known as Class 'A Tanks', they were the second of the two classes to be designed and built by the M&GN and, as with the 0-6-0Ts (Chapter 7), they were classified as rebuilds although in fact they were new. The boiler was very similar to the Johnson boiler used on the 0-6-0s and 4-4-0s, but with a larger firebox and fittings followed Midland practice.

As with the 0-6-0Ts, they took the numbers of the three engines that they replaced, but this time the new engines were numbered in the main not the duplicate list. There was a five-year interval between the first engine and the remaining pair – which hardly suggests any sort of urgent need – and indeed it is hard to establish just why they were built at all. Perhaps it was thought that what amounted to a tank engine version of the passenger 4-4-0s might show savings over the tender equivalent – given the relatively short distances on the M&GN and the lengthy experience with the earlier 4-4-0s – and they did share their driving wheel diameter with the otherwise far more useful Beyer Peacock 4-4-0s. For the record, they were numbered 41, 20 and 9 in order of building and 'replaced' three

of the old Hudswell, Clark 4-4-0Ts. The old No. 41 was withdrawn in 1904 and became a stationery boiler at Melton while the other two 4-4-0Ts went onto the duplicate list as 20A and 9A respectively.

Even when built there were slight differences in all three. The first, No. 41, had a short smokebox and nine-spoke bogie wheels. Both bogie and coupled wheels had rectangular spokes similar to the Beyer Peacock Class 'A', but as that class was still intact and the story goes that Peacock never supplied any spares for these engines it remains a mystery where they came from. The trailing wheels had oval spokes and drawings from the London Tilbury & Southend Railway were used for the trailing axle. There was indeed quite a 'Tilbury' look to these engines and it is possible that the design was influenced by the Whitlegg LTSR 4-4-2Ts.

The principal dimensions for all three were: outside cylinders 17½ inches × 24 inches, bogie wheels 3 feet 0 inches, coupled 6 feet 0 inches and trailing 3 feet 7 inches diameter. Boiler pressure was 160 psi, total heating surface 1232 square feet for No. 41 and 1099 square feet for No's 20 and 9. Grate area was 17.5 square feet. The boilers had the dimensions of the Midland 'B' type but had closed domes and Ramsbottom safety valves. No other Joint engines had this type of boiler and when reboilered the same type was used. Weight in

Plate 1
This picture of No. 9, the final engine to enter service in 1910, was taken at Melton Constable and illustrates the locomotive in its original condition. The imaginative use of the side tank to carry the company name in full was one of the hallmarks of the 'Joint Line'. ALAN WELLS COLLECTION.

working order was 68 tons 9 hundredweight, reduced to 68 tons in 1933–34. Water capacity was 1650 gallons (reduced to 1600 gallons in 1933–34) and coal 2 tons.

No. 41 had a standard numberplate and enclosed safety valves. In contrast, No. 20, built in February 1909, had an extended smokebox and enclosed safety valves as well as large cut out brass numerals. New bogie wheels with ten spokes of oval section were provided and the coupled wheels were also of oval section. No. 9 was built in March 1910 and had the same details as No. 20, except for the safety valves which were open. No. 41 was fitted with an extended smokebox circa 1910 to match the later pair, and its safety valves were now unshrouded, as eventually were those of No. 20. The engines had side doors to the cab and padded seats for the crew, but the lookouts were such that it was necessary for the crew to look over the side. This led Mr Nash to cut the tanks down at the front in 1933–34 but this did not achieve the object. He is reputed to have described them as less than useless! The engines were turned where possible to run chimney first as they tended to run hot if run for any distance bunker first. This was said to be due to a bad distribution of weight that could not be put right.

Deeley smokeboxes were applied from 1929 and the handrail altered at the front. The L&NER applied the prefix '0' in 1937 and later, when Thompson drew up his complete L&NER renumbering scheme in 1943, the two survivors, No's 041 and 09, were allotted numbers 7503 and 7504 but did not survive to carry them. The L&NER continued to use the M&GN classification until 1942 when they became Class 'C17'.

For all that they seem not to have been as useful as may have been hoped, they remained in service for a reasonable period. They were the last 'main line' engines to carry distinctly 'M&GN' looks – as apposed to the 'Derby/Doncaster' lineaments of the rest of the surviving main line locomotives – and added yet another element to the distinctively different character of the M&GN stock. In 1944, when the last one was scrapped, only the 'Melton' 0-6-0Ts remained as reminders of Melton Constable construction, and they were mostly to be found in the yards rather than out on the line. The class was associated with the eastern section; when new No. 41 was employed on passenger trains between Yarmouth Beach and Lowestoft, the Potter Heigham service, and between Cromer Beach and Melton Constable. During the later years after the L&NER takeover they were all allocated to Melton Constable, although No. 020 did spend some time at Yarmouth Beach.

SUMMARY TABLE

M&GN No.	BUILT BY	DATE BUILT	L&NER 1937 No.	MONTH APPLIED	MONTH WITHDRAWN
41	Melton Constable	20/12/1904	041	9/37	1/44
20	Melton Constable	11/2/1909	020	11/37	4/42
9	Melton Constable	15/3/1910	09	5/37	7/44

Plate 2
This picture of No. 9 was also taken at Melton Constable not long after the locomotive was built, and shows the other side of the locomotive to that shown in Plate 1. R.J. ESSERY COLLECTION.

ABOVE: Plate 3
No. 20 is seen in this undated picture which shows the simplified style of company ownership applied in lemon chrome on the dark brown livery from 1929, but the scene dates from before the engine's side tanks were altered in 1933. The picture, taken at Yarmouth Road, also shows the replacement smokebox that was fitted to this class. R.J. ESSERY COLLECTION.

BELOW: Plate 4
This broadside picture of No. 20 has been included to show the side tanks after they had been cut down circa 1933 to improve the visibility for the enginemen. When the engine had been 'well coaled' and was running bunker first the visibility for the driver was not very good. ALAN WELLS COLLECTION.

ABOVE: Plate 5
Photographed at Melton Constable, this undated picture shows No. 41 with a Deeley smokebox and carrying passenger train headlamps, but there does not appear to be anyone on the footplate or any other railway staff to be seen. The ex-L&NWR six wheel luggage brake vans were not transferred to the M&GN until 1936, which helps to date this picture. R.J. ESSERY COLLECTION.

BELOW: Plate 6
This picture of No. 41, photographed when the locomotive was taking water, shows the sloping tank and Deeley smokebox door to good effect; however, what is particularly interesting about this picture is the lagging on the water column, a feature that the author has never seen before. R.J. ESSERY COLLECTION.

Plate 7
No. 41 as built at Melton.

MIDLAND & GREAT NORTHERN

FEET   INS   ALAN M. WELLS. JULY 1986.

Plate 8
This picture of No. 041 was taken at the L&NER works at Stratford where, judging by its condition, the locomotive had been 'through the shops' and lettered L.NER. No. 41 was the first of the class to be built, and ran until withdrawn in 1944.
R.J. ESSERY COLLECTION.

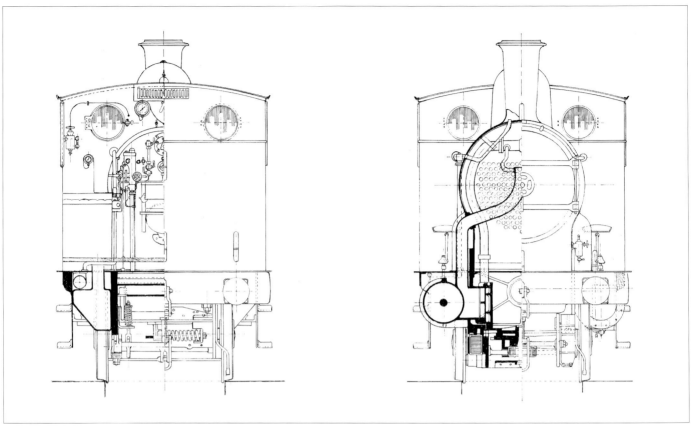

ABOVE: Plate 9
End views with cut away details of Class 'A Tank' engines.

BELOW LEFT: Plate 10
Deeley type smokebox as fitted to Class 'A Tank' engines. It should be noted that No. 41 was one of very few engines to be painted in full yellow livery when carrying this type of smokebox.

BELOW RIGHT: Plate 11
Partial side view of Class 'A Tank' engines No's 20 and 9, as built at Melton Constable and showing extended smokebox.

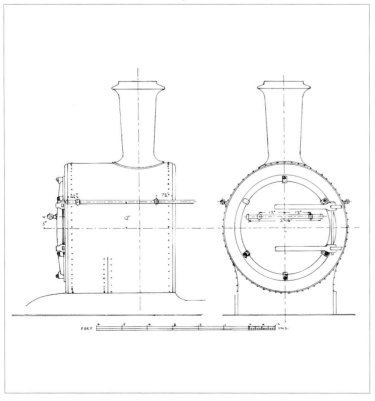

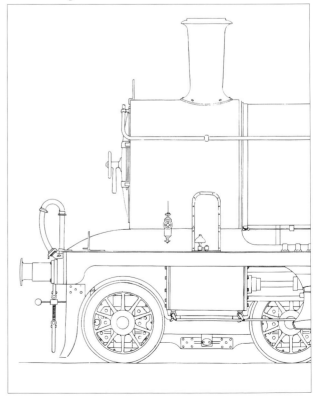

CHAPTER 11

LOCOMOTIVE LIVERIES

PERIOD ONE: YARMOUTH & NORTH NORFOLK AND LYNN & FAKENHAM RAILWAYS 1876–1883

These two railways were designed and built by the contractor Wilkinson & Jarvis. Although nominally separate companies, both railways were under the control of the contractors who regarded them as one entity. This had consequences for the locomotives and their liveries.

The main colour of L&F and Y&NN locomotives was green. It is alleged that the Y&NN green was slightly darker than L&F green, but this seems unlikely considering that the contractor ordered the same types of locomotive from the same builders on behalf of what they regarded as one railway. The actual green used is not definitely known; it has been described as 'Great Central' in shade by R.S. McNaught, but compared to the old North London green by P.C. Dewhurst. Alan Wells researched the Beyer Peacock records and found that it was simply specified as 'green to pattern', which is unhelpful, but he thought that Great Northern green was probably similar. In all cases these are effectively chrome greens manufactured from Prussian blue and chrome yellow. The ex-Cornish Mineral Railway 0-6-0T engines were not green, being delivered in brown lined in black and yellow, allegedly their original CMR colours.

Smokeboxes, cab roofs, footplates, and probably tank and tender tops were black. Valances, cylinders, main frames and outside frames of tenders were 'red-brown to pattern', described by Alan Wells as approximating to Venetian red, a colour used extensively by the Midland Railway and called by them 'chocolate'. Lining was generally in black bands edged in white. Motion, axles and inside surfaces of frames were vermilion, also the levers of safety valves and buffer beams, including buffer castings. Cab interiors are also said to have been vermilion. Engines carried no initials or sign of company ownership.

PERIOD TWO: EASTERN & MIDLANDS RAILWAY 1883–1893

From January 1883 the L&F, the Y&NN and the Yarmouth Union Railways were amalgamated into one entity, the Eastern & Midlands Railway. The contractors, Wilkinson & Jarvis, had been working towards this end since 1878 and with the deposition of the Amalgamation Bill in November 1881 handed over control to the companies. William Marriott was to be Engineer and J.W. Mann was to continue as Locomotive Superintendent, his position on the L&F. However, economies forced Mr Mann to leave and Mr Marriott assumed both rôles.

The livery adopted by the E&MR was a middle brown, sometimes referred to as 'chocolate'. Whether this was the colour carried by the ex-Cornish Minerals engines is debatable, although they certainly carried E&MR lettering on their original paintwork. Engines were now painted middle brown all over, including frames and valances. Smokeboxes, cab roofs, footplates, tank and tender tops and wheel tyres were black. Lining was in black, fine-lined in chrome yellow, possibly lemon chrome as used at Melton for many years. The reported use of red, white and blue lining is thought not to be correct, although at least one engine is believed to have had non-standard lining. Body panels were edged in black and yellow with square corners, and large areas and tenders were also lined into panels, corners being curved normally. Outside cylinders were now

lined with their own panel of lining. Bufferbeams were vermilion, now edged in black only, although the ends of wooden bufferbeams still seem to be lined.

The first lettering style used was 'E & M RY', seen on CMR 0-6-0Ts No's 11 and 13, and 4-4-0 No. 28. The heraldic device was possibly introduced in 1888, but the earliest firmly dated occurrence is 1890. Lettering on tanks and tenders henceforth incorporated the device thus: 'E & [device] M R', except saddletanks, which simply carried 'E & M R'. Lettering was in 6 inch gold sans serif characters, shaded in black. Bufferbeams carried the engine number, in gold seriffed characters, shaded in black, for example, 'No [hook] 19'. Under the 'o' was a dot rather than a line.

The colourful armorial device was not registered with the College of Heralds and so cannot be referred to as a 'coat of arms'. It consisted of the arms of Norwich, Yarmouth, Peterborough and Lynn on a decorated shield within a white garter on which the name 'EASTERN & MIDLANDS RAILWAY' was applied in black sans serif letters. Dimensions were 9¾ inches by 10¾ inches.

The E&MR completed the number list begun by the L&F. The photographic record is very incomplete, but it seems that numbers were carried in a variety of ways, and the elliptical numberplate as used on the Beyer Peacock engines was not generally introduced until circa 1890. The Hudswell, Clark 4-4-0Ts went through the entire E&MR period with numbers on the bufferbeams only, and it seems that all the ex-CMR 0-6-0s and the saddletanks had painted numbers. The numberplates were standardised at 16 inches by 11 inches with 5½ inch numerals, although the plates fitted to the rebuilt 2-4-0s were only about 13 inches by 8 inches.

A number of locomotives were fitted with a pair of jacks to assist in rerailing after minor mishaps, although they were so heavy that they were apparently never used. All the Class 'A' 4-4-0s and Class 'B' 4-4-0Ts had them, some fitted in L&FR days, also at first the ex-Cornish Minerals 0-6-0s. Their colour was vermilion. The base was black, but the ratchet and handle at the top were often kept polished. The locomotive number was often painted in small seriffed numerals on the outer side, possibly in white.

PERIOD THREE: THE EARLY M&GN 1893–1899

From the 1st July 1893 the Eastern & Midlands Railway was vested in the Midland & Great Northern Railways Joint Committee. The first few months of the Joint Committee were ones of experiment, mainly involving the various lettering styles. A Midland Railway photographer was despatched from Derby during 1893 and 1894 to record the various results, probably for review purposes.

The first lettering scheme involved the use of 'MID & G N J R' hand-painted on the garter of the device, with 'M & G N J R' on carriages and locomotives, but the Railway Clearing House stepped in. They were concerned about possible confusion that might arise with number-taking and routing of Joint rolling stock. From December 1893 it was decided that all Joint engines, carriages, wagons and sheets were to be marked 'JT M & G N'. The garter around the device was lettered 'JOINT MIDLAND & GREAT NORTHERN RAILWAY.' However, by about 1896 this lettering had been superseded by 'MIDLAND & GREAT NORTHERN JOINT RAILWAY.'

Decisions had to be made by Melton Constable and Derby regarding the locomotive colour. It seems that Melton expected to use the existing E&MR brown for the new organisation, as it was ordered in December 1893 that the ten engines to be built by Sharp Stewart were to be the same colour as the engines taken over by the Joint Committee. However, there must have been a change of heart, because the new locomotives arrived in a new livery. It is almost certain that many of the ex-E&MR locomotives, particularly those on the duplicate list created in 1894, would not have been repainted by Melton. The average repainting time for locomotives was three years, but there would have been a reluctance to waste time on those engines earmarked for early scrapping. It would also have been sensible to wait until major repairs or rebuildings of the Class 'A' 4-4-0s and Class 'B' 4-4-0Ts were due before repainting. In this way it is likely that E&MR brown was present in dwindling amounts until at least 1899 and, in the case of No. 12A, possibly until 1902.

The new locomotive colour had a variety of names, none of them official, including 'hydrate of iron', 'Quaker green', 'improved willow green', 'autumn leaf', 'golden ochre' and, allegedly, 'golden gorse'. Many of these names have a subjective connotation and, to remove any ambiguity, this chapter will use the description 'light brown', which of course it was. The colour was similar in hue to the E&MR middle brown, but was a lighter shade. 'Hydrate of iron' is actually an accurate description, as both the paints involved consist mainly of that naturally-occurring chemical compound. The process used has been recorded by Jim Miller, a stalwart of the Melton paint shop before the Great War. Put simply, it was two coats of yellow ochre upon a lead grey undercoat, glazed with a top coat of raw sienna, and three coats of varnish. The full amount of preparation is noted below.

The frames, wheels, outside cylinders, valances and steps were painted burnt sienna, a red-brown colour. Smokeboxes, footplates, splasher tops and so on were black. Bufferbeams, motion and inside faces of the frames were vermilion, as were safety valve levers. Salter safety valve spring balances were polished brass. Bufferbeams were edged with black, and the end lips of the buffer castings were also black.

Lining was generally in black (although see below), edged with lemon chrome, in a very similar form to that used by the E&MR. Most body panels were edged ¾ inch black and ¼ inch lemon chrome. Tenders, bunkers and tanks were panelled with 1½ inch black bands, edged on both sides with ¼ inch lemon chrome lines to make the 2 inch lining, usually 3 inches within the edgings. Frames, at least on the Class 'C' 4-4-0s, were edged below the footplate with black fine-lined with lemon chrome, including bogie compensating beams and guard irons.

Wheels had black tyres with a lemon chrome line between the black and the burnt sienna of the wheel. Wheel centres were lined in a circle around the perimeter (not following the shape of the crank) and around the axle end, both with the lemon chrome on the inside only. Spring buckles were also lined. Cab interiors were painted and grained in the upper part, and painted loco light brown in the lower. Firebox backs were black.

The treatment of boiler bands is slightly in question. In most published references and in reported paint shop practice they were black. It has been asserted, at least for the Class 'C' 4-4-0s, that they were 'chocolate', that is, burnt sienna, but this seems highly unlikely and there is no surviving evidence to support it.

The question of how to deal with the initials of the new owning companies was quite a difficult one. The first examples to be relettered simply carried 'M & G N J R', but it must have been deemed necessary to include the device because several photographs exist of experimental arrangements. Three engines were recorded carrying 'M & G [device] N J R', a rather awkward arrangement. Three more carried 'JT M & [device] G N R', but another engine (No. 3A) forecast future practice in having 'M & [device] G N'.

The lettering on the first new locomotives of the M&GN, the Class 'C' 4-4-0s, was in the Midland manner, being gold seriffed characters shaded in blue and white and shadowed in black. The first ten examples actually carried 'JT M & G N R' on the tender, but thereafter the usual form was 'M & G N'. At Melton, meanwhile, locomotives were still being relettered with plain gold sans serif characters shadowed in black, often still on E&MR livery. The last example of this seems to have been Class 'B' 4-4-0T No. 19, which was reboilered in 1903 but still did not yet have the Midland style of initials.

Bufferbeams were lettered in the form 'N⁰ [hook] 19' seriffed in gold. Characters applied at Melton were shadowed in black and had a dot beneath the 'o', but new engines had Midland-type characters shaded in blue and white, shadowed in black, with a dash. Brass numberplates were still used at Melton, standardised at 16 inches by 11 inches whatever the number, with larger 6½ inch numerals in a rather more florid style than the E&MR plates.

On the rear of Midland-type tenders, a short horizontal handrail was fixed centrally. Above the handrail was an elliptical numberplate carrying 'JT MIDLAND &' around the upper edge and 'GT NORTHERN RY' around the lower, with the engine number central and the date of construction below the number. The water capacity was on another plate below the handrail, reading 'WATER CAPACITY' at the top, with '2950' central and 'GALLONS' under it. Both plates were 10½ inches by 6 inches, and had white letters on a black background.

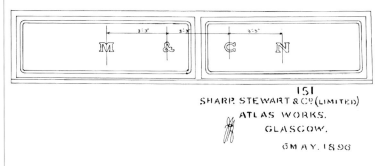

ABOVE: Plate 1
Copy of Sharp Stewart & Co. drawing 13055 that shows the lettering and spacing as applied to the side of the tenders.

RIGHT: Plate 2
A drawing of the letter M with details of shading, letters 6½ inches high with ¾ inch blue and ¾ inch black shading.

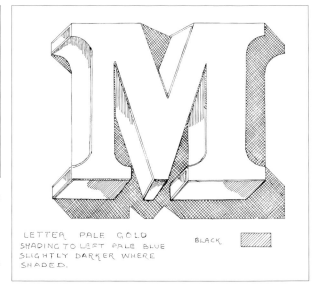

PERIOD FOUR: 'STANDARD' M&GN 1900–1928

This is the period when the liveries and lettering styles appeared which lasted for the majority of the M&GN's independent life. There have been suggestions that the locomotive livery changed around 1904, stemming from a paragraph in *The Locomotive Magazine* in that year stating that M&GN engines were 'now being painted a much brighter yellow'. However, this is a retrospective statement quoted from a much earlier article, and refers to the demise of the E&MR brown. It is known from issues of the same magazine from 1896, 1898 and 1901, in which the locomotive colour is referred to as 'light yellow brown' or 'yellow ochre' or 'the standard yellow of the line', that the lighter colour was introduced almost immediately.

It is almost certain, therefore, that the standard livery of light brown and burnt sienna lined with black and lemon chrome was continued without change. It seems that after the First World War the method of obtaining the light brown was simplified by mixing to a colour board, but otherwise it remained the same hue. Lining on main frames below the footplate was not continued after circa 1900, but one area that persisted was around the edge of Class 'C' bogie compensating beams. Guard irons on these engines were unlined burnt sienna, but on engines where the guard irons were bolted on they were black.

The period was distinguished by Melton Constable rebuilds of several different examples, and new construction of shunting tanks and passenger tanks. These had minor variations of the livery, but the standard was retained until 1922, from which time the Classes 'D' and 'DA' 0-6-0s were finished in a very dark brown. Alan Wells called this a 'red brown', but samples made using the old formula show that there was very little red in it. Two of the Melton-built shunting tanks were also repainted. The other locomotives stayed in the standard light brown until 1929.

The elliptical brass numberplates were used for Melton-built engines up to the end of 1907, but thereafter any rebuilds received Midland-type brass numerals of a much larger size. The Melton numerals were 9 inches instead of 6½ inches. The device was still used on most engines; until 1910 with the usual white garter, but from that date the transfer used a blue garter with gold edging and letters.

All lettering was standardised as the Midland seriffed gold transfers, shaded in blue, light blue and white, and shadowed in black. The only exceptions were the saddletanks and the three Class 'A Tank' 4-4-2T. A drawing issued to the outside builders of the new Midland-type engines specifies tender lettering to be 'M & G N' with an overall dimension of 9 feet 9 inches, and this is how it was spaced on delivery.

For some reason the Melton paint shop preferred a more subtle arrangement. The beading strip on Midland tenders was not exactly central, the rearward panel being slightly longer. Despite this, the 'M' and 'N' of the initials were placed in the centre of these panels, 9 feet 6 inches apart; the '&' and the 'G' were then spaced unequally between. The fact that the middle strip is not exactly central between the two pairs of initials is not noticed by the eye.

A feature in the days of named drivers, which ceased in 1919, was the painted area high up on the right hand side of the cab interior, being a black rectangle about 10 inches by 4½ inches with incurved corners, a white border and the driver's name and last out-shopping date painted on in white.

One other minor development was the adoption of the Midland 2 inch brass power classification numerals. The MR had used these on tender engines since 1905, but the M&GN certainly did not adopt them until about 1923, possibly as a request from the newly-formed London Midland & Scottish Railway. The various groupings were Classes 'A', 'A Tank', 'C' – Power Class 1; Classes 'A Rebuild', 'C Rebuild', 'D', 'DA' – Power Class 2; Class 'D Rebuild' – Power

Class 3. The other types of engine were unclassified. The numerals were fixed high up on the cab side sheets.

PERIOD FIVE: LATER M&GN 1929–1936

From 1929, all the engines that had formerly been painted light brown joined the goods locomotives in being painted dark brown. Lining was much reduced, being a single lemon chrome line around some panels and on the boiler bands, but even so most locomotives were still lined. The old Midland-style transfers or the larger sans serif initials were generally abandoned in favour of 12 inch high lemon chrome seriffed initials. The spacing was as before, being 9 feet 6 inches or 9 feet 0 inches overall depending on class. The lettering and lining turned to a pale orange over time. Brass numerals or numberplates were retained, but the device was not used except on a handful of engines on their first dark brown painting. Subsequently even these were done away with. Valve levers were still vermilion. Bufferbeams were also vermilion, no longer edged with a plain black line, but buffer castings still had a plain black border to their outer edge. Numbers in gold serif transfers, shaded with blue and white and shadowed in black were still applied to the right of the drawhook, but the 'N⁰' was omitted. Later in the period, about 1936, bufferbeam transfers were of a bolder style, still 4½ inches high, but now about 5 inches wide.

One feature that was applied universally and changed the outward appearance of M&GN locomotives was the use of round-headed rivets on smokeboxes, and flat Deeley smokebox doors secured with dog clips. This process had begun around 1927, and so several engines were still running in the light brown but with Deeley smokeboxes while, conversely, quite a number of engines were repainted dark brown with their original smokeboxes.

PERIOD SIX: THE L&NER AND BR PERIOD 1936–1960

From 1st October 1936, the London & North Eastern Railway took over the running and administration of the M&GN, although the Joint Committee still existed. Melton Constable works were closed except for minor repairs in December 1936. Henceforth M&GN locomotives were serviced at Stratford or, in the case of the Class 'DA' 0-6-0s, Doncaster.

At first there was little appreciable alteration in the appearance of M&GN locomotives. However, several were turned out from Melton with the brass numerals removed and large 12 inch painted numbers preceded by a zero applied in lemon chrome. This was the old Stratford method of showing a locomotive on the duplicate list. The same was done on the bufferbeams, using the wide transfers.

Few of these engines were subject to a full repaint, the existing initials (often of duller appearance) remaining on the tender. It is known that some locomotives were actually repainted in varnished black and supplied with standard L&NER transfers at Melton, but this finish was not generally applied until 1937, when M&GN engines were sent to Stratford. Other distinguishing features of this Melton-applied L&NER livery were the final type of M&GN numerals on the bufferbeams, which were themselves painted in standard M&GN style; no lining on the splashers, and the L&NER initials on the tender set closer together than usual. Melton adhered to the 9 feet 6 inches spacing that it had used since 1893.

The standard L&NER painting was varnished black. Most examples were lined in a single vermilion line, sometimes having more lining than they did in the late M&GN period. Valve levers were vermilon. Bufferbeams were vermilion, edged with black and lined with white. Buffer castings were black. Bufferbeam lettering was in the form 'N⁰ [hook] 055' for example, in 4½ inch yellow sans serif characters, shaded in black. Rear bufferbeams were unlined vermilion with no lettering, the buffer castings still being black. The main initials were 'L N E R' in 12 inch yellow sans serif letters, shaded to right and

ABOVE: Plate 3
No. 57 shows the buffer beam lettering in use from 1894 to 1929 'No [hook] 57', where the 'o' is underlined. R.S. CARPENTER COLLECTION.

BELOW: Plate 4
No. 4 shows the buffer beam style for the dark brown engines, with the later wide numeral. R.J. ESSERY COLLECTION.

below in brown and light red, highlighted in white. The extent of the initials applied at Stratford was usually 12 feet 9 inches from the centre of the 'L' to the centre of the 'R'. Numbers were often of the smaller 9 inch transfers, but were sometimes also 12 inch. Initials on the tank engines were also smaller.

The number of ex-M&GN engines rapidly declined, so that only one locomotive ever carried a BR number.

0-4-0ST CONTRACTOR'S ENGINES *ALPHA* AND *VICI*

PERIOD ONE

Green, lined with black fine-lined on each side in white. Lining appeared as a panel on the side of the saddletank, and another panel on the small cab sidesheet which doubled as a bunker. The rear of the engine was also lined in a panel, and there was a small panel on the cylinders. Corners of lining were curved conventionally. Edging in black and white occurred at the front and rear of the saddletank, front and rear of the cylinders, along the lower edge of the footplate valance, around the sandbox, and on the body panels, apparently including the simple cab. The cabside maker's plate and the nameplate were also edged around with black and white. The safety valve cover was polished brass, handrails and coupling and connecting rods were polished steel. Short brass nameplates with raised seriffed letters (probably on vermilion backgrounds) were fixed on the tanks. They were numbered 4 and 5 respectively circa 1881, the brass numerals (about 9 inches high) appearing only on the chimneys, but the nameplates were retained.

PERIOD TWO

Still in lined green. They retained their names and chimney numbers. Coupling and connecting rods were vermilion.

PERIOD THREE

The two engines were used quite a lot on construction work during this period and, although it could be expected that they were painted black by this time, there are enough traces on several photographs to suggest they were still in lined green, although very dirty. Their chimney numbers and their names remained undisturbed. An 'A' was placed below each number in 1894.

PERIOD FOUR

After 1906 the two engines were laid up in Melton Constable yard and not used further. They were apparently still in their original lined green, although very dirty and scruffy. In 1917, *Alpha* was overhauled and repainted black, lined white and vermilion like the other saddletanks, then sold to J. & J. Colman of Norwich. The remains of *Vici* were still observed in the yard in 1932.

0-6-0 SADDLETANKS: *ORMESBY*, *STALHAM*, *HOLT*, *IDA* AND *AYLSHAM*

PERIOD ONE

Almost certainly green, lined out into panels with black and white, the lining having sharply curved corners coming to an inward-facing point. *Stalham* had one panel on the cabside and another on the bunker. The saddletank had a line along its lower edge, which possibly curved over the top to the other side. The front of the tank and the rear of the bunker may also have been lined. The wheel centres were also lined around their perimeters. A photograph of *Aylsham* appears to show a panel of lining with ordinary curved corners on the flat side of the saddletank, but other details are indistinct. There were no numbers, but all carried brass nameplates on the tanks. The Fox, Walker engines had small plates with the name etched in seriffed letters and probably filled with black wax. The others had much larger plates with incurved corners and raised san-serif letters. *Ormesby* and *Stalham* had polished brass domes.

PERIOD TWO

Repainted black, with all names removed and numbers substituted. Lining consisted of a white line, with vermilion fine-lining on the outer side. The Fox, Walker locomotives had panels of lining on the cylinders, round the sandbox filler on the smokebox wrapper, on the cab lower sidesheets, and around the saddletank following the curve up and over to the other side of the engine. The front face of the saddletank was also lined. Domes were polished brass. The Hawthorn locos had a rectangular panel of lining on the tankside, and more lining on the upper and lower cab sidesheets, bunker, footsteps, front sandbox, boiler bands, and on wheel centres and rims. Coupling and connecting rods were vermilion.

At first there was no company lettering. The number appeared on the centre of the tank in the form 'Nᵒ 6' in a small rectangle of lining with incurved corners, a feature also photographed on No. 16. Later, by about 1890, the two Fox, Walker engines No's 15 and 16 were given the initials 'E & M R' in about 4 inch letters (possibly yellow rather than gold) on the side of the saddletank, but the only number was on the bufferbeam. Brass maker's plates occupied the cabsides of all engines, and numberplates were not fitted.

PERIOD THREE

The Black, Hawthorn 0-6-0ST engines No's 6, 7 and 17 were placed on the duplicate list in 1894. The small 'A' being placed beside the painted numbers of the first two, before they were sold later that year. The remaining three engines were black, lined in white, fine-lined vermilion. Brass domes were painted over. Lettering was simply 'M & G N' in the Melton sans serif characters, possibly in yellow rather than gold. Bufferbeam numbers remained in the E&MR style. Elliptical brass numberplates were supplied with vermilion backgrounds. No. 17A was given a small 'A' below. Coupling and connecting rods (and reversing lever of No. 17A) were vermilion. No. 17A was works shunter until 1901, and was scrapped in 1902. No. 15 was sold in 1900.

PERIOD FOUR

The last remaining 0-6-0 saddletank was still painted black lined in white with fine-lining in vermilion. Coupling and connecting rods were vermilion. Lettering was 'M & G N' in 6 inch sans serif initials, possibly yellow rather than gold. Fox, Walker 0-6-0ST No. 16 became works shunter in 1901, remaining so until 1937, and was known as *Black Bess*. It was renumbered 16A in 1905 to make way for the 0-6-0T built in that year. When put on the duplicate list, a small 4½ inch brass 'A' was placed below the elliptical numberplate, and the bufferbeam lettering altered slightly to have a dash below the 'o' in 'Nᵒ [hook] 16'. By 1936, the Melton sans serif letters on the tanks had been replaced by standard shaded seriffed Midland-style transfers, and lining was in vermilion only.

HUDSWELL, CLARK & RODGERS 4-4-0T CLASS 'B'

PERIOD ONE

These locomotives were painted green and lined. Each body panel was edged in black and white, and boiler bands were black with white edging. The tanks had a rectangular panel of conventional type, but the bunkers were lined in a continuous panel from one side around the back onto the other side. This lining style was perpetuated throughout the life of the engines. The lower portions were brown, lined on the L&F engines in black and white. There have been suggestions that the Y&NN engines had the brown portions lined in vermilion, but a recently discovered photograph of *Martham* almost certainly shows white lines. The portion of the main frames above the footplate may have been black. Domes, safety valve seatings and chimney caps were brass. Spectacles and side windows had brass frames. The front bogie wheel also had a small splasher beaded with brass. The slide bars were covered in with a hinged panel, which was possibly brown and lined. The wheels were green with black tyres, with a white line between the black and the green, and the wheel centres were lined around their edges with black and white. The brass nameplates were rectangular with corners an arc of small radius and raised letters and border; most had seriffed lettering of the same size – but *North Walsham* had the initial letters of both words larger in size than the rest – and the background was probably vermilion. Bufferbeams were vermilion, edged in black and lined white and, on *Norwich* and *Martham* at least, white lines formed an inner panel. The only engine of this class fitted with the Westinghouse brake was *Fakenham*, with the pump in front of the tank on the offside. The upper cylinder was trimmed with brass top and bottom, while the bottom cylinder was edged top and bottom with black and white.

PERIOD TWO

The paint colour was middle brown, with black edging lined in yellow. Lining in black and yellow formed a panel on the tank side, and wrapped around the sides and rear of the bunkers as it had in L&F livery. The brass domes and valve seatings were retained, but names were removed and numbers substituted. The number was painted on the bufferbeam only – the elliptical numberplates did not appear on the Class 'B' engines until the M&GN period. The rectangular brass maker's plate remained on the cab side, outlined with lining. Bufferbeams and buffer castings were vermilion, edged in black, although the outer ends seem to have been lined. The position of the bufferbeam number was towards the top of the beam to avoid the safety chains then fitted. The coupling and connecting rods were also vermilion. The standard lettering of 'E & [device] M R' was applied to the tanks. There is no photograph of one carrying the first lettering, but presumably some at least must have carried it.

PERIOD THREE

One of these engines was experimentally relettered 'M & G [device] N J R'. Three others (No's 8, 40 and 41) were reboilered in 1894 with a special boiler having Midland type fittings. The domes remained polished brass. A photograph of rebuilt No. 41 exists showing the lettering 'Jᵀ M & [device] G N R' in the Melton sans serif gold characters, and it is possible that the other two were lettered in the same way. For the first time these engines were given the elliptical brass numberplates, that of No. 41 being placed above the centre line of the lettering. It is strongly suspected that the livery would still be E&MR middle brown at this time, but the light brown and burnt sienna livery would have been applied at their next repaint circa 1897. Frames above the footplate were probably black. The other engines were reboilered in a like manner in 1896 (No. 10), 1899 (No. 9) and 1903 (No's 19 and 20). It is possible that they received Midland-type transfers in the form 'M & [device] G N [number]' at the same time. However No. 19 was clearly photographed after reboilering in 1903 carrying the old Melton style of sans serif letters. The levers of the Salter spring valves were vermilion, as were the coupling rods, although the bosses were left bright. In addition, No's 19 and 41 had their connecting rods painted vermilion.

PERIOD FOUR

Standard light brown livery with brass dome and safety valve cover, lined as described above, the bunker lining being carried round to the rear. Lettering was 'M & [device] G N [number]', the number being carried on the elliptical brass numberplates. No. 41, which had its numberplate positioned above the centre line of the lettering, was withdrawn in 1904, but No's 9 and 20 were put on the duplicate list when the Class 'A' tanks were built. The small 4½ inch brass 'A' was placed to the upper right of the numberplates, and a small 'A' was transferred on the bufferbeams.

The other engines, No's 8, 10, 19 and 40, were loaned to the Midland Railway in 1906. At first the only alteration was the painting-out of the M&GN initials and the substitution of the earlier

Midland device, but in 1907 their numberplates were removed and Midland livery applied. This was the simplified Deeley livery, being alizarin crimson edged with black and yellow, with black wheels and frames. The dome was painted over, and cylinders were crimson. The numbers of the old Pullman cars to which the engines were coupled were applied to the centre of the tanks in 6½ inch brass numerals. The bufferbeam carried the usual 'M [hook] R' in gold sans serif letters shaded in blue, shadowed in black. The four engines were returned to the M&GN in 1912, and a photograph of No. 10 at Cromer Beach would suggest that it was painted grey at Melton. The number was in white numerals shaded black on the former position of the numberplate. These four engines were sold to the Government for War Department use in 1917. The remaining two engines, No's 9A and 20A, were withdrawn in 1932 and 1931 respectively, still in the light brown livery.

SHARP STEWART EX-CMR 0-6-0T+TR CLASS 'D', LATER CLASS 'CM'

PERIOD ONE

These engines arrived in their existing livery; brown lined with black, fine-lined in yellow. Lining on the tanksides and the small tenders supplied specially to the L&F by the original makers had incurved corners. The exact shade of brown is unknown, but it has been referred to as 'red-brown'. However, if, as alleged, it is the same as the later Eastern & Midlands brown then it should be described as 'middle brown'. The chimney was copper-capped, and the brass cleading between boiler and smokebox was kept bright. Alan Wells insisted on dubbing the brown ex-CMR colour as the L&F's 'goods livery' but, as it is by no means certain that these engines were used only for goods trains, and no other engines carried it at this time, this is probably an over-simplification.

The first three had the original CMR numbers removed and rectangular nameplates substituted. These had raised seriffed lettering, probably on a vermilion background. The large elliptical brass maker's plate remained below the name. Numbers were brass numerals about 9 inches high applied only to the front of the chimneys. The subsequent five were not named and retained their large rectangular CMR numberplates.

PERIOD TWO

The E&MR removed names and chimney numbers from No's 1–3. Engines No's 11 and 13 (and possibly others) were lettered in the early style, still carrying their original livery lined with incurved corners. When due for repainting, all of the Class 'D' received the standard livery of middle brown, edged and lined (with normally-curved corners) in black and yellow, with the standard lettering and device on the tender. Engines No's 1 and 11, and therefore probably the rest of the class, had their rectangular CMR numberplates removed and the number painted on the tank instead. The number is also likely to have appeared on the bufferbeam. One unusual aspect of No. 11 is that it is believed to have had lining in green and white at the request of its driver, instead of black and yellow. Coupling and connecting rods were painted vermilion.

No. 18 was rebuilt as a 2-4-0 in 1890, followed by No's 3, 13 and 14. The lining style followed the general standard, with the addition of a brass beading to the driving wheel splashers – except for No. 18. Elliptical numberplates were supplied on the cabside, probably for the first time. The rebuilt engines had their coupling and connecting rods kept bright, and all except No. 3 had Westinghouse pumps, brass trimmed at the top and bottom of both cylinders.

PERIOD THREE

The first locomotive to be withdrawn was No. 2 in 1894, very probably still in E&MR livery. Engine No. 1 was lettered 'M & G N J R' on the tender, almost certainly whilst still in E&MR brown, with a painted

ABOVE: Plate 5
Although the plate says 'rebuilt', 4-4-2T No. 41 was in fact a new engine built in 1904. The photographic grey shows many of the standard M&GN lining details to good effect. R.J. ESSERY COLLECTION.

LEFT: Plate 6
Detail from Plate 5 showing the M&GN crest on the side tanks.

RIGHT: Plate 7
Detail from Plate 5 of the 'rebuilt' works plate on the frames above the cylinders.

number. In 1894 all the survivors were put on the duplicate list and given elliptical brass numberplates. Rebuilt 2-4-0 No. 3A was given a new plate incorporating the small 'A', even though it already had a '3' plate from 1891. The tops of the numeral '3' on No's 3 and 13 were flat. The other plates with two-digit numbers had a small 4½ inch brass 'A' placed to the right hand side. When put on the duplicate list, each engine had its tender lettered 'M & [device] G N' in the sans serif Melton style.

Whether any of the engines received the new light brown livery is a moot point. There is no reason to think that Melton would be keen to spend any more time on them once they had been relettered in 1894, especially since between 1895 and 1899 all but one were scrapped. The last survivor, No. 12A, went in 1902. It may well have been the last engine in E&MR brown, however there is no proof either way.

BEYER PEACOCK 4-4-0 CLASS 'A' AND CLASS 'A REBUILD'

PERIOD ONE

The first four of these famous engines were delivered in green with brown frames, valances and cylinders, lined in black and white. All body panels were edged in black and lined in white. Corners for this edging were mostly square, but on the sandboxes incorporated with the driving wheel splashers the corners were curved. These splashers were decorated with curved brass maker's plates carrying 'BEYER, PEACOCK & Cᵒ MANCHESTER. 1881.', the background of which was probably vermilion. The sector of the splasher under the maker's plate was edged around in black and white. The lower edge of the valance was lined, as were the edges of the tender frames. Wheels were green with black tyres, but no white lining despite the specification supplied to the makers. Smokebox, chimney, footplate, front and top of sandbox and splashers were black, as was the outside steam pipe. The upper part of the main frames above the footplate also seems to have been black. The chimneys were a Beyer Peacock design, and copper-capped.

These engines were the first to carry what became the standard elliptical brass numberplate with vermilion background – but there were no company initials on the tender, which had a small

elliptical maker's plate centrally. Bufferbeams were plain vermilion, and for the first time numbers were applied there in 4½ inch gold seriffed characters, shaded black, in the style 'Nᵒ [hook] 21'. The Westinghouse pump, fitted in front of the cab on the nearside, had the upper cylinder trimmed in brass and the lower one lined.

PERIOD TWO

The second batch of four Peacocks arrived in 1883 painted in the new standard middle brown, but the builder applied lining somewhat differently from the L&F style. Body panels were edged in black, with a yellow line between the black and the brown, but there were no lining panels. Corners were curved rather than square. Cylinders were only lined fore and aft. The tender was still unlettered and had the small elliptical brass maker's plate positioned centrally. Numbers were carried on the elliptical brass plates introduced on the four L&F engines. The driving wheel maker's plate was again present, kept polished. Engine No. 25 was still in this state when photographed in 1887. Domes were now taller, and the chimneys no longer the Beyer Peacock type.

The third and fourth batches, No's 29–31 and 32–35, delivered in 1886 and 1888, carried the proper E&MR livery of middle brown, lined and edged in black and yellow. Edging of black with a yellow (possibly lemon chrome) line between the black and the brown was applied to the sandbox attached to the driving wheel splasher, the curved part of the splasher under the maker's plate, the cab side sheets (lower and upper), cab front and around windows, main tender sides and rear, tender coal flare sides and rear, lower side of valancing, step plates, edges of tender frames and around hornblock castings, and fore and aft and along the top edge of outside cylinders. Each cylinder of the Westinghouse brake pump was trimmed top and bottom with brass. Panels of lining with curved corners were applied to cab sidesheets (again upper and lower), tender sides and rear, and cylinders. Boiler bands were black, edged in yellow, and the bases of the dome and the safety valve seating were also lined in black with one yellow line on the top edge.

Wheels were middle brown with black tyres, there being a yellow line on the inner edge of the tyre. Wheel centres and axle ends were

Plate 8
This view of Class 'D' 0-6-0 No. 68 shows the large brass numerals applied when engines were rebuilt at Melton after 1907. The engine has a stovepipe chimney and an extended smokebox. D. IBBOTSON COLLECTION.

ABOVE: Plate 9
A Johnson tender showing the 12 inch yellow characters applied to the dark brown livery from 1929 and the single yellow line outlining the beading. R.J. ESSERY COLLECTION.

BELOW: Plate 10
A Johnson tender as painted black and lined in vermilion by the L&NER from 1937. R.J. ESSERY COLLECTION.

also lined with black, having yellow lines on the inside edges only. In addition to the usual areas, tops and fronts of sandboxes were black. The outside steam pipes, and probably the main frames above the footplate, were black, but main frames below the footplate were unlined brown. The copper-capped Beyer Peacock chimneys of No's 21–24 were replaced by larger diameter built-up chimneys. Bufferbeams were vermilion, edged with a plain black line. Buffer castings were also vermilion, with the outer lip painted black. Safety valve levers, the backgrounds to the numberplates, and possibly the maker's plates, were also vermilion.

The L&F 4-4-0s No's 21–24 were probably repainted in E&MR livery after about three years, possibly followed by the early E&MR engines. The earliest lettering, 'E & M R^Y', can be seen on No. 28. There was a transitional period after the introduction of the device, as engines No's 25 and 33 were photographed carrying 'E & [device] M R^Y', with the lettering smaller than the later 6 inch standard.

PERIOD THREE

This being the premier class of ex-E&MR engine, it is possible that the change to M&GN light brown was undertaken quite early. Lining was applied generally in the E&MR style. Boilers of Midland design were installed on No's 21–24 from 1895 to 1898. As before, the base of the dome was lined with black, fine-lined with lemon chrome on the top edge only, but the base of the brass safety valve cover was not lined. Engine No. 33 was lettered 'M & G [device] N J R' within a panel of lining (almost certainly on E&MR livery), and No's 28 and 30 carried 'JT M & [device] G N R', all in the Melton sans serif transfers. Even when engine No. 24 was reboilered in 1898, it was given 'M & [device] G N' on the tender, still using Melton transfers. Numberplates were the standard elliptical brass with vermilion background fitted to these engines by the makers. Frames above the footplate were probably black.

PERIOD FOUR

Reboilering with Midland-type boilers continued from 1904 to 1909. The standard light brown livery was applied throughout this period. The elliptical numberplates were retained. From about 1900 the brass

Beyer Peacock lettering on the driving wheel splashers was chiselled out, whether the engine had been reboilered or not. The blank strip was reputedly painted vermilion, but photographs would suggest that some at least were light brown. Lettering was 'M & [device] G N' on the tenders. Three examples were also fitted with tablet apparatus for running tender first, and were given a tender weatherboard with round spectacle windows. These were painted light brown on the forward face, edged in black and lemon chrome, including around the spectacles. It is not clear what the rear face was painted.

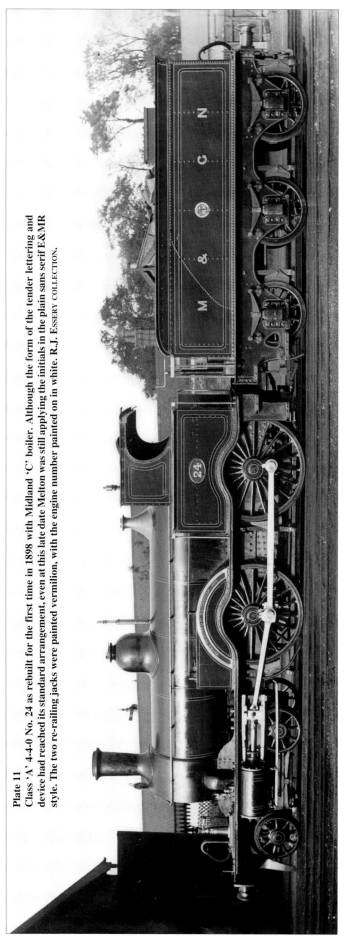

Plate 11
Class 'A' 4-4-0 No. 24 as rebuilt for the first time in 1898 with Midland 'C' boiler. Although the form of the tender lettering and device had reached its standard arrangement, even at this late date Melton was still applying the initials in the plain sans serif E&MR style. The two re-railing jacks were painted vermilion, with the engine number painted on in white. R.J. ESSERY COLLECTION.

Plate 12
Class 'A' 4-4-0 No. 33 was recorded in 1893 as part of a series showing experimental variations on the lettering. This example has had its tender lettering set in a horizontal panel, an awkward arrangement that fortunately was not chosen as the final style. The locomotive is otherwise in E&MR condition, still painted in the mid brown of that railway. R.J. ESSERY COLLECTION.

During the years 1914 to 1927, the first eight Class 'A' engines No's 21–28 were rebuilt again with new boilers, new straight-sided Midland tenders, and new driving wheel splashers incorporating sandboxes for front and rear running. A single brass beading strip was retained on the splasher. The upper parts of the cabs were renewed and the elliptical numberplates were replaced by large brass numerals. There was no change in the livery of the engine, but the tender had the usual Midland beading strip, this time exactly central, which was painted unlined burnt sienna. The device therefore could no longer appear on the tender, and was henceforth not used on these engines. Lettering was now simply 'M & | G N' inside two panels of lining.

PERIOD FIVE
Most of these locomotives were painted dark brown. Three, No's 22, 24 and 27, were painted dark brown while retaining their flush smokeboxes, whereas No. 25 was given a Deeley smokebox while still in the light brown. Three engines, No's 29, 30 and 34, were scrapped in 1933 and may not have been repainted at all. Lining was restricted to panels on the sides and rear of the tender, the boiler bands, the lower edge of the valance, and as a border a short distance from the edges of the upper and lower cab sheets. The brass beading over the driving wheel splasher was still kept unpainted, but apparently no longer polished as assiduously as in earlier times. The large initials were applied, but brass numerals were retained, and brass numberplates on the unrebuilt engines were still painted with vermilion backgrounds. Two engines, No's 21 and 26, had the later wide transfers on the bufferbeams.

There were still three locomotives with tender weatherboards during this period. The front face of the weatherboard was probably painted dark brown and may have been lined in lemon chrome. The rear was probably black.

PERIOD SIX
All except one of the remaining locomotives of this class were withdrawn between 1936 and 1938. Only one, No. 027, is known to have received the temporary painted number, and that was withdrawn in 1937. The last survivor was No. 025, which happened to be turned out of Melton in October 1936 as a combination of two engines, No's 24 and 25. It was painted black, and 'L N E R' and the number '025' were transferred onto the tender and cab side respectively, both in 12 inch size, with the initials closely spaced. The bufferbeam was treated in the normal late Melton style: vermilion with black lip to the buffer castings, and the number on the right hand side of the hook in wide Midland-style seriffed gold transfers shaded in blue and black. No. 025 was lined, the vermilion lines following the same scheme as the former yellow lining, with no lining on the splashers. Engine No. 025 was withdrawn in 1941 without receiving an L&NER classification.

ROTHWELL & CO. EX-L&NWR 2-4-0 CLASS 'C'

PERIOD TWO
These were No's 29 and 30, renumbered 42 and 43 respectively in 1886. These locomotives arrived in 1883, apparently in L&NWR black, but no photographs exist of them at that time. They acquired the standard elliptical numberplates, but probably only after their 1886 renumbering. They were rebuilt in 1891 (No. 43) and 1893 (No. 42).

Livery after 1891 was middle brown, lined and edged in a similar manner to the Class 'A' 4-4-0s. The lower cab side sheets of No. 43 had curved front corners and so the edging at top and bottom was carried round. Because the smokebox wrapper was continued to become the cylinder clothing, an upper yellow line was taken across at the level of the footplate between the fore and aft lining to create a break between the black of the smokebox and brown of the cylinder. Front cylinder covers were polished steel and driving wheel splashers were polished brass. Photographs show only the standard lettering 'E & [device] M R' on the tenders, but in the earlier years they probably carried 'E & M Rᵞ'. It is possible that No. 42 was the first engine to receive M&GN lettering.

PERIOD THREE
The two engines were withdrawn and scrapped in 1895. Engine No. 42 was in the shops shortly before the M&GN came into being and emerged with 'M & G N J R' on its tender, but almost certainly on

Plate 13
No. 34 is seen here at Cromer with Driver Jack Ball on the footplate. The lettering 'E & [crest] E R' is on the tender, and a driver's decoration on the chimney. ALAN WELLS COLLECTION.

E&MR middle brown. Both engines were put on the duplicate list in 1894 and a small 4½ inch brass 'A' placed beneath their elliptical numberplates. Engine No. 43A was still in full E&MR livery when it was scrapped.

Sharp Stewart and Beyer Peacock 4-4-0 Class 'C' and Class 'C Rebuild'

Period Three

The first ten of these engines carried the new M&GN livery of light brown and burnt sienna. The Midland tender had beading outlining the tank area with a central vertical strip and so the device could not be placed centrally; instead it was placed on the driving wheel splasher. Both the main splashers and the small splashers clearing the coupling rod bushes were beaded with polished brass. The beading on the tender, both at the side and at the rear, was painted unlined burnt sienna. On each side of the central beading the tender was lined in two panels in the standard lining method. The rear panel was also lined. On the first batch the lettering was 'JT M & | G N R', in Midland transfers. These were seriffed in gold, 6 inches high, shaded to the left and below with light blue, dark blue and white highlights, shadowed to the right and below in black. Numbers were the standard 6½ inch Midland brass numerals applied to the cab side, the '3' having a flat top at this stage. The tops of the frames above the footplate were painted burnt sienna and lined top and bottom.

Sixteen more arrived in 1894 in the new livery, but the lettering on the tender was now plain 'M & | G N'. A further seven followed in 1896. All had brass numerals, engine No. 53 with a round top to the '3'. Bufferbeam lettering was 'No [hook] 36' in seriffed gold characters about 4½ inches high, shaded in blue like the main initials, shadowed in black.

Seven (No's 74–80) were constructed by Beyer Peacock in 1899 and differed in the livery applied by the makers. As well as the main body panels, those parts which should have been burnt sienna were painted light brown. The front of the tender was also light brown and lined. There was more lining than usual, particularly on the sandboxes, frames, guard irons and brake hangers. Wheels were light brown, tyres were black edged in yellow, but the axle ends were black, encircled with a yellow line. This form of the livery was apparently very difficult to keep smart. It would have been replaced by the standard livery from circa 1902.

Period Four

The livery remained the standard light brown and burnt sienna. The tenders had the beading strips painted unlined burnt sienna as before and were lettered 'M & | G N'. The device remained on the driving wheel splashers. A photograph of No. 47 taken with colour-sensitive film in 1929 indicates that the small subsidiary splashers were painted light brown, edged around the inside of the brass beading with black and lemon chrome. Tender axlebox covers and spring buckles were burnt sienna, but edged with black and lemon chrome.

Two engines, No's 39 and 55, were rebuilt in 1908 with large Midland boilers of Class 'H', with round-topped fireboxes. The coupled wheel splashers were now plain, without the original subsidiary splashers. As usual, the tops of these splashers were painted black. They were edged with brass and a black border, fine-lined lemon chrome. The large Melton brass numerals were applied to the trailing splasher and the driving wheel splasher carried the device enclosed in a square 'shield' of lining. Between 1910 and 1915, No's 45, 46, 51–54, 56 and 57 were rebuilt in a similar fashion but using Midland 'G7' Class boilers with Belpaire fireboxes. They also had plain splashers and large numerals, but the device was enclosed in a new 'lozenge' of lining different from the Class 'A Tanks'. When No's 39 and 55 were rebuilt with 'G7' boilers in 1924 and 1925 respectively, they also received a device within a lozenge. Firebox washout plugs were black. There were no other deviations from the standard light brown livery.

Above: Plate 14
Class 'C' 4-4-0 No. 78, built by Beyer Peacock in 1899, is pictured at Cromer Beach circa 1900 in the anomalous livery as applied by the makers. The driver's embellishments take the form of a polished steel band around the chimney, a cut-out Maltese cross mounted on the smokebox door dart and approximately half an inch of the rear edge of the smokebox wrapper scraped clear of paint and polished. Alan Wells collection.

Right: Plate 15
Detail from Plate 14, showing driver's embellishment on the smokebox door; possibly a Good Templar temperance cross.

PERIOD FIVE

All of these engines were painted dark brown. Two of them, No's 43 and 47, had had Deeley smokeboxes when in light brown; several engines, No's 1, 17, 48, 74 and 76, retained flush-rivetted smokeboxes when they were repainted in dark brown, but these were replaced soon after. Between 1929 and 1931 seven engines (No's 2, 6, 36, 44, 49, 50 and 77) were given 'G6' Class boilers, similar to their previous ones but with Belpaire fireboxes. At the same time they were given Deeley smokeboxes and were painted dark brown.

The dark brown was applied to the entire engine, except for the black smokebox, footplate, cab roof and tender top. Brake hangers and rodding were also black. Lining in lemon chrome was applied to the boiler bands and lower edge of the valance, including the rear step. The splashers were unlined, but the brass beading was polished. The cab above the rear splasher was lined around with a single line near the edge. The tender had a single line around the inner edge of the beading, ignoring the central strip. The tender rear was also lined around the beading. There was no lining on the engine or tender frames, or the wheels. Brass numerals were retained and polished. Four engines, No's 17, 37, 46 and 74, were photographed in dark brown still with the device on the driving wheel splasher, and there may have been more, but the device was lost on the next repaint. No's 4, 12, 36–38, 45, 46, 48, 49 and 74 were seen with the final wide bufferbeam numbers about 1936. Engine No. 54 acquired the straight-sided tender from rebuilt Class 'A' No. 22.

Plate 16
This tender rear elevation of Class 'C' 4-4-0 No. 39 was probably taken as soon as the engine arrived in 1894. Note that the E&MR-type green and white headcode disc has been provided, complete with the engine number. Details on the rear of the tender include the water capacity plate, tender numberplate, horizontal handrail, safety chains and the coupling held by a shackle rather than a hook. R.J. ESSERY COLLECTION.

Plate 17
Class 'C' 4-4-0 No. 53 as rebuilt with a 'G7' boiler in 1910, photographed in works grey. The enclosed splashers were a nuisance when the crew were oiling, so Mr Nash later reinstated slots. Unfortunately for later historians, although the lining is correct, the paint shop has made little attempt to render the engine in an accurate representation of the colours of the running livery.
R.J. ESSERY COLLECTION.

PERIOD SIX

Several of these engines were renumbered with 12 inch lemon chrome numerals at Melton in 1936, noted examples being 01, 02, 05, 06, 050, 052, 054, 056 and 079. Some others were repainted at Melton in black, No's 07, 042, and 078, with L&NER transfers closely spaced on the tender, L&NER numbers and late M&GN bufferbeams. Engine No. 45 was withdrawn in 1936 and fourteen others went in 1937 (including repainted No. 07). From 1937 the other survivors were repainted black at Stratford. Livery was varnished black, lined with vermilion. The lining reproduced the late M&GN style, but also appeared on the splashers for the first time as the brass beading was painted over. The brass safety valve covers were also painted over. Initials were the standard 12 inches, and the majority of the numbers were in 9 inch transfers on the cabside within the rear splasher beading. The Melton-painted examples had 12 inch numerals, as did No's 06 and 043, and parts of these transfers actually went over the beading – although No. 043 had its beading removed. None of them ever seem to have had their L&NER class painted on the front bufferbeam.

NEILSON AND KITSON 0-6-0 CLASS 'D' AND CLASS 'D REBUILD'

PERIOD THREE

The first eight of these engines (No's 58–65) were built by Neilson & Co. and delivered in 1896, the second eight (No's 66–73) by Kitson & Co. and delivered in 1899. They were built to a Midland design and both batches were identical, although their liveries as applied by the makers differed. Colours were light brown and burnt sienna as detailed above, the Midland tender again having raised beading painted unlined burnt sienna. Numerals were 6½ inch brass on the cabside, the top of the '3' on engines No's 63 and 73 being rounded. Numbers on the Neilson engines were positioned considerably above the centre line.

The Neilson engines did not carry what had become the normal lining style. There were two panels of lining on the tender and 'M & | G N' in the usual fashion, but the upper and lower sidesheets of the cab were edged only in black and lemon chrome, corners being rounded rather than square. The Kitson engines had square corners to the panel edging and panels of lining on the upper and lower cab sidesheets, a style to which the Neilson engines were repainted.

All engines carried the device on the driving wheel splasher. Splashers had the outer beading painted black, lined on the inside in lemon chrome. Frames were unlined, but sandboxes were edged with lining. Guard irons were painted black. Upper parts of the frames above the footplate were also apparently black. Coupling rods and the reversing lever were kept bright.

PERIOD FOUR

This class retained the fully-lined light brown and burnt sienna livery until 1922, when a new livery was applied as engines went through the workshops. This was a dark brown livery, sometimes referred to as 'café au lait' or 'chocolate', consisting of burnt umber enriched with burnt sienna. Most of the engine was painted dark brown, including frames and wheels. Smokeboxes, cab roofs, footplates, tender tops and fronts were painted black. Inside faces of frames, motion and bufferbeams were vermilion.

There was limited lemon chrome lining, confined to the cabside, valance, boiler bands and the tender. Boiler bands had one thin line on each edge and cabs had a thin line near the edges of upper and lower panels. The tender was lined in one panel around the inside edge of the beading but ignoring the central strip; the rear of the tender was also lined. The Midland-type lettering was abandoned, larger 10 inch sans serif initials in lemon chrome being applied – the yellow turning more orange over time due to the effects of varnish, cleaning and the atmosphere. The spacing of the letters was the same as before. The device was omitted.

The bufferbeams were now plain vermilion, but still had black ends to the buffer castings. The lettering was altered to omit the 'Nᵒ', but the numerals were still seriffed in gold, shaded in blue and shadowed in black, and applied to the right of the drawhook.

Two engines were rebuilt with Midland 'H' Class boilers, No. 62 in 1906 and No. 69 in 1909. The fully-lined light brown and burnt sienna livery was retained, with the device on the driving wheel splasher. A small elliptical rebuilding plate was fixed on the leading splasher; letters and border were polished brass with a black background. The round-topped firebox now had enclosed Ramsbottom safety valves, the shrouding painted light brown, lined at the top with black and lemon chrome, and capped with a brass beading. Engine No. 62 retained the small 6½ inch numerals but No. 69 was given the 9 inch numerals.

No's 68 and 71 were also rebuilt in 1921, but this time with Midland 'G7' Class boilers with Belpaire fireboxes. They too were given the fully-lined light brown livery, with large brass numerals. The Ramsbottom safety valves were not shrouded and the valve columns were polished brass; valve levers were probably vermilion. Rebuilt engine No. 62 was also given a 'G7' boiler in 1921, large numerals replacing the small ones. The rebuilding plate was now smaller and fixed to the frames below the smokebox saddle. The rebuilt engines had new cabs with curved roof edges, the lining being taken over onto the roof as far as the rainstrip.

In 1924, the other 'H' Class boilered engine, No. 69, was rebuilt with a 'G7' boiler but was now finished in the dark brown livery with limited lining and sans serif tender lettering as detailed above. The other rebuilt engines were also repainted dark brown as they went through the works. The device was not applied, and the 'Nᵒ' was omitted from the bufferbeam.

Plate 18
No. 05 at South Lynn in May 1937, showing the (rather dusty) dark brown livery and the yellow characters, including the '0' prefix to the original number applied at Melton. H.C. CASSERLEY.

Plate 19
An official view of No. 59 in photographic grey taken by the makers Neilson & Co in 1896. The cab side sheets have been lined in an untypical style. R.J. ESSERY COLLECTION.

PERIOD FIVE

There was no change for these engines, which had been dark brown from the early 1920s. The 12 inch seriffed initials replaced the earlier sans serif ones. Lemon chrome lining was applied to the boiler bands, the upper and lower cab sheets, the lower edge of the valance including the rear step, and in one panel around the side of the tender. The rear of the tender was also lined. Brass numerals were retained and polished. Deeley smokeboxes were fitted, a few while the engine was still in the earlier dark brown livery, including No's 59 and 67. Engines No's 61 and 71 had wide bufferbeam transfers by 1936.

PERIOD SIX

Five of these engines are known to have had the large 12 inch temporary numbers painted on their cabsides at Melton; No's 058, 061, 063, 064, and 068. Five engines were withdrawn in 1937 and 1938 (No's 058, 66, 67, 068 and 72), but the survivors were repainted in black. In the usual L&NER livery scheme, goods locomotives would be unlined, but these engines were lined in vermilion, following the scheme used in the late M&GN period plus lining on the splashers. After overhaul at Stratford in 1938, the Class 'D Rebuild' (J41) No. 069 carried the small class lettering on the front bufferbeam 'CLASS [hook] 0.6.0', but seems to be the only engine to have received this feature. The front bufferbeams were lined and carried the usual L&NER lettering. Rear bufferbeams were plain. Tender initials were the standard 12 inches and all engines had 12 inch numerals on the cabside. Two engines were allocated L&NER 1946 numbers but never carried them. The last engine to be scrapped was No. 065 in 1947.

DÜBS & CO. 0-6-0 CLASS 'DA'

PERIOD FOUR

These twelve engines were delivered in 1901 in the light brown and burnt sienna livery. The cab, splashers, sandboxes and steps were edged with black and lemon chrome, and the boiler bands were black, fine-lined with lemon chrome. There was a panel of lining on the tender, and a strip of beading at the top and bottom of the tender side painted unlined burnt sienna. As delivered, 'M & G N' was applied on the tender in the Midland transfers, with the device on the driving wheel splasher. The numbers were also transferred on the cabside in gold, shaded blue and black. The wheel centres were lined around their perimeter and axle ends were black ringed with lemon chrome. The diamond-shaped maker's plate on the leading splasher was lined around. The leading, driving and visible portion of the trailing wheel splashers were beaded with polished brass. At the first repaint the livery was adjusted. Numerals were now 6½ inches and made of brass, and the tender lettering was standardised as 'M & [device] G N', the length being about 12 feet with each element equally spaced. The device was removed from the driving wheel splasher. Lining on the wheel centres was changed to the standard two concentric black rings lined in yellow on the inner edge only. The maker's plate was unlined.

Bufferbeams were vermilion edged in black. The lettering was widely spaced as, unlike the Midland-type engines, safety chains were fitted – for example, 'Nᵒ [chain] [hook] [chain] 88'. The seriffed gold transfers were used, shaded in blue and black.

Between 1920 and 1927, all Class 'DA' engines were rebuilt with large diameter boilers. At the same time they were given large brass numerals, and the Dübs plates and most of the safety chains were removed.

It is believed that the first M&GN engine to be painted dark brown was Class 'DA' No. 92 when it was reboilered in 1921. The others of the class followed rapidly, whether rebuilt or unrebuilt, and were known as 'Coffee Pots' in consequence. As detailed above, the whole engine was painted dark brown including frames and wheels, with the usual black areas, and vermilion between the frames and on bufferbeams. The brass splasher beadings were kept polished and it appears that there was also a polished brass cleading between the boiler and smokebox. From photographs, it is clear that there was no lining. Lettering was in 10 inch lemon chrome sans serif initials 'M & G N' without the device.

PERIOD FIVE

Dark brown, with the larger seriffed initials on the tender. The brass beading on the splashers, which had formerly been polished, was painted over on most engines and in one case (No. 83) removed altogether. The brass cleading to the smokebox was also painted over. The brass numerals were retained and polished, but as before there was no lining at all on these engines. Deeley smokeboxes were fitted and, unusually, the smokebox doors on five engines (No's 82, 85, 87, 89 and 92) were not central but displaced towards the bottom. Uniquely, No. 89 was photographed in colour by H.N. James at Edmonthorpe & Wymondham in this final livery. The slight orange cast of the lettering is evident, also the rather dusty state typical of this era.

PERIOD SIX

Two engines (No's 083 and 092) are known to have received large Melton-applied numbers, and it seems No. 088 was painted unlined black at Melton, with closely-spaced 'L N E R' initials and 12 inch numerals. Because of their Great Northern origin, these locomotives were sent to Doncaster for servicing and most had smaller boilers fitted. They emerged painted unlined black with plain vermilion bufferbeams and black buffer castings. The standard 12 inch L&NER initials were on the tender 11 feet 6 inches in extent, with 9 inch numerals on the cabs. The number was transferred on the bufferbeam in the usual characters, with a choice of position due to the vacuum pipe being located close to the drawhook. Most engines had, for example, 'Nº [pipe] [hook] 084', but No's 090 and 092 were photographed with the 'Nº' between the pipe and the drawhook. Despite being allocated L&NER classes, no photographs show the class painted on the bufferbeam. The remaining large boiler engines, No's 081, 083, 086 and 088, were Class 'J3', the others were Class 'J4'. In 1946 the whole class were allocated new numbers, but No's 090 and 091 were withdrawn without carrying them. The remainder became No's 4156–1464 and 4167. At the time the L&NER were routinely using the shortened version of their initials 'N E', and this was the style used on the survivors of both classes.

The only M&GN locomotive to carry British Railways livery was No. 85, as No. 64160. This engine was painted unlined black and was left to become extremely dirty. Characters were Gill Sans, in pale cream or 'straw' and 9 inches high. The number was on the cabside, with 'BRITISH RAILWAYS' on the tender. The last survivor did not carry its nationalised livery for long, being withdrawn in 1951.

MELTON CONSTABLE 4-4-2T CLASS 'A TANK'

PERIOD FOUR

These three engines carried the standard light brown livery with frames, wheels, cylinders and valancing in burnt sienna. The frames above the footplate were lined burnt sienna but below were unlined. The outside exhaust pipes to the smokebox were black. No. 41 had an elliptical brass numberplate but the other two had the large brass numerals.

Lining of the side tank was in a large panel following the shape of the cab opening, the lining of the bunker was carried round the rear to the other side in a continuous panel. The lettering was not standard, being 'MIDLAND & GREAT NORTHERN' in an arc of 13 feet 6 inches radius over the device, in seriffed gold 6 inch characters shadowed in black to right and below, although an official drawing shows different shading. A decorative lozenge of lining surrounded the device.

PERIOD FIVE

All three were painted dark brown. The large initials were applied to their tanks, and the brass numerals on No's 9 and 20 and the numberplate on No. 41 were retained. Engine No. 41 had a Deeley smokebox when still in light brown, and No. 20 still had a flush-rivetted smokebox when it was repainted. All three eventually received Deeley smokeboxes. Around 1933 their side tanks were trimmed down at an angle towards the front. Lining was applied to boiler bands and lower edge of the valance, but not to the steps. A yellow line also bordered the tankside, curving round to the front before forming a vertical edge, and similarly bordered the bunker, curving around the back of the engine to the other side. The lining followed the shape of the cab cut-out on each side.

PERIOD SIX

All three of this class were repainted in black. Despite being passenger tanks, no lining was applied. Brass numerals and numberplates were removed, leaving visible scars. Lettering was 'L N E R' in the small 7½ inch size along the upper part of the tanks with the number below in 12 inch numerals, '09' for example. For some unknown reason, initials on No's 020 and 041 were about 12 feet in extent, but about 10 feet on No. 09. Front bufferbeams carried the number but were otherwise plain and unlined, as were rear bufferbeams. Buffer castings were black. Despite receiving a classification, it does not appear to have been painted on the front bufferbeam.

MIDLAND RAILWAY 0-4-4T 'No. 6 CLASS'

PERIOD FOUR

During the years 1906 to 1912, three Midland 0-4-4Ts built in 1875 were supplied bearing their MR numbers 142, 143 and 144. They were painted in the full MR alizarin crimson livery, lining and edging being in black and yellow. They retained their MR livery but M&GN initials were applied to the tanks on either side of the number, for example 'M & 142 G N'.

However, the lettering was unusual. From a photograph of No. 142 at Lowestoft it would seem that the central brass numerals are the standard 6½ inch Midland type; but the M&GN initials, while being seriffed and apparently in gold, do not have the usual blue and white shading and are a good inch smaller than the numerals. That gold was used is obliquely confirmed by one observer thinking that the initials were also in brass. Whether they were transfers or applied by hand is unknown. Whether the bufferbeams retained the letters 'M R' is also unknown. On return to the MR they were given the new 1907 numbers, No's 1232–1234 respectively.

MELTON CONSTABLE 0-6-0T CLASS 'SHUNTING'

PERIOD FOUR

Between 1897 and 1905, nine of these engines were built. Apart from the Melton pattern chimney the boiler fittings were Midland, with polished brass safety valve cover. Despite being only shunting and pilot engines, they carried the fully-lined light brown and burnt sienna livery. Tanks, bunkers and cab were edged with black and lemon chrome, and tanks had a panel of lining. The bunker lining was taken around the back to the other side in typical Melton fashion. Cylinders were burnt sienna edged at front, rear and top with black and lemon chrome, and given a small panel of lining. Coupling and connecting rods were kept bright.

Lettering was in the standard Midland-type transfers, with the elliptical brass numberplate central, for example, 'M & 93 G N'. The device was positioned directly above the numberplate. Before renumbering, those engines on the duplicate list had a small 4½ inch brass 'A' placed below the numberplate. These plates were apparently newly-cast – for example, No. 3A did not use the 3A plate already cast for a 2-4-0 in 1894. The numeral '3' for this plate and for No. 93 had a flat top. On the bunker was a small elliptical plate with 'M & G N' around the top edge, 'MELTON CONSTABLE' around the bottom, and 'REBUILT' in the middle with the date below. While most of this class kept their light brown livery until 1929, No's 15 and 98 were painted dark brown before then, having the sans serif yellow initials in a smaller size, about 8 inches. The device was omitted. The lining was simplified as detailed below.

PERIOD FIVE

All were painted dark brown. Lining was a lemon chrome line near the top and bottom edge of tanks and bunker, following the curve of the tanks round to the front, and following the bunker around to the rear and onto the other side of the engine. The only vertical lining was adjacent to the cab door. On the cab the lining was also continuous, following the shape of the cut-out and edging the top and bottom of the side sheet, before being taken around the corner to both front and rear, and onto the other side of the engine.

An interesting feature of the lettering was that the Midland-type transfers were used even when the engines were dark brown. One example, No. 95, was actually given the device in the usual place when in dark brown, no doubt lost at the first repaint. The numberplates were retained and all the class except No. 96 received Deeley smokeboxes. The lettering of No. 96 was also spaced differently.

PERIOD SIX

All were painted unlined black with plain vermilion bufferbeams and black buffer castings front and rear. The initials 'L N E R' were spaced along the upper part of the tank in 7½ inch characters with the number centrally below in 12 inch numerals, all in the standard L&NER yellow, shaded in brown, red and white. Withdrawal started in 1943, leaving five to be allocated new numbers: No. 8488 (094), No. 8485 (095), No. 8484 (096), No. 8482 (098) and No. 8489 (016). These were lettered in the postwar standard, the shortened initials 'N E' being on the upper part of the tank in 7½ inch letters with the number below in 12 inch numerals. The last to be withdrawn was No. 8489 in 1949, without carrying a British Railways number.

MATERIALS USED AT MELTON CONSTABLE FOR PAINTING LOCOMOTIVES

Most of the paints used at Melton Constable were oil based. Oil paint consists of finely-ground pigment mixed with a vehicle or binding medium, usually linseed oil. The pigments were derived from coloured earths or other minerals, or from chemical products. The resulting colours could be transparent, semi-transparent or opaque. The pigments arrived from the paint suppliers as either paste or powder. The paste was already prepared in drums and had only to be rendered into usable paint by the addition of turpentine and linseed oil. The powder arrived in bags and had to be ground in a hand mill with linseed oil and gold size to make a paste before thinning with turpentine. The different powders were kept in boxes in the paint shop. The hand method of mixing could be painfully slow, but always gave a perfect result.

The palette of colours on the M&GN was limited to reds, browns and yellows, with a little blue, and of course black and white. Vermilion (mercury (II) sulphide) was the Victorian equivalent of high-visibility paint. It was a brilliant red colour, but could be liable to darkening and was poisonous. Its primary use was between frames, on the axles and motion and on bufferbeams. Another colour at the red end of the spectrum was burnt sienna which, as its name suggests, was made by taking sienna, a natural earth pigment, and calcining it in a furnace. The result was a rich red-brown which was used on the lower portions of M&GN engines. A much darker brown was burnt umber, again a calcined natural earth. It did not see a great deal of use until engines were painted dark brown, when it was mixed in equal proportions with burnt sienna. In the yellow-brown

family were raw sienna and yellow ochre. Both of these natural earth pigments were of similar chemical composition, containing 'iron hydrate' or hydrated iron (III) oxide, and were a slightly greenish, brownish yellow – but raw sienna contained more manganese and was darker. Raw sienna was also transparent, unlike yellow ochre, which was opaque. Buff was a variable mixture, made up from white and yellow ochre, which was used as the base coat on the painted and grained cab interiors. The brightest yellow, used on the lining, was lemon chrome. This was a pale yellow, made from lead (II) chromate, the palest shade of a range progressing through deeper yellows to orange. Under varnish it would have looked less orange than standard chrome yellow.

There were three sorts of black in use. Japan black was a black varnish used to produce an acid-resistant gloss finish on metal, particularly smokeboxes, where ordinary varnish would crack. Drop black was the best industrial grade of carbon black, used for the more visible areas of black required, said to be named after the shape of the lumps in which it was once delivered. Vegetable black, on the other hand, was an inferior (and cheaper) grade of carbon black, used for less visible areas and brake hangers.

White was obtained by the use of white lead, which was manufactured from basic lead (II) carbonate. It was an opaque, brilliant white with good covering qualities, but was poisonous and darkened on exposure to sulphurous air. Its primary function, as far as locomotive painting went, was to make up lead grey, a mixture of lead white and drop black in a variety of shades, also called 'lead colour'. On the M&GN, lead colour was made from approximately two to one proportions of white to black, and was the basic undercoat for all operations.

Finally, no engine would be complete without several coats of varnish. There were two grades available at Melton, hard drying varnish and finishing varnish. They were both oil based copal varnishes made by melting various hard resins in hot linseed oil. The hard drying variety was meant to dry quickly and then be rubbed down or 'flatted' and contained relatively little linseed oil. Finishing varnish contained more oil and dried more slowly to give a hard, glossy shine. They were by no means colourless, imparting a yellow tinge to paints below them and they turned darker with age and could crack.

Turpentine was used in large quantities, both as a thinner and as a drying agent, making the normally slow-drying oil paint harden overnight, allowing one coat a day. Turpentine was kept in a tank in the paint shop, as were the varnishes.

PAINTING METHODS

One of the first areas of an engine to be painted was that between the frames. This could be done in the Erecting Shop while the engine was in pieces, so the inner faces of the frames, the axles, motion and big ends could be painted easily with two coats of vermilion, followed by one coat of varnish.

Once the reassembled loco and tender were in the paint shop, the painter's mates took over, removing loose paint and grease, and giving the bare metal a coat of lead colour. This was rubbed smooth, then the complete loco and tender painted in lead colour. All holes and scratches were filled with 'stopping', which was dry white lead mixed with gold size. Three coats of brush filler were then applied to the surfaces that had been scraped fully, and then rubbed down with composition blocks – a process which took a full two days for two men and two boys. The surfaces of the engine were now perfectly smooth.

A further coat of lead colour was applied as a primer, followed by three coats of the finish paint applied to the upper parts of the engine and tender. Before about 1920, this consisted of two coats of yellow ochre, and then one coat of raw sienna glazed over the top. After that time, the paint was pre-mixed to a colour board in the paintshop by the chargehand painter, using yellow ochre, burnt umber and burnt

LEFT: Plate 20
Detail from Plate 22 of the M&GN crest on side tanks of No. 41.

RIGHT: Plate 21
Detail from Plate 22 showing the jack with the engine number on it.

BELOW: Plate 22
Originally No. 32, 4-4-0T No. 41 was renumbered in 1886. This photograph was taken in 1894, after the Railway Clearing House had insisted on the use of the prefix 'Joint'. The arrangement is more balanced than the earlier experiments, but it is still a rather ponderous way of lettering a locomotive. As usual, the dome is polished brass. R.J. ESSERY COLLECTION.

sienna to secure the correct shade. The lower parts of the engine and tender were painted with three coats of burnt sienna. Bufferbeams, safety valve arms and sometimes coupling or connecting rods, depending on the engine, were painted vermilion.

At this stage, the black lining on body panels, boiler bands and wheels was carried out. A coat of hard drying varnish followed, flatted down with pumice powder and water. The ¼ inch lemon chrome lining was then applied very skilfully to engine and wheels, using chalk lines as a guide. The company transfers were then applied. These were self-coloured and came from Derby stores. If for some reason there were none of the initials left, senior painter Jimmy Platten was able to copy them by hand. One more coat of hard drying varnish was applied, flatted down again, and finally one coat of finishing varnish.

The smokebox had a coat of drop black followed by a topcoat of black japan varnish. The cab was painted buff and comb grained at the top to resemble wood, but the bottom received the same painting as the rest of the engine. The engine and tender were left for two days for the paint to get hard, then loco men applied thick grease with rags.

From 1929, all locos were painted dark brown. The painters called this 'chocolate', and it was made by enriching burnt umber with burnt sienna. Unlike the previous era the batches could vary slightly. The mates still scraped off loose paint and other dirt, and painted the metal they had prepared with lead colour, but there was very little stopping up of holes and no filling. The engine and tender were then painted one coat of lead colour, one coat of chocolate and then one coat of half paint (chocolate) and half varnish. This latter coat was called an enamel and was increasingly used in railway paintshops, having the advantage of being self-levelling.

At this stage the lemon chrome lining was applied to the upper parts of the engine. No transfers were now used, except that the device was applied on a few examples. The initials 'M & G N' on the tender were now hand-painted 12 inch letters in lemon chrome. Their outline was placed on the surface by pinpricks through a drawing, using a chalk dust bag. Finally, there was one coat of finishing varnish.

The bufferbeams and motion were still vermilion red, and the interior of the cab was still painted and grained as before. The brass rims on the coupled wheel splashers of passenger engines remained polished.

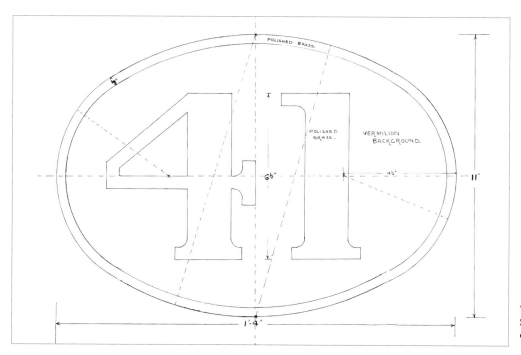

TOP LEFT: Plate 23
Standard M&GN number plate No. 41, copied from the official drawing.

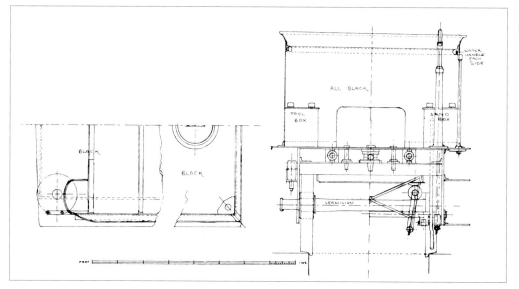

BOTTOM LEFT: Plate 24
Painting details for Class 'A' tender.

APPENDIX A: LOCOMOTIVE LOANS TO AND FROM THE M&GNJR

During the early years of the Edwardian period, the loss of traffic to tramways caused some of the mainline companies to examine alternative ways of operating, while in rural areas there was a need to contain or reduce expenses relative to traffic receipts. The Midland Railway's first essay was in 1904, with two steam motor carriages that were used on the Lancaster, Morecambe and Heysham line. Towards the end of 1905, it was proposed to undertake trials with what were described as 'auto-cars', and on the 22nd December the M&GN agreed to recommend that four locomotives be transferred to the Midland Company for experimental auto-car services. In return, the M&GN were to receive three Midland 0-4-4 tank engines. The basis of three for four was that the capital value of the three Midland engines equalled the four M&GN locomotives. The Midland locomotives were old numbers 142–144, which upon their return to the Midland received the numbers allocated to them under the 1907 renumbering, namely 1232–1234. Most sources give 1912 as being the date when the Midland returned the 4-4-0 tank engines to the M&GN and their three 0-4-4Ts were went home, but unfortunately it has not been possible to confirm the precise date.

The Midland Railway received M&GN No's 8, 10, 19 and 40 in 1906. They were coupled to old American Pullman coaches that were owned by the Midland Railway. When propelling the coach, communication between the driver and the fireman was by means of an endless rope which ran from the driving compartment in the coach to a 'ship's telegraph dial' at the end of the locomotive cab. The dial was marked, 'Full gear', 'Notch up' and 'Reverse', and these controls were duplicated in the driving compartment, together with control of the vacuum brake. They were used on a number of services, namely between Hemel Hempstead and Harpenden, Derby and Ripley, Derby and Wirksworth, and Wellingborough and Higham Ferrers. There can be no doubt that they were successful, leading the way to the wider use of motor trains on the Midland Railway and later to the adoption of the Midland vacuum controlled regulator by the LM&SR for this class of train. When the locomotives went to the Midland they retained their numbers for a time, before being altered to carry the number of the Pullman car they were coupled to – so M&GN No. 8 became No. 2, M&GN No. 10 became No. 5, M&GN No. 19 became No. 1 and M&GN No. 40 became No. 10.

The engine is in the bay at Harpenden, the platform used by the Hemel Hempstead branch train. This was one of the first lines to be used by the combination of a M&GN 4-4-0T coupled to a Midland Railway Pullman car equipped for use on auto-car service. No. 19, originally *Great Yarmouth*, was built for the Yarmouth & North Norfolk Railway. The locomotive still carried M&GN livery, but a transfer of the Midland device had been applied to the tanks. P.C. DEWHURST.

ABOVE: Taken at South Lynn on the 1st July 1936, this photograph shows LM&S 3P 4-4-0 No. 758, on loan to the M&GN, in the station at the head of an express passenger train with what can only be described as a 'full load of coal'. Presumably No. 758 would work through to Leicester and return without taking coal at Leicester, although the fire would have to be cleaned before the return journey began. H.C. CASSERLEY.

BELOW: When this picture was taken at Kentish Town shed, former M&GN 4-4-0T No. 40 had been renumbered with standard Midland brass numerals to match the number of the Pullman carriage to which it was coupled. No. 40 had been supplied to the Yarmouth & North Norfolk Railway in 1881 and was named *Martham*. Under the E&MR it was numbered 31. The material on the cab floor appears to be wood, but it is rather more than one would expect to see if it was for fire lighting purposes. ALAN WELLS COLLECTION.

In 1908, two locomotives received new boilers; the Derby Locomotive Works order 3442, dated 3rd February 1908, reads, *'Autocars Nos 2 and 10. Please put in hand at once two new boilers for engines of autocars Nos 2 and 10'*. The boiler drawing was numbered 08-7490. When the boilers were ready, two further Derby orders were issued; dated 28th May 1908, they were for the rebuilding work and were numbered 3478 for No. 2 and 3479 for No. 10. Although there are references to both No's 5 and 8 being rebuilt at Derby, the orders for this work have not survived in the Derby Locomotive Works records held at the National Archive at Kew.

Some further general notes about loans from the Midland and Great Northern Railways appear elsewhere in this book, in particular in Chapter 6.

Although not strictly locomotives, it should be noted that three steam railcars were loaned briefly to the M&GN at different periods. The first was in 1922, when Midland Railway steam railcar No. 2233 appeared at Cromer. This was a trial run for the conductor-guard services on the Norfolk & Suffolk Joint, introduced when staff numbers at intermediate stations were reduced and signalboxes closed. Apparently the railcar was not a success and could not pull its trailer car up the Mundesley line.

The minutes also mention the loan of a second steam railcar from the LM&SR in 1925; this is believed to have been an ex-Lancashire & Yorkshire example, but no further details are known.

The third railcar was a Sentinel-Cammel steam railcar of the L&NER, No. 248 *Tantivy*. A series of summer-only halts were opened between Stalham and Yarmouth Beach in 1933 for tourists staying at the local holiday camps, and the plan was that *Tantivy* would provide a frequent service for these halts in between the regular trains. The service was so successful that passenger numbers exceeded the capabilities of the railcar to cope and the following year it was replaced by a locomotive and two carriages fitted with retractable steps for the low platforms. However, the halts services were forever known as 'The Tantivy'.

In 1936, two LM&SR engines were stationed at South Lynn to help the M&GN to work the heavy expresses. These were Johnson Belpaire '3P' 4-4-0s, No's 758 and 759, and were a great success. The M&GN men believed that they were the best engines they had ever had. When the L&NER took responsibility for the Joint line's locomotives in October of that year, the LM&SR engines were returned and replaced by a variety of L&NER types of dubious benefit. The enginemen's comment is not surprising; the 'Belpaires' – as they were known on the Midland – could take a heavier load than the other classes of 4-4-0 working over the Joint line. Between Saxby and Bourne a Power Class 1 could take 160 tons, a Power Class 2 maximum load was 220 tons and Power Class 3 could load to 260 tons. Fortunately there are pictures of both locomotives at South Lynn in July 1936.

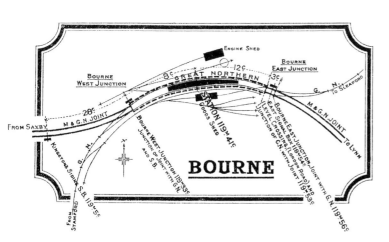

This broadside view shows M&GN No. 8, originally L&FR *Hillington*, when it was at Derby and coupled to Pullman No. 10. The picture was probably taken prior to the motor train entering service, although it could have been used on the Wirksworth branch, which was one of the lines where the M&GN locomotives were used. On the original picture it is possible to see the control wires that ran between the driving position at the end of the car and the locomotive. The locomotive is still in M&GN livery, but with the Midland device applied to the tanks. R.J. ESSERY COLLECTION.

ABOVE: When the author was in the Control Link at Saltley, his driver, Charlie Smith, who was born in London, had spent some time as a fireman at Bourne before he transferred to Saltley. Unfortunately, most of the stories Charlie told were of his exploits on the express freight trains from London, but there were some references to work over the Joint line. This picture of Midland Railway No. 323 shows the locomotive on Bourne shed. Judging by the well coaled tender, express headlamp code and reporting number, it is about to take over an express train working. This locomotive was the only Midland 4-4-0 to be rebuilt in this manner, with new frames, 'B' Class boiler but an extended smokebox. R.J. ESSERY COLLECTION.

Another picture taken at South Lynn on the 1st July 1936, this one showing the other loaned LM&S 3P 4-4-0, No. 759, on shed. The locomotive has again been well coaled in readiness for its next working, probably to Leicester and return. H.C. CASSERLEY.

APPENDIX B: THE WHITTAKER TABLET APPARATUS AND THE M&GNJR

The Whitaker apparatus was installed on the M&GN during 1907 and proved to be extremely reliable in use. The automatic tablet exchanging apparatus had four main features: a combined receiver and deliverer on the locomotive or tender; a deliverer placed by the side of the track at the beginning of a single line section; a receiver placed by the side of the track at the end of a single line section; and a combination receiver and deliverer placed at each intermediate crossing place. The Norfolk & Suffolk line from North Walsham to Cromer was never fitted with the automatic apparatus, and remained hand exchange.

There were several patterns of engine exchanger – ranging from the original with a brass jaw, double front triggers, pneumatic buffer and spring locking bolt in the sliding bar, to the final turnover type. In addition, the lineside apparatus was also developed over the years.

Most locomotives were fitted with the apparatus, except the saddletank No. 16A and the Melton Constable-built 0-6-0T shunting engines. The primary fitting was on the nearside (for tender engines running in forward gear) on the tender side near the front handrails. The apparatus could be mounted on a slide or a special swing arm. Tank engines were fitted with the apparatus on the nearside bunker for forward running, and on the offside cab for running in reverse gear; this included the three Class 'A' 4-4-2T, the four remaining Class 'B' 4-4-0T and the three loaned Midland 'No. 6 Class' 0-4-4T locomotives.

For working the Norfolk & Suffolk lines, where turning was not often an option, three of the Class 'A' 4-4-0s (No's 30, 33, 34) were fitted with tablet apparatus and tender weatherboards for reverse running circa 1906. The apparatus was fitted to the cab side sheets on the offside. In about 1933 the engines fitted changed, to No's 32, 33, and 35 – No's 30 and 34 being withdrawn. In about 1935 several of the Class 'C' 4-4-0s were also fitted with the apparatus for reverse running, but not with weatherboards; observed examples were No's 1, 7, 12, 42, 49, 76 and 78. In these cases, the apparatus was fitted on the offside of the tender in a corresponding position to the forward-facing apparatus on the other side of the engine.

ABOVE: This shows the tablet exchange apparatus on the tender of No. 24, one of the 'Peacocks'. R.S. CARPENTER COLLECTION.

BELOW LEFT: Detail from the plate on page 192, showing the tablet exchange apparatus fitted to 4-4-2T No. 9. R.J. ESSERY COLLECTION.

BELOW RIGHT: Detail from the plate on page 191, showing No. 077 with the tablet exchange apparatus on the tender. The new cab fitted in 1930 and the horizontal rail on the tender can also be clearly seen. R.J. ESSERY COLLECTION.

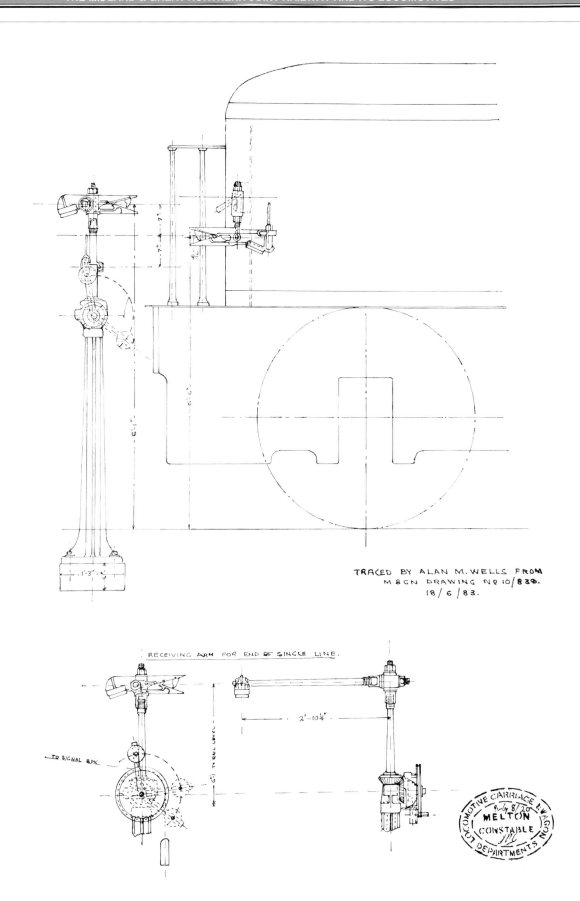

TRACED BY ALAN M. WELLS FROM
M & GN DRAWING № 10/830.
18/6/83.

RECEIVING ARM FOR END OF SINGLE LINE.

TO SIGNAL BOX

2'-10¼"

Traced from an original Melton Constable drawing dated 8th July 1920, these drawings show the interaction of the equipment at the lineside and on the locomotive, as well as the delivery arm at the start of a single line section and the receiver arm at the end of a single line.

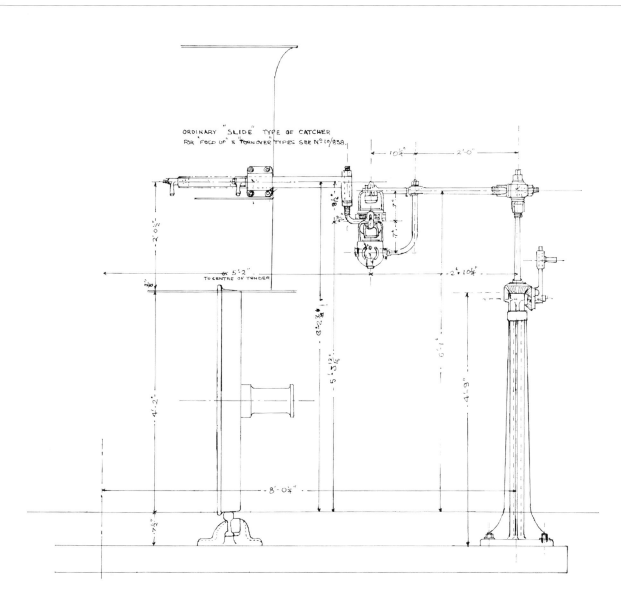

ORDINARY "SLIDE" TYPE OF CATCHER
FOR "FOLD UP" & "TURNOVER" TYPES SEE Nº 10/858.

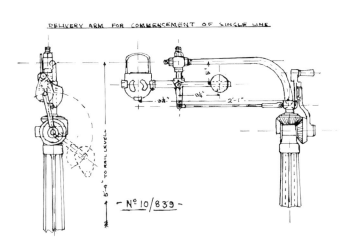

DELIVERY ARM FOR COMMENCEMENT OF SINGLE LINE

~ Nº 10/839 ~

Above: Detail from Plate 2 on page 50, showing the tablet exchanger in the extended position on Johnson 4-4-0 No. 13 in the 1930s. R.S. Carpenter.

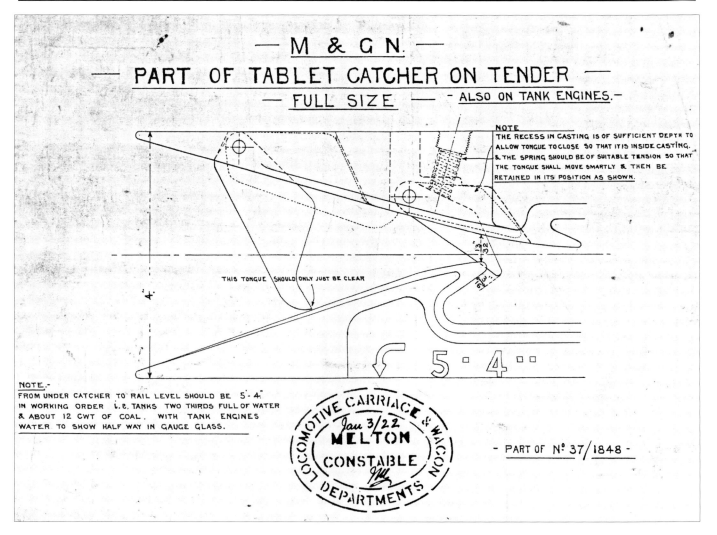

— M & G N. —
— PART OF TABLET CATCHER ON TENDER —
— FULL SIZE —   — ALSO ON TANK ENGINES. —

NOTE
THE RECESS IN CASTING IS OF SUFFICIENT DEPTH TO
ALLOW TONGUE TO CLOSE SO THAT IT IS INSIDE CASTING.
& THE SPRING SHOULD BE OF SUITABLE TENSION SO THAT
THE TONGUE SHALL MOVE SMARTLY & THEN BE
RETAINED IN ITS POSITION AS SHOWN.

THIS TONGUE SHOULD ONLY JUST BE CLEAR

5·4··

NOTE.-
FROM UNDER CATCHER TO RAIL LEVEL SHOULD BE 5·4"
IN WORKING ORDER i.e. TANKS TWO THIRDS FULL OF WATER
& ABOUT 12 CWT OF COAL. WITH TANK ENGINES
WATER TO SHOW HALF WAY IN GAUGE GLASS.

LOCOMOTIVE CARRIAGE & WAGON
Jan 3/22
MELTON
CONSTABLE
DEPARTMENTS

— PART OF Nº 37/1848 —

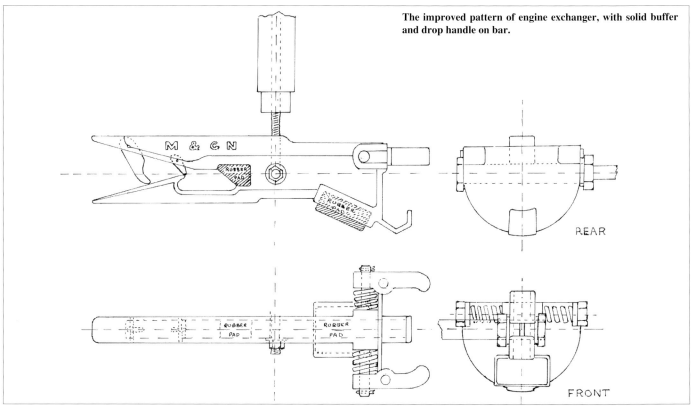

The improved pattern of engine exchanger, with solid buffer
and drop handle on bar.

M & G N

RUBBER PAD

RUBBER PAD

REAR

RUBBER PAD

RUBBER PAD

FRONT

APPENDIX C: M&GNJR LOCOMOTIVE NUMBERING AND STOCK LIST: 1893–1936

The M&GN numbering system, though at first sight somewhat confusing at its lower end, was really quite straightforward. It followed the traditional 'lowest available vacant number' principle and actually continued from the previous Eastern & Midlands scheme, itself a continuation of the old Lynn & Fakenham system. The Yarmouth & North Norfolk had merely named its engines.

The first L&F engines were merely named, but by March 1882, when the first four Beyer Peacock 4-4-0s were delivered, an attempt had been made by the contractors to start a number list. This probably began with the numbering of the ex-CMR arrivals (No's 1–3) in December 1880. When the rest arrived in March 1881 they were allowed to retain their CMR numbers (No's 11–14, 17 and 18). Subsequent engines had to slot into the vacant places thus created. However, apart from the contractor's engines (No's 4 and 5) and the Beyer Peacock 4-4-0s (No's 21–24), it is not known if any more of the locomotives actually carried their allocated numbers during the L&F period, the original names remaining in place.

On formation of the E&MR most names were removed, and the ex-Y&NNR and remaining unnumbered ex-L&F engines were either integrated at random into the gaps between 1 and 20 in the fledgling L&F list or added at the end. This was from No. 31 upwards since the L&F list had already allowed the range 21–30 for the new Beyer Peacock 4-4-0s though not all were yet built. In the event, the 4-4-0 series went to No. 35 and this caused a little further upward adjustment of No's 31 and 32 (ex-Y&NNR) which were then allocated No's 40 and 41, followed by No's 42 and 43 for the newly acquired ex-L&NWR 2-4-0s which had formerly been No's 29 and 30. This left a gap (36–39) in the number series of the 39 engines handed over to the new M&GN Committee.

On its formation, the M&GN clearly decided to institute its own version of the well-known pre-group practice of 'main' and 'duplicate' lists, the former usually being those engines charged to capital stock. This began in 1894 when, after the first four new Johnson Class 'C' 4-4-0s had been given the natural 36–39 number gap at the end of the Beyer Peacock series, the class then continued upwards from No. 42 to No. 50. Thus, two of the new Class 'C' 4-4-0s were given numbers of the old L&NWR 2-4-0s which were destined to be withdrawn shortly. This was soon to be followed by a major incursion into the 1–20 number series for the new 4-4-0s, and all the original engines thereby affected went onto the duplicate list with the 'A' suffix added to their old numbers. The only mildly surprising thing about this 1894 activity was that the whole of the 1–20 number series was not reused for new Class 'C' 4-4-0s. Seven old engines retained their original numbers, presumably it had been decided that they remain in capital stock; five of them were 4-4-0Ts and clearly main line engines, so this probably made some sense, but why two of the older 0-6-0STs were thus distinguished (No's 15 and 16) when most of their equally aged contemporaries were 'duplicated' is not known. As it turned out, three of these seven numbers on the capital stock list (8, 10 and 19) were never used again after their original holders (all 4-4-0Ts) had been scrapped.

Thereafter, all the new engines of either Derby or Doncaster design were merely added from No. 51 upwards in order of their appearance on the system. The new Melton-built engines, however, were different. Here it would seem that they were regarded as a mixture of capital and duplicate stock. It is suspected that this may be why they are alleged to have been 'rebuilds' in some sources, even though they were self evidently new engines apart, maybe, from a very limited

reuse of older parts. The 4-4-2Ts were clearly, by their very nature, 'capital' stock and given gap-filling numbers in the main series, as were two of the 'Melton' 0-6-0Ts, thus adding a few more numbers to the duplicate list in compensation. But the other examples of the 0-6-0T series were originally given duplicate numbers from new. These were maybe regarded as 'accountancy rebuilds' and numbered accordingly – but it did cause some degree of confusion in the number lists (especially in relation to the old 'Cornwall Mineral' engines). It does seem that as the new 0-6-0Ts gradually appeared, so an old duplicate engine was simultaneously withdrawn – having officially been rebuilt. In 1907, this nonsense was terminated by giving the 'duplicated' 0-6-0Ts their proper place in the main list as No's 93–99. It is mildly surprising that once again the opportunity was not taken to reallocate the three 'old' numbers in the main list (8, 10 and 19) to these 0-6-0Ts and 'duplicate' their original holders – but this was never done. This information is tabulated below, with enough detail to enable the engines concerned to be identified but without including very much by way of technical data. It is hoped that it will also serve as a useful index to the engines described in the main part of the book.

On taking over responsibility for locomotives, the L&NER carried out all major repairs at Stratford. They appeared concerned at the condition of many of the boilers of all classes and draughted a series of drawings relating to boiler patches. Perhaps a full assessment of the condition of all the locomotive stock was undertaken; a document that records the average age of boilers and mileage run is included here, suggesting this was the reason which led to the early withdrawal of many M&GN locos.

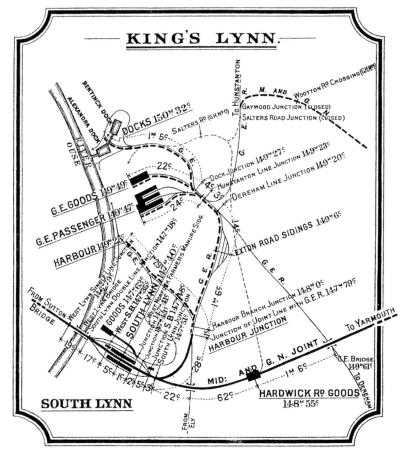

— STATEMENT GIVING AGE OF BOILERS IN
— ALSO MILEAGE

YEARS	1	2	3	4	5	6	7	8	9	10	11	12	13	14
ENGINE Nº			9.46	2 20	6.41	16.16^	15.47	27 42	14. 17	3,5,13	1. 12	4 7	93.	38.58
			51.	49.	44.52	36.50	95.99	43 69	45,85	28 55	37. 39	11. 18		65.66
					54.57	56.37		81. 86	89 90	87	53 64	26 61		68.71
					77. 94			96.98	91.		76 84	62 70		82 83
											BEING FITTED			92

✕ NOTE Nºs 38. 42. FITTED WITH L.M.S SECOND HAND BOILERS IN 1931.
      1. 3.12   - 1932
      4 . 7. 11   - 1933   AVERAGE AGE
         14   - 1934
      5 . 17.   - 1935

ENGINE Nº	TYPE BOILER	AGE OF BOILER	MILEAGE 1934	1935	ENGINE Nº	TYPE BOILER	AGE OF BOILER	MILEAGE 1934	1935
✕ 1	B	$11\frac{2}{12}$ YEARS	195132	221613	28	C	$10\frac{11}{12}$ YEARS	181313	193919
2	G6	$4\frac{8}{12}$ "	92827	119921	32	"	$28\frac{11}{12}$ "	327459	353681
✕ 3	B	$10\frac{11}{12}$ "	174189	201479	35	"	$26\frac{3}{12}$ "	428288	458509
✕ 4	"	$12\frac{8}{12}$ "	192909	221275	36	G6	$6\frac{8}{12}$ "	133373	160307
✕ 5	"	$10\frac{10}{12}$ "	99013	126887	37	B	$11\frac{9}{12}$ "	298480	329990
6	G6	$5\frac{5}{12}$ "	116424	139064	✕ 38		14 "	258057	286407
✕ 7	B	$12\frac{5}{12}$ "	190614	218839	39	G7	$11\frac{11}{12}$ "	275961	306722
9	"	$3\frac{10}{12}$ "	50892	69913	41	B	$5\frac{9}{12}$ "	109659	136293
✕ 11	"	$12\frac{7}{12}$ "	181991	211870	✕ 42	"	$8\frac{9}{12}$ "	160774	193895
✕ 12	"	$11\frac{4}{12}$ "	186774	212232	43	"	$8\frac{6}{12}$ "	196146	218896
13	"	$10\frac{5}{12}$ "	265180	293047	44	G6	$5\frac{7}{12}$ "	130013	159022
✕ 14	"	$9\frac{8}{12}$ "	58089	86965	45	G7	$9\frac{6}{12}$ "	246386	283294
15	SE	$7\frac{8}{12}$ "	87231	100819	46	"	$3\frac{6}{12}$ "	83836	118582
16	"	$6\frac{3}{12}$ "	58163	69709	47	B	$7\frac{5}{12}$ "	162344	193408
✕ 17	B	$9\frac{5}{12}$ "	86201	110277	48	"	$23\frac{2}{12}$ "	453886	476950
18	"	$12\frac{8}{12}$ "	275931	306715	49	G6	$4\frac{10}{12}$ "	95220	112998
20	"	$4\frac{10}{12}$ "	93867	115555	50	"	$6\frac{1}{12}$ "	120088	149503
23	C	$16\frac{1}{12}$ "	273854	291736	51	G7	$3\frac{4}{12}$ "	48606	69159
25	"	$15\frac{6}{12}$ "	283652	301.278	52	"	$5\frac{10}{12}$ "	164799	195328
26	"	$12\frac{8}{12}$ "	239658	258106	53	"	11 "	304404	327487
27	"	$8\frac{9}{12}$ "	153511	180096	54	"	5 "	127743	162384
					55	"	$10\frac{5}{12}$ "	289679	317688

LOCOMOTIVES TO JANUARY 1ST 1936 —
1934 - 1935 —

15	16	17	18	19	20	21	22	23	24	25	26	27	28	YEARS
25.59 72 88	23.63 80	73.74	67 79	60.75 78				48			35		32	ENGINE Nº

OF BOILERS $11\frac{3}{12}$ YEARS · OF · 10 C CLASS REBᴰ (G7) $7\frac{3}{12}$ YEARS
4 D · · · $12\frac{3}{12}$ ·

ENGINE Nº	AGE OF BOILER	MILEAGE 1934	1935	ENGINE Nº	AGE OF BOILER	MILEAGE 1934	1935
56 TYPE BOILER G7	$6\frac{6}{12}$ YEARS	182169	218653	78 TYPE BOILER B	$19\frac{7}{12}$ YEARS	498113	521814
57 "	$5\frac{6}{12}$ "	146054	181145	79 ·	$18\frac{1}{12}$ "	384136	416542
58 B	$14\frac{10}{12}$ ·	234584	254455	80 ·	$16\frac{7}{12}$ "	344103	368712
59 ·	$15\frac{3}{12}$ "	249963	268123	81 G.N.R	$8\frac{7}{12}$ ·	150797	168835
60 · ·	$19\frac{2}{12}$ "	315248	331561	82 ·	$14\frac{5}{12}$ "	232506	250171
61 ·	$12\frac{5}{12}$ "	184889	204204	83 ·	$14\frac{11}{12}$ ·	259754	277947
62 G7	12 ·	273687	291096	84 ·	11 ·	188475	210294
63 B	$16\frac{5}{12}$ ·	290756	310345	85 ·	$9\frac{8}{12}$ ·	171493	183995
64 ·	$11\frac{1}{2}$ ·	169001	187677	86 ·	$8\frac{2}{12}$ ·	135394	147848
65 ·	$14\frac{11}{12}$ ·	263667	282373	87 ·	$10\frac{8}{12}$ ·	183099	200548
66 ·	$14\frac{2}{12}$ ·	240919	260349	88 ·	$15\frac{2}{12}$ ·	244205	259671
67 ·	$18\frac{1}{12}$ ·	293131	311447	89 ·	$9\frac{11}{12}$ ·	172812	190555
68 G7	$14\frac{5}{12}$ ·	352474	380984	90 ·	$9\frac{1}{12}$ ·	144683	160215
69 ·	8 ·	216176	250603	91 ·	9 ·	150034	169786
70 B	$12\frac{2}{12}$ ·	208985	218685	92 ·	$14\frac{3}{12}$ ·	247206	260231
71 G7	$14\frac{7}{12}$ ·	352769	386297	93 SE	$13\frac{8}{12}$ ·	89499	110674
72 B	$15\frac{6}{12}$ ·	275103	293484	94 ·	$5\frac{8}{12}$ ·	79481	89622
73 ·	$17\frac{7}{12}$ ·	295517	314265	95 ·	$7\frac{3}{12}$ ·	77572	88504
74 ·	$17\frac{3}{12}$ ·	419378	444060	96 ·	$8\frac{11}{12}$ ·	125860	151591
75 ·	$19\frac{1}{12}$ ·	395095	417311	97 ·	$6\frac{6}{12}$ ·	88354	99253
76 · FROM L.M.S.	$11\frac{3}{12}$ ·	FROM L.M.S.	123589	98 ·	$8\frac{2}{12}$ ·	141609	152429
77 G6	$5\frac{1}{12}$ ·	106222	129914	99 ·	7 ·	145831	157782
				DEPARTMENTAL ENGᴱ 16ᴬ	$6\frac{10}{12}$ ·	49324	57446

M&GNJR LOCOMOTIVES 1893–1936

Final M&GN Number	Origin	Type	Remarks	Disposal
1	M&GN (MR)	4-4-0 Class 'C'	Replaced CMR 0-6-0T+TR (1A)	to L&NER
2	M&GN (MR)	4-4-0 Class 'C'	Replaced CMR 0-6-0T+TR (2A) – Rebuilt 'G6'	to L&NER
3	M&GN (MR)	4-4-0 Class 'C'	Replaced CMR 2-4-0 (3A)	to L&NER
4	M&GN (MR)	4-4-0 Class 'C'	Replaced 0-4-0ST (4A)	to L&NER
5	M&GN (MR)	4-4-0 Class 'C'	Replaced 0-4-0ST (5A)	to L&NER
6	M&GN (MR)	4-4-0 Class 'C'	Replaced 0-6-0ST (sold) – Rebuilt 'G6'	to L&NER
7	M&GN (MR)	4-4-0 Class 'C'	Replaced 0-6-0ST (7A)	to L&NER
8	E&MR (L&F)	4-4-0T (originally *Hillington*)	On loan to MR 1906–12 (as No. 2)	sold 1917
9	M&GN (Melton)	4-4-2T Class 'A Tank'	Replaced 4-4-0T (9A)	to L&NER
10	E&MR (L&F)	4-4-0T (originally *Norwich*)	On loan to MR 1906–12 (as No. 5)	sold 1917
11	M&GN (MR)	4-4-0 Class 'C'	Replaced CMR 0-6-0T+TR (11A)	to L&NER
12	M&GN (MR)	4-4-0 Class 'C'	Replaced CMR 0-6-0T+TR (12A)	to L&NER
13	M&GN (MR)	4-4-0 Class 'C'	Replaced CMR 2-4-0 (13A)	to L&NER
14	M&GN (MR)	4-4-0 Class 'C'	Replaced CMR 2-4-0 (14A)	to L&NER
15	M&GN (Melton)	0-6-0T 'Shunting'	Replaced 0-6-0ST (sold)	to L&NER
16	M&GN (Melton)	0-6-0T 'Shunting'	Replaced 0-6-0ST (16A)	to L&NER
17	M&GN (MR)	4-4-0 Class 'C'	Replaced 0-6-0ST (17A)	to L&NER
18	M&GN (MR)	4-4-0 Class 'C'	Replaced CMR 2-4-0 (18A)	to L&NER
19	E&MR (Y&NN)	4-4-0T (originally *Great Yarmouth*)	On Loan to MR 1906–12 (as No. 1)	scrapped?
20	M&GN (Melton)	4-4-2T Class 'A Tank'	Replaced 4-4-0T (20A)	to L&NER
21	E&MR (L&F)	4-4-0 Class 'A'	Rebuilt (boiler/tender/cab)	scrapped 1936
22	E&MR (L&F)	4-4-0 Class 'A'	Rebuilt (boiler/tender/cab)	scrapped 1936
23	E&MR (L&F)	4-4-0 Class 'A'	Rebuilt (boiler/tender/cab)	to L&NER
24	E&MR (L&F)	4-4-0 Class 'A'	Rebuilt (boiler/tender/cab)	scrapped 1936
25	E&MR	4-4-0 Class 'A'	Rebuilt (boiler/tender/cab)	to L&NER
26	E&MR	4-4-0 Class 'A'	Rebuilt (boiler/tender/cab)	scrapped 1936
27	E&MR	4-4-0 Class 'A'	Rebuilt (boiler/tender/cab)	to L&NER
28	E&MR	4-4-0 Class 'A'	Rebuilt (boiler/tender/cab)	to L&NER
29	E&MR	4-4-0 Class 'A'	Displaced L&NWR 2-4-0 (42)	scrapped 1931
30	E&MR	4-4-0 Class 'A'	Displaced L&NWR 2-4-0 (43)	scrapped 1933
31	E&MR	4-4-0 Class 'A'	Displaced 4-4-0T (40)	scrapped 1933
32	E&MR	4-4-0 Class 'A'	Displaced 4-4-0T (41)	scrapped 1933
33	E&MR	4-4-0 Class 'A'		scrapped 1936
34	E&MR	4-4-0 Class 'A'		scrapped 1936
35	E&MR	4-4-0 Class 'A'		scrapped 1933
36	M&GN (MR)	4-4-0 Class 'C'	Rebuilt 'G6'	to L&NER
37	M&GN (MR)	4-4-0 Class 'C'		to L&NER
38	M&GN (MR)	4-4-0 Class 'C'		to L&NER
39	M&GN (MR)	4-4-0 Class 'C'	Rebuilt 'H' – Rebuilt 'G7'	to L&NER
40	E&MR (Y&NN)	4-4-0T (originally *Martham*)	On loan to MR 1906–12 (as No. 10)	sold 1917
41	M&GN (Melton)	4-4-2T Class 'A Tank'	Replaced 4-4-0T (withdrawn)	to L&NER
42	M&GN (MR)	4-4-0 Class 'C'	Replaced L&NWR 2-4-0 (42A)	to L&NER
43	M&GN (MR)	4-4-0 Class 'C'	Replaced L&NWR 2-4-0 (43A)	to L&NER
44	M&GN (MR)	4-4-0 Class 'C'	Rebuilt 'G6'	to L&NER
45	M&GN (MR)	4-4-0 Class 'C'	Rebuilt 'G7'	to L&NER

Final M&GN Number	Origin	Type	Remarks	Disposal
46	M&GN (MR)	4-4-0 Class 'C'	Rebuilt 'G7'	to L&NER
47	M&GN (MR)	4-4-0 Class 'C'		to L&NER
48	M&GN (MR)	4-4-0 Class 'C'		to L&NER
49	M&GN (MR)	4-4-0 Class 'C'	Rebuilt 'G6'	to L&NER
50	M&GN (MR)	4-4-0 Class 'C'	Rebuilt 'G6'	to L&NER
51	M&GN (MR)	4-4-0 Class 'C'	Rebuilt 'G7'	to L&NER
52	M&GN (MR)	4-4-0 Class 'C'	Rebuilt 'G7'	to L&NER
53	M&GN (MR)	4-4-0 Class 'C'	Rebuilt 'G7'	to L&NER
54	M&GN (MR)	4-4-0 Class 'C'	Rebuilt 'G7'	to L&NER
55	M&GN (MR)	4-4-0 Class 'C'	Rebuilt 'H' – Rebuilt 'G7'	to L&NER
56	M&GN (MR)	4-4-0 Class 'C'	Rebuilt 'G7'	to L&NER
57	M&GN (MR)	4-4-0 Class 'C'	Rebuilt 'G7'	to L&NER
58	M&GN (MR)	0-6-0 Class 'D'		to L&NER
59	M&GN (MR)	0-6-0 Class 'D'		to L&NER
60	M&GN (MR)	0-6-0 Class 'D'		to L&NER
61	M&GN (MR)	0-6-0 Class 'D'		to L&NER
62	M&GN (MR)	0-6-0 Class 'D'	Rebuilt 'H' – Rebuilt 'G7'	to L&NER
63	M&GN (MR)	0-6-0 Class 'D'		to L&NER
64	M&GN (MR)	0-6-0 Class 'D'		to L&NER
65	M&GN (MR)	0-6-0 Class 'D'		to L&NER
66	M&GN (MR)	0-6-0 Class 'D'		to L&NER
67	M&GN (MR)	0-6-0 Class 'D'		to L&NER
68	M&GN (MR)	0-6-0 Class 'D'	Rebuilt 'G7'	to L&NER
69	M&GN (MR)	0-6-0 Class 'D'	Rebuilt 'H' – Rebuilt 'G7'	to L&NER
70	M&GN (MR)	0-6-0 Class 'D'		to L&NER
71	M&GN (MR)	0-6-0 Class 'D'	Rebuilt 'G7'	to L&NER
72	M&GN (MR)	0-6-0 Class 'D'		to L&NER
73	M&GN (MR)	0-6-0 Class 'D'		to L&NER
74	M&GN (MR)	4-4-0 Class 'C'		to L&NER
75	M&GN (MR)	4-4-0 Class 'C'		to L&NER
76	M&GN (MR)	4-4-0 Class 'C'		to L&NER
77	M&GN (MR)	4-4-0 Class 'C'	Rebuilt 'G6'	to L&NER
78	M&GN (MR)	4-4-0 Class 'C'		to L&NER
79	M&GN (MR)	4-4-0 Class 'C'		to L&NER
80	M&GN (MR)	4-4-0 Class 'C'		to L&NER
81	M&GN (GN)	0-6-0 Class 'DA'	Rebuilt larger boiler	to L&NER
82	M&GN (GN)	0-6-0 Class 'DA'	Rebuilt larger boiler	to L&NER
83	M&GN (GN)	0-6-0 Class 'DA'	Rebuilt larger boiler	to L&NER
84	M&GN (GN)	0-6-0 Class 'DA'	Rebuilt larger boiler	to L&NER
85	M&GN (GN)	0-6-0 Class 'DA'	Rebuilt larger boiler	to L&NER
86	M&GN (GN)	0-6-0 Class 'DA'	Rebuilt larger boiler	to L&NER
87	M&GN (GN)	0-6-0 Class 'DA'	Rebuilt larger boiler	to L&NER
88	M&GN (GN)	0-6-0 Class 'DA'	Rebuilt larger boiler	to L&NER
89	M&GN (GN)	0-6-0 Class 'DA'	Rebuilt larger boiler	to L&NER
90	M&GN (GN)	0-6-0 Class 'DA'	Rebuilt larger boiler	to L&NER
91	M&GN (GN)	0-6-0 Class 'DA'	Rebuilt larger boiler	to L&NER

FINAL M&GN NUMBER	ORIGIN	TYPE	REMARKS	DISPOSAL
92	M&GN (GN)	0-6-0 Class 'DA'	Rebuilt larger boiler	to L&NER
93	M&GN (Melton)	0-6-0T 'Shunting'	Ex 1A replacing CMR 0-6-0T+TR	to L&NER
94	M&GN (Melton)	0-6-0T 'Shunting'	Ex 2A replacing CMR 0-6-0T+TR	to L&NER
95	M&GN (Melton)	0-6-0T 'Shunting'	Ex 3A replacing CMR 2-4-0	to L&NER
96	M&GN (Melton)	0-6-0T 'Shunting'	Ex 11A replacing CMR 0-6-0T+TR	to L&NER
97	M&GN (Melton)	0-6-0T 'Shunting'	Ex 12A replacing CMR 0-6-0T+TR	to L&NER
98	M&GN (Melton)	0-6-0T 'Shunting'	Ex 14A replacing CMR 2-4-0	to L&NER
99	M&GN (Melton)	0-6-0T 'Shunting'	Ex 17A replacing 0-6-0ST 17A	to L&NER

DUPLICATE LIST

FINAL M&GN NUMBER	ORIGIN	TYPE	REMARKS	DISPOSAL
1A	E&MR (CMR)	0-6-0T+TR (originally *Melton Constable*)	Replaced by 0-6-0T, then 4-4-0 Class 'C'	scrapped 1898
2A	E&MR (CMR)	0-6-0T+TR (originally *Reepham*)	Replaced by 0-6-0T, then 4-4-0 Class 'C'	scrapped 1894
3A	E&MR (CMR)	2-4-0 (ex-0-6-0T+TR) (originally *Blakeney*)	Replaced by 0-6-0T, then 4-4-0 Class 'C'	scrapped 1899
4A	E&MR (L&F)	0-4-0ST (*Alpha*)	Displaced by 4-4-0 Class 'C'	sold 1917
5A	E&MR (L&F)	0-4-0ST (*Vici*)	Displaced by 4-4-0 Class 'C'	scrapped circa 1932
6	E&MR (L&F)	0-6-0ST (originally *Holt/Chairman*)		† sold 1894
7A	E&MR (GY&S)	0-6-0ST (originally *Ida*)	Displaced by 4-4-0 Class 'C'	sold 1894
9A	E&MR (L&F)	4-4-0T (originally *Fakenham*)	Displaced by 4-4-2T Class 'A Tank'	scrapped 1933
11A	E&MR (CMR)	0-6-0T+TR	Replaced by 0-6-0T, then 4-4-0 Class 'C'	scrapped 1899
12A	E&MR (CMR)	0-6-0T+TR	Replaced by 0-6-0T, then 4-4-0 Class 'C'	scrapped 1902
13A	E&MR (CMR)	2-4-0 (ex-0-6-0T+TR)	Displaced by 4-4-0 Class 'C'	scrapped 1898
14A	E&MR (CMR)	2-4-0 (ex-0-6-0T+TR)	Replaced by 0-6-0T, then 4-4-0 Class 'C'	scrapped 1897
15	E&MR (GY&S)	0-6-0ST (originally *Ormesby*)		† sold 1900
16A	E&MR (GY&S)	0-6-0ST (originally *Stalham*)	Replaced by 0-6-0T	to L&NER
17A	E&MR (Y&NN)	0-6-0ST (originally *Aylsham*)	Replaced by 0-6-0T, then 4-4-0 Class 'C'	scrapped 1902
18A	E&MR (CMR)	2-4-0 (ex-0-6-0T+TR)	Displaced by 4-4-0 Class 'C'	scrapped 1895
20A	E&MR (L&F)	4-4-0T (originally *King's Lynn*)	Displaced by 4-4-2T Class 'A Tank'	scrapped 1931
41	E&MR (Y&NN)	4-4-0T (originally *North Walsham*)		† withdrawn 1904
42A	E&MR (L&NWR)	2-4-0	Displaced by 4-4-0 Class 'C'	scrapped 1895
43A	E&MR (L&NWR)	2-4-0	Displaced by 4-4-0 Class 'C'	scrapped 1899

NOTES:

In case of replaced or displaced locomotives, the new number (if any) is given in parentheses. If a new number is not quoted, then the locomotive was sold or withdrawn.

†=Sold or withdrawn without receiving a Duplicate number.

L&F=Lynn & Fakenham Railway, GY&S=Great Yarmouth & Stalham Light Railway, CMR=Cornish Mineral Railway, L&NWR=London & North Western Railway, E&MR=Eastern & Midlands Railway, Melton=built or rebuilt at Melton Constable.

H=large boiler with round-topped firebox, G6=small boiler with Belpaire firebox, G7=large boiler with Belpaire firebox.

T+TR=tank engine with additional tender.

APPENDIX D: LOCOMOTIVE SHEDS

M&GN LOCOMOTIVE SERVICING

At each shed there needed to be coal, water and lubrication, as well as the men to clean, service and operate the locomotives. There were varying degrees of facilities for servicing. All sheds had inspection pits between the rails; lifting gear was provided at Melton, Norwich and South Lynn, and also the Midland shed at Peterborough. All sheds would have had at the very least a fitter's bench, but most had a fitter's shop attached.

Coaling was usually achieved from simple brick platforms, the coal being delivered into tenders and bunkers by iron tubs lifted by hand cranes. South Lynn was the only covered M&GN coal stage, but Peterborough had a Midland 'coal shed'. Mundesley and Bourne had no coal stages – the former being coaled from the end of one platform, and the latter being coaled direct from a loco coal wagon. South Lynn and Yarmouth later acquired electrically operated coaling plants, where the coal would be loaded into small wagons before being hoisted up and tipped. The coal was stored in coal stacks, skilfully built up from an outer wall of brick sized coal lumps, with loose coal within. It is not known if coal was ordered yearly or half yearly, but sometimes these coal stacks had to be used.

The coal came direct from the collieries, there being two or three preferred suppliers, so quality could vary from day to day. The coal was mostly received in GN or MR 'loco coal' wagons. There were also a number of M&GN loco coal wagons and these were routed from South Lynn to Shirebrook Colliery. This was considered the best coal and was mixed with the other hard coals in the proportion two hard to one best. All loco coal was labelled to South Lynn and there would be relabelled as required for the eastern section sheds. The wagons would usually arrive ten or twenty in number on a mineral train, but sometimes occupied almost a whole train which caused congestion in the West Yard. Storage was a problem and wagons would be sent on to eastern section stations until needed, often utilising Bawsey sidings or the Down refuge at Raynham Park. Storage of the loco coal empties was also a problem, but they were useful in making up load for special trains to Peterborough and the west. All engines leaving South Lynn were expected to take as much coal as possible, especially those returning to the eastern sheds. This was intended to save wagon trips.

Water was kept in large tanks, which were invariably made up from cast iron panels bolted together. There were several designs, including a Midland example at Wisbech, but the most common involved panels of 4 feet 6 inches by 3 feet 6 inches. These had a raised beading with incurved corners moulded onto each panel and, for those built after 1893, a smaller central panel containing the initials 'M&GN'. At Melton, Norwich, Yarmouth, Cromer and Aylsham the tanks were built on brick bases, all of them except Yarmouth having swing-out arms to water the engines. Grimston Road also had a similar style, probably dating from L&F times, but with smaller cast iron tank sections, while Massingham had a wooden tank on piles, but both these two fell out of use for locomotive purposes. The brick bases housed a pump, usually a small 'gas' engine, with the well nearby. Yarmouth had trouble with brackish water, so a second tank was supplied with Corporation water, and this became the rule at most sheds except South Lynn which was supplied from the nearby River Nar. South Lynn tank (1895) and Mundesley tank (1899) were mounted on timber piles, but the usual method after brick bases were abandoned was to have cast iron columns.

Apart from the swing arms referred to above, there were several designs of water column, which could be seen at some stations as well as at the sheds themselves. The earliest on the eastern section were plain standpipes where the leather bag hung unsupported. A firing shovel was usually required for support when watering from these. A similar design was used by the E&MR, again with a standpipe, but this time with a system of folding arms to lift the bag, operated by a weighted arm. The usual M&GN design was of a long swing arm balanced by a water filled ball. This arm was pivoted by an elbow tube to the main column. There were also several examples of both Midland and GN water columns dotted around the system. An M&GN type seen at only a few locations was similar to the Midland column but used smaller section materials. During frosty weather, braziers and tall chimneyed stoves were trolleyed out into position and kept burning at most locations, but on the platforms at South Lynn the M&GN columns were kept frost free by integral gas flames.

Turntables were all hand operated and to similar designs. Many of them seem to have been supplied by the Isca Foundry, Newport. The sizes were originally small: 42 feet (Sutton Bridge), 45 feet (Bourne, Fakenham and Norwich), 46 feet (Yarmouth), 47 feet (South Lynn, Melton and Cromer). Bourne, South Lynn, Norwich and Yarmouth were given 60 foot replacements in the years 1929–31, built by Ransomes & Rapier.

The oils arrived in barrels or drums and had to be hand pumped into storage tanks in the stores area of each shed. There were three oils in common usage: heavy engine oil, rape oil, and cleaning oil. The rape oil was highly prized by drivers for use in the cylinders and on the motion; there was a great deal of grumbling when its use was discontinued in the 1930s. The 'cleaning' oil was actually used in the cleaners' lamps when cleaning the locomotives, not for lubrication. Rape oil was also used in gauge glass lamps, whilst paraffin, which was also referred to as petroleum, was used in the locomotive head and tail lamps.

Loco sand was dried off in special sand furnaces before use, their location betrayed by short brick chimneys. All M&GN loco sand came from a pit at Yarmouth Beach and was delivered in low-sided wagons from time to time. The furnace was often used for unofficial cooking purposes by the shed staff.

Flint stones were used by Joint loco staff on the firebars in order to keep the fires open, free of clinker and free burning. Midland men used broken up firebrick for the same purpose. A wagon of flints would arrive from time to time from Kelling or Holt ballast pits. The used stones were discarded as glassy, congealed lumps. The practice was slightly frowned upon in the 1930s, but still carried on in Joint sheds.

Ash was shovelled from the disposal pits into low-sided wagons shunted nearby. The ash was saved for use on railway premises or sold to local builders and farmers. Smokebox clinker or 'loco dirt' was kept separately in its own wagon. Every week or so when the wagon was full it would be sent to Cromer Electricity Works.

MELTON CONSTABLE SHED

Melton Constable shed was built in 1881 and opened with the Lynn & Fakenham line through to Guestwick in 1882. In anticipation of the location's importance as the crossroads of the railway, it was the largest so far built and was the first of a series of sheds with similar design features.

Melton was a three road shed for nine tender locomotives, built of brick with deeply panelled walls and large, probably cast iron, windows. The roof was low pitched and clad in pantiles, the gables being filled with vertical boarding. The bargeboards were of the usual curved type used by the contractor Wilkinson & Jarvis, with pendant ends and central finial. There were no gable ventilators, but

A small mechanical coaling stage was installed at South
Lynn in 1930, and this picture shows 0-6-0 No. 87 being
coaled there. Compared with the concrete coaling plants
installed on the parent companies' systems it was a simple
affair. ALAN WELLS COLLECTION.

each road had a number of large wooden smoke chimneys spaced above them, connected to smoke troughs. Inside the shed each road had full length inspection pits and there were two ash pits outside. Behind the shed was a lean-to building housing the boilermaker's room, fitter's shop and tool store. On the north side of the shed were a sheer-legs and inspection pit, but these were installed circa 1906. Prior to this there was a lifting frame behind the loco office at the end of the road serving the coal stage.

On opposite sides of the single road approach to the shed were the coal stage and water tank. The coal stage was a simple brick platform with a hand-operated wooden jib crane for lifting tubs of coal. Coaling was done laboriously by hand and the cleaners on coal duty were often to be found sheltering in the dark recesses under the tank, where there was a gas engine for pumping. Nearby were the coal stack and two timber and corrugated iron buildings. The larger was the loco office or 'Wicka', with the smaller mess room adjacent. Between all the various running lines, the staff were pleased to make gardens, bordered by stones, to cheer up the smoky atmosphere a little.

Between the shed and the platform was the 47-foot turntable. Unusually, there was an end-loading dock here, which could only be reached by shunting across the turntable. The 'breakdown' vehicles were stationed here. Nearby was a pleasant little wooded knoll, a remnant of the original topography before the railway came. This was swept away when the new 70-foot turntable was installed in 1952.

Watering facilities were a swing-out arm from the water tank, an E&MR lifting type crane nearby, an original L&F standpipe on the turntable road and two M&GN swinging arm cranes for the platform. Lighting of the yard was by tall swan-neck lamp posts carrying large pendant gas lamps.

In 1914 there were twenty-five engines allocated to Melton Shed, plus a further fourteen in the Works.

Norwich City Shed

Norwich City shed was opened with the rest of the station at the end of 1882. It was built in brick, with the slate roof and curved bargeboards typical of the contractor's structures, and bore a strong resemblance to Melton shed. There were two lantern ventilators on the ridge with bargeboards and finials, and several additional chimneys over the rest of the roof area. The overall dimensions of the shed were 156 by 43 feet, the sides being deeply panelled and fitted with eighteen windows, apparently in cast iron. Each of the three roads could take two engines, six in all, and each had an inspection pit. The central road also had an ashpit outside the shed. At the rear was a small fitter's area, partitioned off from the main body of the shed with timber; although fitted with internal windows to allow more light penetration, it must have been a gloomy place. In the rear gable was a circular window and the front gable, originally boarded, was fitted with glazing between 1901 and 1912.

The three loco roads converged into one, which led to the 45-foot turntable, turned by hand. The turntable pit was only a few feet from the bank of the River Wensum, strengthened here by a brick retaining wall. Between the turntable and the shed points were the water tank and coaling stage. The tank and its brick base were the same as at Melton, although the Norwich tank never had a roof. The water was delivered from a swing-out arm. The coal stage was a simple brick platform with a hand crane to lift small tubs of coal. The stage was supplied from the rear by a road for loco coal wagons. Originally this siding was taken off the third shed road, but after a sheer-legs was ordered from Derby in 1897, access was from a new sheer-legs road which curved round the back of the shed. A second ashpit was put in this road. After 1893 an old North London Railway carriage body was supplied as the enginemen's mess room, surviving until at least 1907. A brick messroom was built near the water tank in 1900.

In 1929 it was proposed to replace the 45-foot turntable with a 60-foot one, which was brought into use in January 1931. The new turntable road was taken off the former dead-end spur in front of Norwich South signalbox. The old turntable pit was filled in and plain line carried over it. Unlike Yarmouth Beach and South Lynn, an electric coal hoist was not supplied.

The Norwich allocation in 1914 was seven engines. It was apparently usual to have two pilot engines, 0-6-0Ts No's 96 and 97 being prominent.

South Lynn Shed

South Lynn shed was built as part of the Eastern & Midlands Railway 'Lynn loop' construction. Opened in 1885, it was to become the largest and most documented shed on the M&GN. The first part of the shed was only two roads, holding four engines. It was a 'through' shed, both roads extending through doors at the rear. The exterior was weatherboarded in panels between vertical frame members, with one large cast iron window to a panel. The large pitched roof was slated, with four smoke vents per side and two large ridge ventilators. All gables had the contractor's standard curved bargeboards and finials.

In order that the shed could cover the larger number of engines required when the M&GN began supplying the motive power for all trains on the western section, it was extended to more than double its former size. A new two-road shed was joined to the original and exactly copied its construction. This part of the shed could hold six engines, making ten in all. However, the growing levels of traffic meant that there were still over a dozen engines that had to stand outside. There were inspection pits the entire length of each road in the shed. A lean-to fitter's shop and stores was at the rear. The open part at the rear of the original shed was used for a sheer-legs, and in 1901 this part was enclosed. To clear the top of the sheer-legs the extension was made slightly higher than the rest of the shed and given a pitched roof with its ridge at right angles to the normal ridge line.

The coaling stage was the usual brick platform, with a large open-fronted timber shed over it to provide a wind screen in this rather draughty location, and a hand crane. In 1930 it was replaced by an electric coaling plant of the same type as at Yarmouth Beach.

Water was supplied from a very large tank of M&GN cast iron panels standing on timber piles adjacent to Saddlebow Road. This tank was supplied from the nearby River Nar by a water syphon into a cistern. The water ran by gravity into another cistern outside the loco office. A float in the cistern was connected to a semaphore signal above so that the staff could tell the state of the water supply and when to go and 'prime the water'. The tank was then filled by a pump, originally steam but later electric. There were six water cranes; two large M&GN swing types on the platforms, two E&MR lifting types by the coal stage with a third by No. 1 shed road, and a smaller M&GN swing type by the sheer legs road. When the new electric coal stage was erected, one of the E&MR types was lost, replaced by a small M&GN swing type on the new turntable road. The original 47-foot turntable was adjacent to the coaling stage, but in 1930 a new 60-foot turntable was brought into use in a new position, partially using 'the pit', an old ballast pit which had become part of the site drainage.

There were twenty-three engines allocated here in 1914. In addition, during the day a large proportion of the rest of the M&GN locomotive stock would call here, making it an extremely busy place indeed.

Mundesley Shed

Mundesley was a relatively late destination for Joint engines. It was located to the north of the road overbridge at Mundesley station. Authorised in November 1898, it was erected in 1899 as a 'temporary' structure, its construction reflecting this concept. A sturdy timber frame was clad on the outside with corrugated iron and lined on the inside with 6 inch boarding. There were two roads, each able to hold one tank engine with the doors closed. There were two large windows per side, with one at the rear. The pitched roof, also of corrugated iron, had a ridge ventilator supplemented by timber smoke vents. There does not seem to have been any additional building for fitters or stores, and there may have just been a bench inside the shed. There was no coal stage or turntable. The shed was closed and demolished in 1929, its materials being sold by public auction on New Year's Day 1930.

Much nearer the road overbridge on its north side was the water tank. This was of M&GN cast iron sections supported on large section timber posts and covered with twin corrugated iron pitched roofs. The water was supplied by the local authority, with a charge of one shilling per 1000 gallons. The water supply was not copious and would trickle into the tank for a long time after the water column was used. The position of the water column changed at some point. Originally it was in the 'six foot' north of the road bridge, not far from either tank or shed, but by the time of the 1913 Appendix it had been moved to the island platform, south of the bridge, probably a more convenient spot. The crane was of a swing type used occasionally by the M&GN, similar to the Midland design but apparently made at Melton. By the 1950s a makeshift coaling area had been provided next to the water crane.

There was only one M&GN engine allocated to Mundesley, usually a Class 'B' 4-4-0T. The Great Eastern also stationed an engine here, invariably a 2-4-2T.

CROMER BEACH SHED

Despite the intensive service provided on the Cromer branch, it is astonishing to find that even in 1914 there were only three engines allocated to Cromer Beach shed. In fact, Cromer had the smallest shed on the Joint and in many ways it could be considered as a sub-shed of Melton. The building was a one-road version of the contractor's 'standard' design such as Melton, constructed from panelled brick with a slated roof. There was a ridge ventilator along

the entire length, later supplemented by a timber smoke vent. The front gable was brick, whereas the rear gable had glazing in vertical strips, possibly not an original feature. A small timber lean-to fitter's shop and stores was provided at the rear.

The shed was approached across the 47-foot turntable and there was a second engine road beside the shed. Enterprising staff housed chickens and grew vegetables on the unused ground between the shed and the goods yard. The water tower and coaling stage were on the shed approach road; the coaling stage was the typical brick platform, possibly with a hand crane, but photographs are few and inconclusive. The coaling facilities do not appear to have been used a great deal, Melton being the preferred coaling point; a wagon of loco coal was unloaded here at roughly fortnightly intervals. Opposite was the brick-based water tower, fitted with a swing-out arm. The water tank was originally open to the sky, the brick base housing a steam water pump. From about 1902, however, the Corporation supplied the water and the tank was roofed to cover the regulating equipment. The ashpit was nearby.

As far as is known there was no loco office; a messroom was provided from circa 1920, apparently a redundant signalbox of the contractor's platform type. The only other major change occurred in 1953, when the original turntable was replaced by a 60-foot example in a new position on the south side of the shed.

In 1914 there were three engines allocated to Cromer, one required for working of the Norfolk & Suffolk.

YARMOUTH BEACH SHED

Yarmouth Beach originally had only a small shed, demolished in the extensive alterations at Yarmouth resulting from the opening of the Lowestoft line in 1903. The first shed, built circa 1877, was of concrete block with large rectangular windows and arched corrugated iron roof. There was a lantern ventilator, again with a curved roof, and several wooden smoke vents. There were two roads within, probably only long enough for one tender engine or two tank engines on each. The turntable and coaling area were completely separate from the shed. The 46-foot turntable, reached by a trailing connection crossing the goods yard entry road, had to be

The single road shed at Cromer had a small brick stage where locomotives were coaled by hand. The original turntable was 47 feet in diameter, replaced in 1953 with a 60-foot table. This picture was taken on the 29th March 1937 and shows 4-4-2T No. 20 on shed. B. ROBERTS.

An overall view of the Yarmouth Beach shed, probably taken during the mid 1930s. Unfortunately, none of the locomotives were identified by the photographer. The locomotive at the left of the picture is a Class 'C' 4-4-0 as rebuilt with a 'G6' boiler, on the right is a Melton 0-6-0T shunting tank, and in the far distance a Class 'D' 0-6-0. W.A. CAMWELL.

crossed by loco coal wagons in order to restock the coal stage beyond. In common with the other M&GN coal stages, it was a simple brick platform. It is not known if a hand crane was supplied for coaling. Unusually, the cattle pens were combined with the coal stage – a most unusual arrangement.

At the rear of the site were the old workshops of the Yarmouth & North Norfolk Railway, built in the same materials as the loco shed – concrete block with large rectangular windows – but this time with two arched corrugated iron roofs. The workshops were used for sheet making and for stabling the collection and delivery horses. At the north-west corner of this building there was a water tank of M&GN cast iron panels on a brick base housing a pumping engine, built circa 1893. The well itself was near the southern corner of the building and was tapped into an underground stream of brackish water. An anti-foaming chemical had to be used to prevent priming, and it is thought that the high domes of the later batches of 'Peacock' 4-4-0s were to avoid this. A second water tank, for fresh Corporation water, was provided in 1903, on iron posts. Both tanks were roofed in corrugated iron. South of the workshops was the locomen's mess room, an old North London Railway carriage body. It is possible that the sand furnace and yard lavatories were also present at this time.

The site was considerably remodelled in 1903 and the old workshops were converted into the new running shed. The first shed was demolished in 1905 following a short period where it had stood isolated with its connections severed. The turntable and coal stage were resited in a much better arrangement, reached by lines separate from the running lines. Inside the shed, the two halves were divided off by a wooden screen, the eastern half still being used to make and repair wagon sheets and stable the horses. The running shed had two roads with full-length inspection pits and there was room for four tender engines. The old turntable was replaced by a 60-foot one in 1930 and the coal stage was replaced by an electric coil hoist in 1931.

In 1914 the allocated number of locos was ten.

PETERBOROUGH SHED

Peterborough shed was owned not by the Joint but by the Midland Railway. Consequently, it was always referred to either as the 'Derby Loco' or the 'Spital' shed, being adjacent to the old Spital Bridge. The shed was opened in 1872, being one of the Midland's standard square 'round-houses'. It was in brick with extensive decoration and picturesque round-topped windows. Originally it had an internal central 42-foot turntable, replaced by a 50-foot one in 1899. The shed had a sandhouse with chimney, and offices on

the front (south) elevation, with a standard MR 'outstation' fitting shop at the rear. A watertank was nearby. The north-facing exit from the loco yard was by Spital Bridge signalbox, the south exit was controlled by Crescent Sidings signalbox. The shed was Midland No. 9, with Bourne as sub-shed No. 9A. Later, in 1935, Peterborough became LM&SR 16B.

Inside the shed were twenty-two stabling roads and the straight-through line. On the corner road (usually No. 16) there would have been a sheer-legs. Another sheer-legs was erected in the yard outside at some date between 1900 and 1923. The whole floor and a wide area outside was brick paved. Coal was supplied from the Midland's earlier design of ground-level coal shed. It had one internal supply road, an open front and a central pedestal for the coaling crane. This was replaced circa 1936. There were two water cranes of MR swing type, and one more near Crescent box.

All the M&GN Peterborough engines were stationed here, sharing facilities with over forty MR engines. There were nine M&GN engines here in 1914. It seems they were all Midland types.

BOURNE SHED

The history of Bourne shed is quite an involved one. A small shed, about which little is known, was erected by the Great Northern in the 1860s, but this was swept away by the new shed of 1893. This two-road shed was by the northern boundary of the site; 75 feet long, it provided space for two tender locos or four tank engines. In order to provide accommodation for M&GN engines after the Joint took over the working of most of the services from 1895, the structure was extended by 90 feet to allow the shed to house six engines, three on each road. The north road was used by Midland locos. The building, now 165 feet by 36 feet 9 inches, was large and distinctive with a 'northlight' roof over panelled brick walls. The shed was formally transferred to the Joint Committee in 1897.

Adjacent to the shed was a large brick-based water tank, built in 1893. The messroom and loco office were between the shed and the tank. There is some controversy over watering facilities at Bourne, but the general opinion is that the GN owned the large swing-arm water cranes at each end of the island platform and foreign drivers were charged for their use by the usual ticket system. Free water was obtained from a Midland swing arm crane on the Down main line near Bourne West signalbox, and from a standpipe at the east end of the loco yard. M&GN engines obtained further watering three quarters of a mile down the line at Four Cross Roads, where two GN-type swing arm cranes were provided, fed by a natural spring.

There was a 45-foot turntable but no coaling facilities. M&GN

engines would take coal at Spalding and Midland engines obtained their coal direct from a loco coal wagon. A new 60-foot turntable was installed in 1929.

In 1914 it was recorded that there were five M&GN and five Midland engines stationed here.

SPALDING SHED

This shed was opened by the Spalding & Bourn (sic) Railway in 1866. The building was a sturdy brick affair with two through roads, each with a semi-circular arched doorway. The pitched roof was slated, with a ridge ventilator and additional circular vents in the apex of each gable. Its size was only sufficient to take two tank engines and it was not possible to shut the doors if tender engines were in the shed. The doors were later removed altogether, probably after a mishap with a 'K2' 2-6-0 in 1949.

Although worked by the Great Northern and considered by them as 'their' shed, it was actually owned by the S&B and the GN paid rent. The shed was subsequently owned by the Midlands & Eastern

Railway (administered as the Bourn & Lynn Joint) and then the M&GN. On the opening of the line from Bourne to Saxby the shed became home to two Midland engines as well. It was not until February 1895 that the last GN and MR engines were transferred away and the shed became the sole domain of Joint engines.

The loco office was attached to the north-west corner of the shed and the water tank was just beyond. The tank was made up of M&GN cast iron panels mounted on iron posts and was covered with an arched corrugated iron roof. This had been removed by 1936.

A wooden coaling stage was provided in 1891, with hand crane and ten-hundredweight tub. A fitter's shop and store was provided inside the shed in 1896. Water was obtained from a swing-arm water column on the shed approach road, but there was no turntable; engines used either the GN station turntable or ran round the 'avoiding line' triangle. The water crane was the same M&GN type as at Mundesley – similar to a Midland column, but slenderer. Unaccountably, it was left out of the list of facilities in the 1913 Appendix to the Working Timetables, but surely must already have been installed. In 1914 there were six engines at this shed.

LOCOMOTIVE FACILITIES (1913)

LOCATION	WATER COLUMN	TURNTABLE	COALING
Wisbech	7ins MR swing, Up Platform 7ins MR swing, Down Platform		
Bourne	Standpipe, Loco Sidings 8ins GN swing, West Platform 8ins GN swing, East Platform 7ins MR swing, Down Main	45ft (60 ft 1929)	Coal taken from wagons
Four Cross Roads	8ins GN swing, Up Main 8ins GN swing, Down Main		
Spalding	6ins swing, Loco Sidings	44ft 7ins (at GN station)	Hand, timber stage
Sutton Bridge		42ft (in goods yard)	
South Lynn	8ins swing, Up Platform 8ins swing, Down Platform 6ins E&MR lift, West Yard 6ins swing, East Yard 6ins E&MR lift, Coal Stage 6ins E&MR lift, Coal Stage 6ins E&MR lift, Ash Pits	47ft (60ft 1931)	Hand, timber stage (Electric 1931)
Grimston Road	Tank arm, Down Platform		
Fakenham	L&F standpipe, Down Platform L&F standpipe, Shunting Road Tank arm, Turntable Road	45ft (in goods yard)	
Melton Constable	8ins swing, Up Platform 8ins swing, Down Platform L&F standpipe, Turntable Road 6ins E&MR lift, Loco Depot Tank arm, Coal Stage	47ft (70 ft 1953)	Hand, brick stage
Aylsham	6ins E&MR lift, Down Platform Tank arm, Up Platform		
Stalham	6ins E&MR lift, Up Platform 6ins E&MR lift, Down Platform		
Yarmouth Beach	8ins GN swing, Loco Depot 6ins E&MR lift, Shed Road 8ins GN swing, No.1 Platform	46ft (60ft 1931)	Hand, brick stage (Electric 1931)
Norwich City	Tank arm, Loco Depot	45ft (60ft 1931)	Hand, brick stage
Sheringham	6ins E&MR lift, Up Platform 6ins E&MR lift, Down Platform		
Cromer Beach	Tank arm, Loco Depot	47ft (60ft 1953)	Hand, brick stage
Mundesley	6ins swing, Platform		Coal taken from wagons

APPENDIX E: ENGINE LAMP HEADCODES

Until the delivery of the Beyer Peacock 4-4-0s, locomotives carried only one lamp bracket at the base of the chimney. The Peacocks were supplied with three brackets: one at the base of the chimney and one over each of the buffers, and this became the standard arrangement of the E&MR. The codes involved discs by day and green or white lights at night. The rule seems to have been to store the lamps and discs on the brackets even when out of use. Discs were 12 inches diameter and green with a white border on one side, white with a blue border and a red 'X' on the other. The green side had the engine number painted in small white numerals in the upper portion, above the staple into which the lamp iron was inserted. It is difficult to see from photographs if the lampcases were black or the loco colour. The lamps probably had a removable shade to change the colour of the light from white to green.

From 1894 the M&GN used a five-position headlamp code, based on the Midland standard. This involved a lamp iron on the smokebox top just under the chimney, another under it on the top of the smokebox door, one over the left hand buffer, and two over the right hand buffer (looking at the front of the engine).

The five position headlamp code was superseded by a new Railway Clearing House national standard, introduced in February 1903, detailed in Supplement B to the M&GN No. 1 Appendix, January 1904. It had only four positions; one on the smokebox top, one over each buffer and one central between them. On the M&GN the lamps themselves were painted loco light brown and lined in black and yellow, with the driver's name and the engine number painted on during the days when engines had one named driver. After that era had ceased in 1919, lamps were painted black with the depot name on a brass plate.

There was a further revision in 1918, when the former headlamp code for empty coaching stock was combined with that of parcels trains (more correctly express goods, newspaper or parcels trains composed of passenger stock), the codes for through goods and stopping goods were simplified to one lamp position (on left and right sides of the bufferbeam respectively) and the light engine code became one lamp central on the bufferbeam.

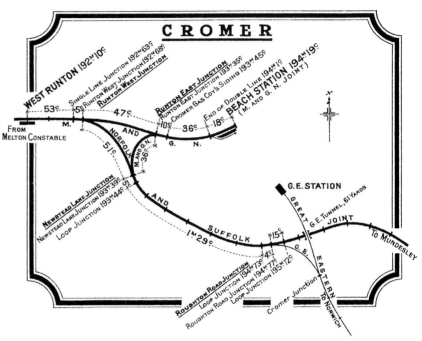

	By day	By night	
Ordinary passenger trains and all trains over M&GN and GE lines into Lynn	A	A	green light
Special passenger trains	AC	A	green light
		C	white light
Ordinary goods or cattle trains	A	A	white light
Special goods or cattle trains	AC	AC	white lights
Ordinary fast goods or fish trains	AC	A	white light
		C	green light
Special fast goods or fish trains	BC	B	white light
		C	green light
Ballast trains	BC	BC	green lights
Shunting	A	A	purple light

Evidence of the earliest practice showing engine headlamp codes on the M&GN was published in George Dow, *Midland Style*, but although the lamp positions are correct, the period was prior to 1894 and not as stated. The codes were those that had been employed by the Eastern & Midlands Railway which were adopted by the M&GN until their own new codes came into service.

ENGINE HEAD LAMPS.

In order that Station-masters, Signalmen, Platelayers, Gatemen, Porters, and all other servants may be able to distinguish the kind of train that is approaching by the head lamps on the engine, all engines working over the Midland and Great Northern Joint Railways must, except where instructions to the contrary are given, carry head lamps as follows :—

1. Engines of Express Passenger trains and Break-Down Van trains when going to clear the line .... A White Light over the Left Hand Buffer, and a White Light at the Foot of the Chimney, thus :—

2. Engines of Excursion, Officials, and Special Passenger trains, booked to stop at principal stations only .... A White Light over the Right Hand Buffer, and a White Light at the Foot of the Chimney, thus :—

3. Engines of Ordinary, Passenger, Excursion, Officials, and other Special Passenger trains, booked to stop at other than principal stations, Break-Down Van trains when not going to clear the line, and Empty Coaching Stock trains .... A White Light over the Left Hand Buffer, thus :—

4. Engines of Cattle, Fish, Meat, Fruit, and Milk trains A Blue Light over the Left Hand Buffer, and a White Light at the Foot of the Chimney, thus :—

5. Light Engines .... A White Light at the Foot of the Chimney, thus :—

6. Engines of Through Goods, Mineral and Ballast trains .... Two White Lights at the Foot of the Chimney, thus :—

7. Engines of Stopping Goods and Mineral trains, Ballast trains requiring to run short distance, and Ballast trains requiring to do work in the Section................... Two White Lights over the Left Hand Buffer, thus :—

8. Shunting Engines employed exclusively in Station Yards and Sidings must, after sunset or in foggy weather or during falling snow, carry both Head and Tail Lamps shewing a Red Light.

9. The Head Lamps must always be carried in their ordinary positions, whether they are lighted or not.

LOADS OF ENGINES.

The following loads, in addition to the brake, can be taken over the Midland and Great Northern Joint Lines, with joint engines, wind and weather permitting.

Class.	Engine Numbers.	WESTERN SECTION.				EASTERN SECTION.			
		Minerals.	Cattle.	Goods.	Empties.	Minerals.	Cattle.	Goods.	Empties.
A	21 to 35	27	30	40	50	24	28	35	46
B	8, 9, 10, 19, 20, 40 and 41	15	16	22	33	13	14	20	30
C	1 to 7, 11 to 14, 17, 18, 36 to 39, 42 to 57 ...	32	34	45	50	27	30	40	50
D†	58 to 65	40	40	50	50	30	35	45	50
Duplic'ts	1A, 2A, 3A, 11A, 12A,	20	24	30	40	18	20	27	38
„	14A Shunting Engine ...								

† Until further advised these engines will only work between Lynn and Melton Constable and on the Western Section.

50 wagons, excluding the brake, to be maximum number taken over any portion of the Joint Line.

Cromer Branch only : 5 minerals, 7 goods, and 10 empties less.

Up Trains between Melton Constable and South Lynn must not consist of more than 40 vehicles, engine and brake included.

In mixed loads, 3 loaded goods to be taken as equal to 2 minerals, and 3 empties to be taken as equal to 2 loaded goods. (Cattle and Great Northern Railway sleeper wagons excepted.)

Three loaded cattle to be reckoned as equal to 4 loaded goods.

One empty cattle wagon to be taken as equal to 1 loaded goods.

In reckoning Great Northern Railway sleeper wagons, an 8-wheel wagon loaded to be counted as 2½ loaded minerals, and a 6-wheel wagon to be counted as 2 loaded minerals, and either an 8 or 6-wheel sleeper wagon empty to count as 1 loaded mineral.

Coke, pig iron, iron ore, salt, stone, sand, ballast, heavy machinery, plate or scrap iron, loaded rail wagons, slates, tiles, pipes, clay, grain and compressed Esparto grass, all to be reckoned as minerals.

Wherever engines cannot start their Trains, or when there is a probability that they will lose much time on the road owing to severe frost or very bad weather, the loads may be reduced by the Station Master or Foreman in charge. Guards and Drivers must specially report each case, the Guards on their journals, and Drivers at the Locomotive Office, before signing off duty, stating the exact numbers and class of wagons on the Train left behind.

APPENDIX F: ORDERS PLACED AT DERBY WORKS
FOR MATERIALS TO BE SUPPLIED TO THE M&GNJR

Some years ago, Phil Chopping and the author transcribed the existing Derby Locomotive Works Order Books for the Johnson and later period that are held at the Public Record Office (now the National Archive) at Kew. The records are not complete – the first order book for the period is missing; and although when the orders were hand written the records are complete, with the advent of the typewriter the practice changed. Orders were typewritten on loose sheets and there are many gaps. The author has searched the records and has set out below what was recorded. In the majority of cases this is a *précis* of the actual order and a certain amount of 'shorthand' has been used. This was done in the days before digital cameras were allowed in the reading room so it was a case of transcribing the orders in the PRO. These are all the entries that were found.

ORDER NUMBER	DATE	SUMMARY OF THE ORDER
1278	6/07/1893	Cast iron water tank 32ft × 16ft × 3ft, capacity 9,600 gallons, with nine girders as per tracing, also 7in water crane and 20yds 10in main to connect for Bourne station, M&GNJR.
1312	20/10/1893	Four 'A' Class boilers for rebuilds M&GNJR, wp 140lbs.
1313	20/10/1893	Four 'B' Class boilers for rebuilds M&GNJR, wp 140lbs.
1380	5/07/1894	Materials for a set of shear legs to Melton Constable.
1381	9/07/1894	170yds of 3in main, etc., for fire protection in passenger and goods stations at Melton Mowbray.
1441	23/04/1895	Three new boilers 'B' Class for rebuilds, wp 140lbs, same as O/N 1313 M&GNJR.
1501	9/12/1895	Hydraulic spring testing machine for Melton Constable.
1528	23/04/1896	Two steel boilers for 'D' Class engines M&GNJR, Drg 96-4249.
1581	1/10/1896	Material for shear legs at Melton Constable.
1701	11/11/1897	Three steel boilers for shunting engines for M&GNJR, drg 96-4249.
1980	5/09/1899	One set of three throw pumps for hydraulic wheel press at Melton Constable.
2450	11/09/1902	Two fixed store holders to drg for the proposed oil gas works at Melton Constable.
2521	16/12/1902	Fittings belonging to Haycock's system of Carriage Warming Apparatus off Leeds engine 1331 and Nottingham engines 1863 and 1865 to be forwarded to Mr Marriott at Melton Constable for use on M&GNJR.
2621	22/06/1903	Two new 'C' Class boilers for M&GNJR. These are same as our 'B' Class and stock boilers No's 2087/2088, made to O/N 2397 are to be appropriated, mountings are not required, no tubes, photo print S-222.
2622	16/03/1903	One new 'D' Class boiler (this is the same as our 'H' Class), and one of our stock boilers is to be appropriated for the purpose, mountings not required, no tubes. [Pencil notes: taken from O/N 2646 No H/81, photo print S-223]. This should be 'One new boiler for rebuilding M&GNJR 'D' Class engines, these are the same as our 'M' Class standard goods.'
2931	15/02/1905	50 Whitaker's patent water level indicators. The above were ordered from Messrs Taite & Carlton on the 7th instant. Please note that 30 will be supplied to the M&GNJR in response to their requisition.
	2/06/1905	14 indicators for tank engines were ordered on the 1st to be delivered to Melton Constable.
	17/04/1905	Please note that 54 further indicators have been ordered for the M&GNJR for delivery to Melton Constable.
	14/04/1905	Please note that 200 indicators have been ordered for use on our own engines (MR).
2951	15/04/1905	Two standard boilers for M&GNJR 'C' Class. Please put your work in hand-.
3033	11/10/1905	'H' Class boilers for Melton Constable. Please note, two of the boilers to be taken out of O/N 2969 and appropriated for Melton Constable. They will be used for rebuilding M&GNJR 'C' Class passenger engines.
3053	21/12/1905	Combined tank engines and carriages as motor cars. Please note it has been agreed to fit up four tank engines for this work and arrangements are being made for four M&GNJR tank engines to be provided for this purpose.

FACING PAGE: During the period from 1894 until 1902 the headlamp codes were as shown here, which is a copy of page 42 in the M&GNJR *Appendix to the Book of Rules and Regulations and to the Working Time Tables*, this copy is dated 1st February 1898.

In 1903 the headlamp positions were largely standardised for British railway companies. After comparing the M&GN codes for the period 1903–18, as shown in Nigel Digby, *Liveries of the Midland & Great Northern Railways Joint Committee and its Constituents. M&GN Circle Booklets No. 17*, with the Midland Railway codes in the company's 1904 Appendix, it is clear they are identical. A further change came in 1918 when, with the exception of the Royal Train, all British railway lamp codes were shown by the use of two lamps and those codes requiring three lamps were altered. In making this statement we should be aware that over some lines where the traffic was intense, discs were used to indicate route rather than class of train, but since this did not apply to the M&GN it need not be considered further.

ORDER NUMBER	DATE	SUMMARY OF THE ORDER
	22/02/1906	Two more of these engines have been received from Melton Constable. Please therefore push on as fast as possible with the necessary works. The drgs are now in the shops.
memo	25/05/1906	From Henry Fowler. Telegraph & Regulator Gear for Auto Car. Please fit up another auto car with telegraph and regulator gear similar to the four previously done.
	29/05/1906	Please carry out this work to O/N 3053.
	27/09/1906	Combined tank engines and carriages as motor cars. Carriage Warming Apparatus, the necessary drawings for fitting the four auto cars with Johnson & Bain Carriage Warming Appartaus have been issued. Please carry out this work.
3331	18/07/1907	'H' Class boiler for M&GNJR. Please put in hand one boiler for the M&GNJR Joint line.
3331	18/07/1907	'H' Class boiler for M&GNJR. Please put in hand one boiler for the M&GNJR Joint line.
3442	3/02/1908	Autocars No's 2 and 10. Please put in hand at once two new boilers for engines of autocars No's 2 and 10. The boiler drawing was numbered 08-7490.
3471	3/06/1908	Two boilers for M&GNJR. Please put your work in hand for 'C' Class passenger engines.
3478	28/05/1908	This order was issued to cover the rebuilding of No. 2 as in order number 3442.
3479	28/05/1908	This order was issued to cover the rebuilding of No. 10 as in order number 3442.
3619	31/08/1909	Boilers for M&GNJR. Please put in hand ... four boilers without tubes or mounting for rebuilding 'C' Class passenger engines. These to be made to the same dimensions as MR 'B' Class boilers but to have small fire hole rings 15in × 12in as shewn on drg 09/7929 with stays arranged to suit. To be delivered this year. Fire box drg 09-7929.
3702	16/03/1910	Four boilers for M&GNJR committee. Please put your work in hand, M&GNJR 'C' Class (same as MR 'B' Class) with alterations asked for by Mr Marriott and shewn on drg. Firebox drg 09-7929. Two boilers required early and the other two within eight months.
3704	22/03/1910	Cylinders for M&GNJR. Please put your work in hand- 18½in × 26in × 2ft-4in centres for M&GNJR 'C' Class engines. Drgs 93-3903B, 93-3904B, 98-4489.
3800	7/10/1910	Cylinders for M&GNJR. Please put your work in hand– four cylinder castings right hand being issued. The engine No's are shewn on S1581. 17in × 24in and four left hand 17in × 24in for M&GNJR 'A' Class engines. Patterns are being sent by Melton Constable, drgs 10-8122/23/24.
3801	7/10/1910	Cylinders for M&GNJR. Please put your work in hand– four pairs for M&GNJR 'C' Class.
3870	31/01/1911	Cylinders for M&GNJR. Please put your work in hand–.
3989	11/10/1911	Two 'G7' Class boilers for M&GNJR. Please put your work in hand– for 'C' Class engines. No tubes or mountings are required. Take from O/N 3591 and delver to Melton Constable in December 1911.
4005	6/11/1911	Cylinders for M&GNJR. Please put you work- two pairs of engine cylinders, finished 18in × 26in × 28in centres, for 'D' Class engines.
4006	31/10/1911	Cylinders for M&GNJR. Four pairs, finished 18½in × 26in × 2ft-4in for 'C' Class engines, similar to O/N 3870, drgs 93-3903B/3904B/ 4489.
4036	11/01/1912	Cylinders for M&GNJR. Two pairs for 'D' Class engines, drgs 92-3694/3695/3696 and 88-3041.
4138	18/09/1912	Two 'G7' boilers for 'C' Class rebuilds (less tubes and mountings) to be delivered December 1913.
4235	14/03/1913	Two pairs of cylinders for 'C' Class M&GNJR engines.
4243	2/04/1913	Small vertical boiler for M&GNJR to drg 10-8002.
4278	3/06/1913	Two pairs of cylinders 18½in × 26in × 28in for 'C' Class M&GNJR engines.
4314	9/08/1913	Two pairs of cylinders for M&GNJR 'D' Class goods engines to MR pattern S.7.
	12/08/1913	'to be held in abeyance'.
	18/08/1913	Order reinstated to MR pattern R.3, drg 09-7946.
4428	12/03/1914	Four new 'G7' Class boilers for M&GNJR. [Pencil note: No MR boiler numbers given].
4477	5/05/1914	Two pairs of cylinders for M&GNJR Class 'C' passenger engines, no covers required.
4649	6/04/1915	Two pairs of cylinders for M&GNJR 'C' Class engines.
4771	22/10/1915	Two pairs of cylinders for M&GNJR 'D' Class goods engines to drg 09-7946.
4818	27/01/1916	Two pairs of cylinders for M&GNJR 'D' Class goods engines.
4917	13/07/1916	Cylinders for M&GNJR. Please put your work in hand– four cylinder castings 17in × 24in for M&GNJR Class 'A' to patterns sent from Melton Constable Drgs 10-8122/3/4.

Order Number	Date	Summary of the Order
5095	27/09/1917	Two pairs cylinders for M&GNJR Drg CF15/949. Please put your work in hand– two pairs goods engine cylinders 18in × 26in × 2ft-4in centres M&GNJR 'D' Class. [*Pencil note: This order should have been issued in a similar way to O/N 4818.*]
5145	17/01/1918	Two pairs cylinders for M&GNJR Please put your work in hand– 18in × 26in × 2ft-4in centres for 'D' Class goods engines.
5527	18/11/1920	16in × 20in cylinder castings for M&GNJR shunting engines. Please put your work in hand– two left hand 16in × 20in, one right hand 16in × 20in. Patterns are supplied by Melton Constable. [*Pencil note: casting made by Clayton & Shuttleworth.*]
	17/02/1921	Please note steel one cancelled. Casting made by Clayton & Shuttleworth.
5684	13/02/1922	Two pairs of cylinders for M&GNJR 'C' Class passenger engines, to MR pattern T2, similar to O/N 4649.
5709	23/03/1922	Motor coach No. 2233 to be loaned to the M&GNJR. All charges to this O/N.
5832	13/12/1922	10 new 'G7' Class boilers, No's 5481–5490.
	25/01/1923	A note states, send first two boilers to M&GNJR.
6080	10/12/1923	Two pairs of cylinders, 18in × 26in, for M&GNJR.
6268	11/07/1924	Melton Constable requisition No 744 2/11/1923. Tender frames to drg S-1718.
6425	3/04/1925	Two pairs of cylinders, 18½in × 26in × 28in, for M&GNJR, requisition C.F. 16/949 20/03/1923.
6451	14/05/1925	Cylinders for M&GNJR similar to O/N's 3800 and 4917.
6584	23/12/1925	Cylinders for M&GNJR Class 'C' engines, Melton Constable requisition No. 50 dated 11/12/1925. Please put your work in hand– two pairs of cylinders (finished) 18½in × 26in × 28in centres.
6593	6/02/1926	One 'G7' standard saturated boiler for M&GN No. 45 (without tubes or mountings) to drawing 07-7361 as requested by Melton Constable 29/01 1926.
6630	9/03/1926	Cylinders for 'C' Class M&GNJR passenger engines, Melton Constable requisition No. 83 dated 26/02/1926. Please put your work in hand– two pairs of cylinders (finished) 18½in × 26in stroke × 28in centres, similar to O/N 6584.
6844	22/02/1927	One 'G7' Class saturated boiler for M&GNJR 'D' Class without tubes or mountings. Stock requisition No. 226 Jan. 1927. Similar to O/N 6593, Drgs boiler 07-7361, firebox 07-7362, please complete within three months.
6855	8/03/1927	Two pairs of finished cylinders, no covers, for 'C' Class M&GNJR engines, 18½in × 26in × 28in centres, requisition CF 17/230 dated 25/02/1927, to drg 12-8390.
7052	15/03/1928	Four pairs of cylinders, 18½in × 26in × 28in, for M&GNJR.
7152	8/06/1928	Order was for VCR gear for M&GNJR, cancelled.
	30/06/1928	Parts sent to Melton Constable returned to Derby.
7171	21/07/1928	Two 'G6' standard saturated boilers for M&GNJR 'C' Class passenger engines, Melton Constable requisition No. CF 17/451 of 29/06/1928, boiler drg 16-9769 and firebox drg 17-9925, drgs marked 1/08/1928.
7172	21/07/1928	Two 'G7' standard saturated boilers for M&GNJR 'C' Class passenger engines, to be supplied without tubes or mountings. O/N is similar to O/N 6593/6844, boiler drg 07-7391 and firebox drg 07-7362, drgs marked 30/07/1928.
7463	1/08/1929	S1- Please put your work in hand– in connection with repairing five 'G6' Class boilers to be supplied to M&GNJR, Melton Constable. These boilers are to have the new standard 'G6' smokebox tubeplates 2ft-11½in deep below boiler centre but closed at the bottom to suit frames, drg 16-9769, similar to the boilers to O/N 7171. Three of these boilers have been selected, D7056 (ex engine No. 3545), D6652 (ex engine No. 259), D7182 (ex engine No. 3134).
7500	8/10/1929	Five new 'G6' Class boilers for M&GNJR, similar to O/N 7171, delivery is not required until early 1930.
7541	15/11/1929	Two new G7 Class saturated boilers for M&GNJR Class 'C' passenger engines.
7601	17/02/1930	Two cylinder castings, 16in × 20in for M&GNJR 0-6-0 side tank shunting engines.
8054	21/12/1931	S1- Five new 'G7' saturated boilers, two for M&GNJR and three for LMSR (Derby). [*Pencil note: The two M&GNJR to O/N 8059.*] Please put your work in hand– five 'G7' saturated boilers without tubes or mounting for disposal as above and charge to O/N 8054. The mud plug holes at sides of fireboxes are to be drilled and tapped 1-7/16in diameter × 12 threads as usual; the plugs will be provided by Melton Constable for their boilers. Boiler No's D8255–D8259 have been allocated and the drg(s) will be marked by the locomotive drawing office (Midland division) in due course. The central order office will deal with this order.
8059	29/12/1931	Two saturated 'G7' Class boilers for M&GNJR [see O/N 8054].
	6/01/1932	S2- Please note the domes of these boilers are to be to arrangement 'A' as usual for Melton Constable, similar to O/N 7541.

ORDER NUMBER	DATE	SUMMARY OF THE ORDER
8084	22/02/1932	Second-hand 'B' Class boilers for the M&GNJR. It has been agreed for the undermentioned unrepaired 'B' Class boilers to disposed of to M&GNJR: Boiler No's (ex engine No.) 5509 (2791), 5934 (3175), 5939 (2762). These are to be loaded up and despatched forthwith to W.E. Newman Esq, Resident Mechanical Engineer, M&GN Joint Line, Melton Constable.
8144	8/07/1932	Two pairs, 18½in × 26in × 28in centres for M&GNJR 'C' Class engines, no covers are required but studs are to be fitted as usual.
8169	13/08/1932	Spare wheels and cranks for M&GNJR. Please put your work in hand– recondition a set of coupled wheels and axles for use on the M&GNJR. The coupled wheels and axles ex No 336, which is due in shops for breaking up are to be utilised for this purpose. The wheels and axles when finished are to be forwarded to A.H. Nash at Melton Constable.
8173	23/08/1932	Three unrepaired 'B' Class boilers for the M&GNJR. It has been agreed to supply to the M&GNJR three unrepaired 'B' Class boilers for stationary purposes. Boiler No's (ex engine No.) 5370 (2584), 5584 (2637) have already been selected.
8236	10/11/1932	Spare wheels and cranks for M&GNJR from reconditioned items off engine No. 390 which has been broken up. Forward to A.H. Nash at Melton Constable.
8239	10/11/1932	One left hand cylinder casting, 16in × 20in, for M&GNJR 0-6-0 side tank shunting engine.
8240	10/11/1932	One right hand and one left hand cylinder casting for M&GNJR Class 'A' 4-4-2T engines to drgs 10-8122, 10-8123, 10-8124. Castings are required to patterns, core boxes, etc., being sent to Derby in L&NER box wagon No. 75101.
8446	7/07/1933	Second-hand 'B' Class boiler for M&GNJR. Please note it has been agreed for the undermentioned unrepaired 'B' Class boilers to be disposed of to the M&GNJR: Boiler No's (ex engine No.) 5464 (2476), 5470 (2706). To be loaded up and sent to Mr A.H. Nash at Melton Constable.
8398	16/05/1933	One pair of cylinders, 18½in × 26in × 28in, for M&GNJR 'C' Class engines.
8446	7/07/1933	Second-hand 'B' Class boiler for M&GNJR. Please note it has been agreed for the undermentioned unrepaired 'B' Class boilers to be disposed of to the M&GNJR: Boiler No's (ex engine No.) 5464 (2476), 5470 (2706). To be loaded up and sent to Mr A.H. Nash at Melton Constable.
8665	7/02/1934	One pair of cylinders, 18½in × 26in × 28in, for M&GNJR 'C' Class passenger engines.
8710	5/04/1934	'B' Class boiler No. 6237 ex engine No. 2661 to be sent to M&GNJR as a second-hand boiler to A.H. Nash at Melton Constable.
8727	8/05/1934	Load and despatch second-hand B boiler No. D5942 ex engine No. 2511 to M&GNJR for Mr A.H. Nash, Melton Constable.
8929	7/11/1934	Wheel centre and tyre boring gauges for M&GNJR to drgs D23-W221, WS-189, D33-W476.
9098	29/04/1935	Three second-hand 'B' Class boilers for M&GNJR. Boiler (ex engine No.) 5413 (2748), 5502 (2634), 5053 (2654). Please despatch to A.H. Nash, resident mechanical engineer at Melton Constable.
9496	9/03/1936	10 sets of tablet catching apparatus for M&GNJR.

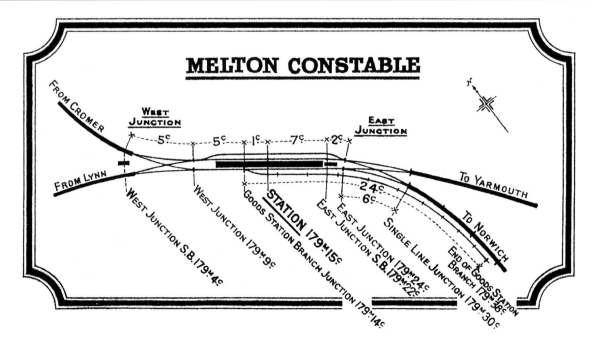

APPENDIX G: SOURCES AND REFERENCES

Derby Locomotive Works Order Books held at the National Archive, Kew.
Midland Railway Gradient Sections. The Engineers Department, Derby, 1902.
Midland Railway Distance Diagrams. Various editions.

Locomotives of the LNER, various parts, RCTS.
Official Handbook of Stations etc., Railway Clearing House, 1938.
Railway Magazine, various editions, in particular 1908.
Railway Returns of the Railway Companies of Great Britain for the year 1922, HMSO, 1923.
Trains Illustrated, various editions, Ian Allan.

Beckett, C. (ed.), *Forty Years of a Norfolk Railway*, Midland & Great Northern Joint Railway Society, 1974.
Butt, R.V.J., *The Directory of Railway Stations*, Patrick Stephens Ltd., 1995.
Cattermole, P.E., *Alfred Whitaker and the Tablet Apparatus*, The Somerset and Dorset Railway Trust, 1982.
Clark, Ronald H., *An Illustrated History of M&GNJR Locomotives*, OPC, 1990.
Digby, Nigel J.L., *A Guide To The Midland & Great Northern Joint Railway*, Ian Allan, 1993.
Digby, Nigel J.L., *Liveries of the M&GN and its Constituents*, M&GN Circle, 2002.
Dow, George, *Midland Style*, HMRS 1975.
Essery, R.J. & D.Jenkinson, *An Illustrated Review of Midland Locomotives Volume Two*, Wild Swan Publications, 1988.
Essery, R.J. & D.Jenkinson, *An Illustrated Review of Midland Locomotives Volume Four*, Wild Swan Publications, 1989.
Essery, Bob, 'Midland Railway Motor Trains', *Midland Record*, Preview Issue, Wild Swan Publications, 1994.
Quick, M.E., *Railway Passenger Stations in England Scotland and Wales – A Chronology* (2nd edition), RCHS, 2007.
Summerson, Stephen, *Midland Railway Locomotives Volume 3*, Irwell Press, 2002.
Wells, Alan, *Locomotives of the M&GN*, HMRS/M&GN Circle 1981.
Wells, Alan, *The Cornwall Minerals Railway and its Locomotives*, M&GN Circle Booklet 7, 1984.
Wells, Alan, *The Peacock 'A' Class Locomotives of the Lynn & Fakenham Railway*, M&GN Circle Booklet 11, 1990.

By the time this picture was taken, sometime after 1939, No. 77 had been rebuilt (in 1930) with a 'G6' boiler and new cab and was in L&NER stock classified as D53. Other changes that can be seen are the steam sanders for running in reverse and the horizontal rail on the tender where a tarpaulin sheet could be attached, either to give protection to the enginemen when running tender first, or it could have been in connection with wartime black-out requirements. The tablet exchange apparatus can be seen on the tender. R.J. ESSERY COLLECTION.

This ex-works picture of 4-4-2T No. 9 in photographic grey shows the form of the lining used by the M&GN but, as usual, not the colour differences. Everything not painted black above the locomotive platform (footplate) was painted in the light yellow-brown, and below in burnt sienna, including the wheels. The tablet exchange apparatus and the open Ramsbottom safety valves can be compared with those shown in the ex-works picture of No. 41, on page 151. R.J. ESSERY COLLECTION.